PHIL H. RUESCHHOFF, Ed.D., The Pennsylvania State University, is Professor and Chairman of the Department of Art Education at the University of Kansas. He has taught at the University of Nebraska and The Pennsylvania State University. Dr. Rueschhoff has been a Western Arts Council member and is a past president of the Kansas Art Education Association.

M. EVELYN SWARTZ, Ed.D., University of Kansas, is Associate Professor of Education at that institution. She has had extensive teaching experience at several different grade levels in elementary schools.

Teaching Art in the Elementary School

Enhancing Visual Perception

Phil H. Rueschhoff

M. Evelyn Swartz

Both University of Kansas

THE RONALD PRESS COMPANY • NEW YORK

Library of Congress Catalog Card Number: 78–75641

PRINTED IN THE UNITED STATES OF AMERICA

Preface

Education is facing a challenge to provide learning experiences for children that will develop well-informed citizens capable of coping with our rapidly changing world. Considerable attention has been given to the understanding of technological change, but much less has been done toward the development of people who are well informed about art and capable of intelligent empathic responses to the world of art.

The art education program presented in this book is an answer to the challenge. It is a program designed to nurture knowledgeable consumers of art by bridging the gap between the two main existing kinds of art programs—those primarily concerned with media processes and those devoted to the study of art history. It is built upon the conviction that there are basic concepts in the arts, comparable to those in science and mathematics, which can be presented in a meaningful progression of multisensory experiences leading to understanding and enhanced visual perception.

A program such as this utilizes the potential of children and the possibilities within art education by emphasizing the knowledge that can be acquired about art through learning experiences which take into account both the child and art. The foundation thus laid will help prepare children to understand the work of architects, city planners, artists, and designer-craftsmen and to recognize the contributions they themselves may make both as producers and consumers of art.

The book is designed for courses in the teaching of art in the elementary school, for prospective teachers and art supervisors.

Part I presents the theoretical foundation, drawn from many sources including research conducted by the authors. The basic structure of art and the reasons for presenting this to children provide the background for implementing this approach; together they show the possibilities of art education as a dynamic force in school and in the whole of society.

Part II consists of sample learning experiences—episodes—which show how the theory can be implemented in the classroom. These are teaching strategies which are structured but which are flexible enough to be modified for use in many different classroom situations. The sample experiences suggest possibilities for the construction of other art learning experiences. The suggested teacher background which precedes each episode gives prospective teachers and those who work with them an idea of what must be understood before the episode can be presented effectively to children.

Part III consists mainly of practical suggestions considered to be helpful in using this program. They are the result of the authors' experiences in elementary schools and of their work in teacher education and in-service education.

This book has been made possible by the work of more people than can be acknowledged here—graduate students, teachers, art supervisors and consultants, and hundreds of children, all of whom were a part of research which led to the development of the episodes. Acknowledgments are given to those artists, designer-craftsmen, and museums whose work and selections exemplify the approach presented here. Finally, we would especially like to thank Rosemary Beymer of the Kansas City, Missouri, Public Schools and Elaine La Tronico of the Denver Public Schools for their generous assistance and counsel.

PHIL H. RUESCHHOFF
M. EVELYN SWARTZ

Lawrence, Kansas
February, 1969

Contents

I

A THEORY FOR
TEACHING ART

1

Art for Today's Children

The way to learn to read is to read. While the construction of the language, the prosody as it were, may be unfamiliar, the vocabulary which comes out of the artist's experience as a human being is already known. This, in large degree, is shared with him. Just as we construct with words a world of consciousness parallel to but different from the objective world we live in, so the artist uses his symbolic forms to construct a world analogous to but different from the world he knows through his senses. These other worlds lie close at hand, ours for the entering.[1]

PURPOSES OF
ART EDUCATION

Art education has a major responsibility of providing children with experiences which will enable them to enter the worlds created by artists and designer-craftsmen. In this respect art is unique, for it is the only part of the elementary school curriculum designed specifically to help children make the symbolic worlds created by others a part of their world. Through art education children can learn to react empathically, intelligently, and aesthetically to the world of art.

---

[1] Roberta M. Capers and Jerrold Maddox, *Images and Imagination* (New York: The Ronald Press Co., 1965), p. 3.

The responsibility of art education to help children develop aesthetic behavior and make aesthetic responses to the natural and man-made environment is a major one, but it is one that can be met. And it is important that the responsibility be met in the elementary school since this is the last experience many children may have with art. Whether or not children have additional experiences in art on higher levels, the foundations laid in the elementary school are those upon which a lifetime of learning and of designing for living with developed tastes is based.

The purpose of this book is to present ways for prospective and experienced teachers to help children develop aesthetic behavior. There are many contributing factors, but the one stressed here is to help children learn to "see" and understand what they see in works of art and nature. When children are able to see more because they know more, when they have developed *enhanced visual perception,* they have acquired a foundation for making intelligent and evaluative observations of the visual world and for forming aesthetic judgments and discriminations about it.

The theoretical foundation of visual perception and the learning experiences for its enhancement presented in this book are based on the premise that every subject taught in school must consider the children being taught, the society in which they live and to which they will contribute as adults, and the integrity of the subject itself. The theoretical foundation and its application include a process of learning which is based on what children can learn and their ways of learning, a scope of content which is derived from the whole realm of children's experiences and from the world of art, and an orientation of the teaching–learning process toward the world that today's children will live in as adults.

The process of enhancing visual perception is based on art learning experiences designed to increase children's perceptiveness. Two types of learning experiences have been found to be effective—creative art activities and selected experiences with works of art and nature. Creative activities provide children with opportunities for creative growth and perceptual development, and also help them develop a frame of reference for understanding the works of artists and designer-craftsmen.

Selected experiences with works of art also provide opportunities for growth in perceptiveness and for the development of sensitivity to the visual world. A balanced use of both kinds of experiences helps children to experience the world of art and to become astute observers of their environment.

THE CONTRIBUTIONS ART MAKES TO THE CHILD

The procedures for enhancing visual perception presented in this book make significant contributions to the lives of children and to the adults they will become. These are based on the assumption that there is much to be learned in and about art, and these learnings can help children to become sensitively aware of art and more creative, and to achieve more understanding of themselves and others.

Development of Sensitive Awareness

Through sculpture, painting, architecture, and other artistic endeavors, man has left a legacy of knowledge and experience which can be shared by all if opportunities are provided. Art education can provide these opportunities and can help children develop a high degree of awareness to this visual legacy. By giving children purposeful activities through which they learn to see and understand the structural design qualities in nature, and to discriminate and interpret the visual symbols used by artists and designer-craftsmen, a sensitivity to and awareness of the world of nature and art can be developed.

Understanding Others

Art can never be removed from the persons who produced it. Through art people have expressed themselves—their feelings, beliefs, attitudes, values, and understandings—and have reflected and added to their culture. Part of the learnings in and about art are learnings about the people and culture from which works of art have come; insights into people and understanding of culture are a significant part of the enhancing of visual perception. Cultural and even world understanding can be important outcomes of art education.

Creative Self-Expression

Art is one of the areas in the elementary school curriculum which provide children with the opportunity to create something that is meaningful and satisfying to them. It is an area which affords children the time and resources to develop their creative potential, a potential which exists to some degree in every child.   The self-expression which is made possible through art activities is vital to the development of the individual and to society.   The process of enhancing visual perception capitalizes on the individual need to create, and uses it as both means and end: the means is a greater sensitivity to the creative expression of others; the end is knowledge, enjoyment, satisfaction, and self-realization.

FOUNDATION FOR THE PROGRAM

In developing the basis for the program presented in succeeding chapters, one must first acknowledge the trends in art education and in society as a whole which have provided a foundation on which to build. These include art programs, past and present, and the interest of certain segments of our society.

Art Programs

Creative art activities which have been well developed as a result of research and innovation by many art educators provide a source of the content for enhancing visual perception and a part of the foundation of this program.   Creative activities do not, of course, mean those which call upon children to fill in outlines or to copy work done by others, but they do include those experiences with media which are valuable for children's intellectual and emotional growth.

Past attempts to present children with "art appreciation" courses or "picture studies" are also a part of the foundation.   Although these have not been as successful as was hoped, they indicated the concern for acquainting children with works of art and with providing them with a widened horizon for aesthetic education.   Although the authors do not accept the procedures used for such activities, they do accept the underlying concern for using works of art with children.

Interest of Educators

Professional art educators have often stressed the importance of developing art programs which will meet the challenge of growing interest in the arts and which will expand the learning possibilities within the area of art. Their interest is supported by other educators, including school administrators and supervisors. Although art is still regarded by many as a "frill" of modern education, more time, attention, and money are being spent on this "frill" than ever before. It is not at all uncommon for money to be spent on reproductions of great works of art for use in classroom, for trips to museums and galleries, or even for special art teachers and supervisors.

This interest has increased as a result of research on children and their processes of learning. These studies indicate that even young children are capable of learning more than we have given them credit for, and this includes learning about art. The adult is the product of what the child learns and experiences, and many educators are interested in developing adults who are as knowledgeable about art as about science or mathematics.

Interest of Others

Since schools reflect the society they serve, it is obvious that our society is becoming increasingly concerned with art. In fact, we find ourselves today in the midst of a "culture boom"—more and more people are becoming actively engaged in the arts, either as producers or as consumers. Although for some people involvement in the arts is merely one more status symbol, for many it shows a recognition of the value of art to life. The culture boom has caught up not only individuals, but industries, businesses, philanthropic organizations, and churches. Our society has often been criticized for its seeming lack of regard for aesthetics. Current trends indicate a change in this cultural pattern and the development of a pattern in which art is becoming an integral part of our daily lives. In one way or another the extent of participation in the arts has greatly increased.

As our culture changes, it behooves schools to try to develop knowledgeable art consumers. Everyone is constantly confronted with choices that involve the ability to make aesthetic responses. Because aesthetic responses must be made, whether one is buying a car, a painting, or a coffeepot, society recognizes the responsibility of the schools for educating persons as intelligent consumers.

A particularly striking example of current interest in some aspects of art can be found in urban renewal projects. Many people, saturated

Figure 1

Figure 2

with scenes such as the one shown in Figure 1, have agitated for legislation and education which will produce scenes comparable to that shown in Figure 2. Here man has corrected the non-aesthetic environment superimposed on nature. It is possible to achieve this through legislation, but it is more probable that lasting effects and achievements can be made only through education. Our society is showing an interest in art education programs which will help develop adults who are capable of living as comfortably in a world of art as in a world of technology.

OBJECTIVES OF ART EDUCATION

The preceding discussion has given the purpose and rationale of this book. Embodied in this discussion are the objectives for the art education program explained in the remainder of the book. These objectives have been developed with consideration given to children, society, and the subject being learned. Meeting these objectives should contribute to the personal growth of children, to an increased and sustained interest in art, and to the improvement of society. Specifically, there are four objectives, all of which may be grouped under a single heading:

1 To help elementary school children develop enhanced visual perception.
   a To help children express ideas, attitudes, feelings, values, and imagination through art activities which contribute to their personal growth.
   b To help children see, discover, and understand visual relationships in the environment—natural and man-made.
   c To help children acquire an understanding of man's visual art heritage, and the roles of artists and designer-craftsmen.
   d To help children use intelligent judgments and discriminations in personal and community life.

FURTHER READINGS

Blake, Peter. *God's Own Junkyard*. New York: Holt, Rinehart and Winston, Inc., 1964.
    A pictorial critique of the nonaesthetic environment created by man. Contrasts are made between this and the aesthetic environment.

Conant, Howard. *Seminar on Elementary and Secondary School Education in the Visual Arts.* Cooperative Research Project No. V-003. New York: New York University Press, 1965.

Report of a symposium which provides impetus for an examination of existing art programs. See pp. 57–70, 148, 156–62.

Jefferson, Blanche. *Teaching Art to Children.* Boston: Allyn and Bacon, Inc., 1963.

Chapter 1 gives an evaluation of various methods used for teaching art in elementary schools.

Kaufman, Irving. *Art and Education in Contemporary Culture.* New York: The Macmillan Co., 1966.

Chapter 15, "Redirection in Art Education," presents the need for redirection in art education for elementary schools.

McFee, June King. *Preparation for Art.* Belmont, Calif.: Wadsworth Publishing Co., Inc., 1961.

Chapter 8, "Establishing Objectives for Art Activities," gives the sources from which objectives for art education programs may be drawn.

Miller, Richard I. (Ed.). *Perspectives on Educational Change.* New York: Appleton-Century-Crofts, 1967.

Chapter 1, "An Overview of Educational Change," presents the factors that foster and inhibit change, and the process of change in education.

Osborn, Robert C. "Art Gets the Tag End of Friday," *American Education.* Washington, D. C.: U. S. Office of Education, 1965. Pp. 5–8.

An impetus and plea for a new direction in art education.

2

Selecting Content for the Teaching of Art

To meet the main objective presented in this book, that of enhancing the visual perception of children, specific art programs should be designed. In planning these programs children, art, and art experiences should be kept in such a relationship that enhanced visual perception is the inevitable outcome. Before such a program can be planned, it is necessary to: (1) identify the body of knowledge of art, (2) select content from this knowledge for use in nursery and elementary schools, and (3) structure a framework for the content so that it can be taught.

IDENTIFYING THE BODY OF ART KNOWLEDGE

Because the body of art knowledge is so encompassing, it is important that clarification be made concerning the knowledge that is to be used in nursery and elementary schools. As defined here, this body of knowledge consists of four separate but related parts:

1 Knowledge of art elements.
2 Knowledge of production.

3   Knowledge of art vocabulary.
4   Knowledge of the works of artists and designer-craftsmen and the natural environment.

Art Elements

Visual art elements are the simplest components of art and constitute what may be considered the "visual language" of art. When the child experiences and learns to "read" this visual language, he can more easily respond with feeling and understanding to the world of art.

Production

The learnings which the child acquires from his use of art media and tools in creative activities give him a knowledge of production. Included in this knowledge are an understanding of media and techniques and a development of skills through experimentation and innovation with the visual art elements in problem-solving art activities.

Art Vocabulary

An art vocabulary includes words which explain tools, techniques, and processes used in creative activities, and words which are used in connection with works of art. Although there are aspects of art which cannot be expressed verbally, words can add meaning to art and can facilitate learning. As the child acquires an understanding of the vocabulary of art, he can express ideas and feelings about art more clearly, and can use words as tools for gaining deeper understandings.

Works of Artists and Designer-Craftsmen and the Natural Environment

Throughout history man has met the challenges of his culture and time and has enriched his environment through art. As a result, man has left a part of himself and his culture in the categories of painting, sculpture, architecture, textiles, ceramics, silversmithing, photography, commercial layout, industrial design, city planning, and landscape design. Acquiring knowledge in this area helps the child to develop a better understanding of man and his culture at various places and stages in history, and to become sensitive to works of art and to the people who produced them. The child can also become sensitively aware of the natural environment and can be prepared to make aesthetic contributions to this environment in the future.

SELECTING CONTENT

The body of knowledge of art includes more than can be mastered by anyone in a lifetime. Even dividing this knowledge into four parts does not give teachers enough guidance in selecting content. Greater specificity than this is needed if an appropriate balance is to be maintained in selecting from these four parts and if the relationship which exists among the parts is to receive attention. The questions of what to choose as content for children can never be completely and conclusively answered. However, it is possible to suggest a procedure for selecting content for art education.

Many educators have grappled with the problem of choosing content which can be handled by the child but which can also provide a foundation for future learnings. Again and again, educators have proposed that the content consist of the main ideas or major concepts of each subject taught in school. This approach, advocated by many today, is not a new one. Dewey [1] suggested that disciplines could be organized around their main ideas, and Charles Judd [2] believed that the main lines of thought could be organized for presentation to children. Jerome Bruner [3] is one of the more recent educators to suggest this, postulating that for every subject taught in school there is a basic structure made up of the key or fundamental ideas which are drawn from the knowledge of the subject. He further states that once these are identified, they can be presented in an intellectually honest way to any child at any age.[4]

[1] John Dewey, *Democracy and Education* (New York: The Macmillan Co., 1916).

[2] Charles Hubbard Judd, *Education and Social Progress* (New York: Harcourt, Brace & World, Inc., 1934).

[3] Jerome S. Bruner, *The Process of Education* (Cambridge, Mass.: Harvard University Press, 1960).

[4] *Ibid.,* p. 12.

Although identifying the fundamental ideas or major concepts in a subject is a difficult task, such an approach makes the education of the child more effective in a number of ways. First, it limits the scope or coverage of a subject so that it can be dealt with realistically in schools; concern about covering a certain part of knowledge is eliminated by allowing attention to be focused on the core of the subject. Second, by using major concepts as the content, it is possible to develop hierarchical learnings; that is, simplified forms of the concepts can be presented to the young child, with increasingly complex versions introduced as he becomes capable of handling them. Third, by concentrating on the major concepts, one may be more assured that economical and permanent learnings result. As the child forms these concepts, he develops a framework into which new learnings can be placed and is able to see relationships among learnings. Last, by using major concepts as the content it is possible for the child to build a foundation upon which future learnings may be based.

STRUCTURING A CONTENT FRAMEWORK

Identifying certain concepts as the content for use in elementary schools has been done for science, mathematics, and social studies; and what has been done in these subjects can be done in art. When these are identified, a framework of the content can be structured. Selecting as the main concepts for art certain elements which can then be used in developing a basic structure or framework for the content is extremely difficult. Few psychologists, educators, artists, or art historians can reach a consensus about this basic structure, and it is doubtful if any group could reach a consensus within itself. The reason is rather simple. A concept which may be simple to a child, such as "line," could mean—depending on the artist—shape, form, pattern, or texture. To the art historian it might mean a basis for a critical analysis of composition, abstractions, or techniques, and to the educator it could be equated with line in mathematics, a time line, or direction. These groups have failed to reach an agreement on "line" because each person and/or each group has a concept of line and a frame of reference which has been developed from personal experiences, either informal or directed.

In spite of the lack of agreement on a basic structure of art, or even on whether there *is* a basic structure, one finds such a structure being used. Curricula exist, sometimes rigidly so, in art schools, colleges, institutes, and even some high schools. Careful examination shows that these curricula are based on what each school considers to be a basic structure of experience and knowledge applicable to the attainment of its goals and objectives for the students. Since only a very small percentage of our young people will ever be involved in experiences leading toward the attainment of such knowledge, it would be feasible—even vital—to identify the basic structure for art which can be used on the elementary level.

FOUNDATION OF THE BASIC STRUCTURE

To make the whole thing easier, though possibly not less controversial, it would seem wise to start with the basis for all experiences and learnings in art—that is, with line and color. It has been said that art is the most universal of all languages and that this language is made up primarily of line and color, coupled with a developed technique. The authors have selected these two elements as the major art concepts and as the foundation for the basic structure with the recognition that one must begin somewhere. However, justification for using line and color can also be found in (1) the history of man and his art, and (2) the development of children.

The History of Man and His Art

Men in various cultures employed line and color in recording their first visual expressions. The graphics of primitive man were linear expressions which were enhanced by color. Man has used color for thousands of years, even though for a part of that time he did not know much about how color was perceived. However, the fact that color cannot be seen without light did not escape early man, for he lighted his caves with torches while he applied color to his linear representations. Early man seemed to have an emotional need for color, and this need led him to discoveries about color and its uses.

The Development of Children

A child is involved in kinesthetic movement from the moment of birth. This movement results in the child's first attempt at graphic expression, known as scribbling. Such an expression forms a meaningful beginning of a basic structure of learning in art for the child. Quite often the scribbles are enhanced by color. Just as the caveman had an emotional need for color so the child has this need, and it is expressed very early in his life. The very young child reacts to the color of a rattle or ball or other objects around him.

A BASIC STRUCTURE FOR ART

From the foundation of line and color described above, a basic structure for teaching art in nursery and elementary schools has been developed. [In this basic structure line and color have been identified as the major art concepts from which all other art concepts are derived. This basic structure, shown in Figure 3, is a framework of concepts which may be used as the content for teaching art to children.]

It should be noted that the terms used to label the concepts in the basic structure may be different from terms that other art educators use. For example, size and shape may be designated as dominance and space, and pattern referred to as rhythm. However, because of the relationships which exist between the basic structure and other curriculum areas and because of the procedures used in helping children with these concepts, the terms used in this basic structure are preferred by the authors. As a child progresses along the concept enrichment continuum, the more sophisticated terms (dominance, space, and rhythm) can be used.

CONCEPTS DERIVED FROM
THE MAJOR ART CONCEPTS

As can be seen in Figure 3, shape, size, texture, and solid form are derived from the major concept of line, as are other art concepts. Shape is derived from a closure of line, and sizes (big, little) are developed from different-sized shapes. A repetition of shapes leads to a repeat pattern, while different sizes lead into perspective, and from perspective into concepts of space. Thus, innovations with line develop other concepts used in art. All of these can be enhanced by the use of color and its related theories. The enrichment of the concepts of line and

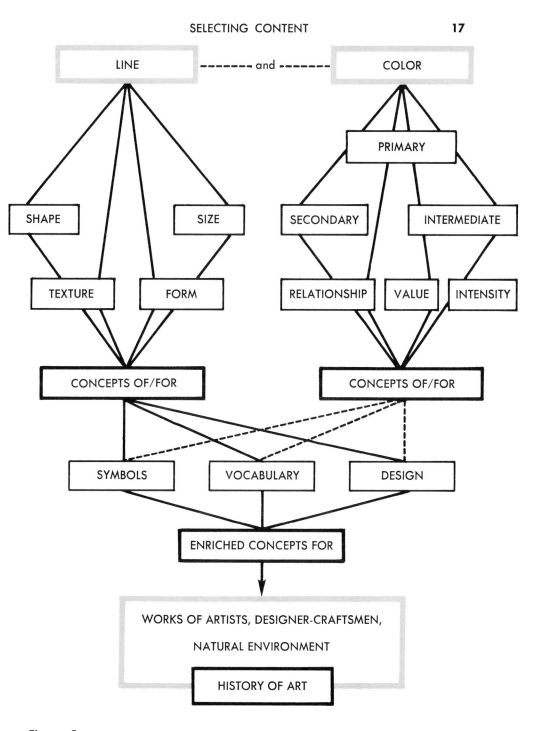

Figure 3
Basic Structure in Art for Nursery and Elementary Schools

color, and of the concepts emanating from them, can help the child enrich concepts of and for symbols and design. Symbols are the representations that the child uses for man, tree, dog, etc., while design is the organization of all components into a pleasing arrangement. As the child engages in activities which will help him enrich all these concepts, he will learn an art vocabulary. The enriched concepts that the child develops enable him to interact with works of artists and designer-craftsmen drawn from the history of art, and with the natural environment.

The art concepts formed by the young child may be very rudimentary ones, but as the child engages in learning experiences which are specifically planned to enrich the concepts that make up the basic structure, his conceptual framework is expanded. Because of his limited experience, the young child interacts with works of art in a rather simple way compared with adults; but as the art concepts are dealt with in a spiral fashion throughout the child's school experience, he becomes able to understand the more sophisticated innovations of the artist. Thus, the child at the intermediate level may be able to understand the innovations that the artist makes from line: linear textures, linear shapes, structural elements, motion, composition, and abstractions, which are enhanced by innovations with color: color theories, symbolism, transparency, and emotion.

The use of a basic structure is, admittedly, a cognitive approach to art education, but this approach does not rule out the creative or media approach. While the expressive intent of the child must be given attention, consideration should also be given to the expressive intent of artists and designer-craftsmen. For, just as the child is an innovator in the use of line, color, and other concepts, so the artist is an innovator. The innovations of artists have produced different modes of expression in objects which represent a part of man's cultural heritage and which encompass knowledge to be acquired by children. A cognitive approach which recognizes the importance of the creative aspects of art can help the child to become more aware of his own work and to make intelligent judgments and discriminations about the works of others.

THE NUCLEUS OF COMMONALITIES

Certain concepts in the basic structure for art can be said to form a nucleus of commonalities for other disciplines as well. At the early primary level, the visual perception and understanding of line, shape, size, and color are as basic to reading, mathematics, science, music, and social studies as they are to art. This nucleus of commonalities is a foundation upon which future learnings in various areas are based. Figure 4 shows this foundation and the relationships among various disciplines at the early primary level.

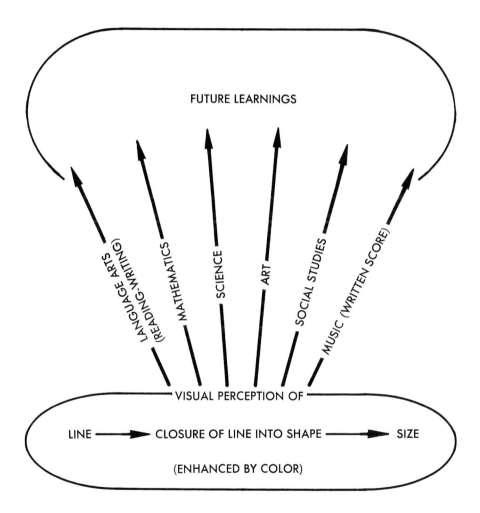

Figure 4
The Nucleus of Commonalities

Several examples of the use of the foundation can be found in materials developed for use with four and five year old children. In the approaches used in modern mathematics the child at the early primary level is confronted with lines, the closure of lines into shapes, sizes, and comparisons and discriminations of shape and size.[5] Another program [6] uses shape and color in helping young children develop a foundation for understanding mathematical concepts.

A current science series [7] not only gives the primary child learning experiences to help him understand seasonal changes, air, earth and sky, and living things, but also gives him his initial experience in the theory of light and color. The child learns about the complexities of color and about the way colors are developed from primary ones. Concepts of light and color developed and used in science can also be used for interacting with works of art from the Impressionist School. The use of such works is not foreign to the study of science or art at the primary level. Also in the area of science, the AAAS program [8] uses recognition and discrimination of color, shape, texture, and size to help children develop basic skills in science.

It can be further noted that at the early primary level the child is given experiences with size, shape, and color as a part of the foundation on which learning to read is based.[9]

The designation of a nucleus of commonalities is not an attempt to integrate all subjects taught in school, but is a way of showing that the child is developing similar concepts in different areas of the curriculum. Classroom teachers readily grasp this idea of the nucleus of commonalities because of their familiarity with programs in mathematics, reading, science, etc. These teachers understand the interrelationships between basic learnings in these disciplines. Special art teachers need to have this kind of working knowledge so that they too can see the relationships and can understand that concepts formed in one discipline can

---

[5] Ernest R. Duncan, *et al.*, *Modern School Mathematics: Structure and Use* (Boston: Houghton Mifflin Co., 1967).

[6] James S. Lucas and Evelyn Neufeld, *Developing Pre-Number Ideas* (New York: Holt, Rinehart and Winston, Inc., 1965).

[7] John Navarra and Joseph Zafforoni, *Today's Basic Science, Book One* (New York: Harper & Row, 1963).

[8] *Science—A Process Approach, Part One A* (American Association for the Advancement of Science, 1965).

[9] Ralph Scott, *Fun at the Pond* (New York: Harper & Row, 1966).

be used in others. All teachers need to understand that the basic procedures used to help children form and enrich concepts are similar. When teachers understand the nucleus of commonalities as a foundation for future learnings, they can make teaching and learning more efficient and effective.

FURTHER READINGS

Anderson, Donald M. *Elements of Design*. New York: Holt, Rinehart and Winston, Inc., 1961.
Identification of the visual elements in art and their use.

Bruner, Jerome S. *The Process of Education*. Cambridge, Mass.: Harvard University Press, 1960.
A proposal for selecting content for use in schools.

Duncan, Ernest R., *et al. Modern School Mathematics Structure and Use*. (K) Boston: Houghton Mifflin Co., 1967.

Hunt, J. McV. *Intelligence and Experience*. New York: The Ronald Press Co., 1961.
An analysis of studies which show the relationship between experience and intelligence. Evidence against the idea of predetermined intelligence.

Navarra, John, and Joseph Zafforoni. *Today's Basic Science 1*. New York: Harper & Row, 1963.

Pepper, Stephen C. *Principles of Art Appreciation*. New York: Harcourt, Brace & World, Inc., 1949.
Chapter 3, "The Principles of Design," Chapter 8, "Color," Chapter 9, "Line." Presentation of visual art elements.

Wilson, Robert C. *An Alphabet of Visual Experience*. Scranton, Pa.: International Textbook Co., 1956.
A visual presentation of all visual art elements.

3

The Formation and
Enrichment of
Art Concepts

*Let the main ideas which are introduced into a child's education be few
and important, and let them be thrown into every combination possible.
The child should make them his own, and should understand their application here and now in the circumstances of his actual life. From the very
beginning of his education, the child should experience the joy of discovery.
The discovery which he has to make is that general ideas give an understanding of that stream of events which pours through his life, which is
his life.*[1]

The basic structure for teaching art given in the preceding chapter
was designed to provide a logical and coherent source of content from
which learning experiences could be developed. Use of the basic structure provides an opportunity for efficient learning: the child acquires
a conceptual framework which can be built on in later years and which
will facilitate future learnings. The use of the basic structure also
enables teachers to make better use of their teaching time by giving a

---

[1] Alfred North Whitehead, *The Aims of Education and Other Essays* (New
York: The Macmillan Co., 1929), p. 3.

direction and purpose to art activities. However, efficient learning and effective teaching depend upon the ways that the concepts from the structure are presented to the child. If, for example, he is taught these concepts in a formal way and is required to memorize works of art, artists, or vocabulary, his responses will probably be on the verbal level only and he may develop only superficial understandings. If, however, he is motivated to explore and discover relationships and understandings, his aesthetic responses and behavior will more likely be on a higher level. To help the child reach a high level of intelligent empathic response, teaching procedures should make use of the basic structure in directed learning experiences based on the child's natural curiosity to learn and his own learning strategies. Such procedures are inherent in the process of enhancing visual perception.

The process of enhancing visual perception involves (1) concept formation, (2) concept enrichment, and (3) the development and use of a frame of reference. These are all interacting parts of the whole process and should not be regarded as discrete units. However, to show how each one interacts with the others, the parts will be discussed separately. And, in order that the objective of the process may be kept in mind throughout the following discussion, an explanation of enhanced visual perception will be given first.

ENHANCED VISUAL PERCEPTION

Simply stated, *enhanced visual perception means that one has the ability to see and feel more because one knows and understands more.* Excluding those who are visually handicapped, everyone has the ability to see, but what is seen depends, in part, upon what is known and understood. For example, educators are familiar with the need for understanding in the act of reading; although a child may be able to read words, they are meaningless to him unless he brings understanding to the word symbols. The same is true in art. It is possible to look at a painting or a piece of sculpture and to notice certain characteristics of it, but an intelligent empathic response is not likely to be made unless the viewer has had some experiences which enable him to interact with the sculpture. The aesthetic judgments and discriminations which a person should be capable of making result from an enhanced visual perception, which, in turn, is based on understanding. Aesthetic judgment and sensitivity depend, in part, on a cognitive approach to art.

CONCEPT FORMATION

The importance of concept formation has been increasingly affirmed by educators and scholars who recognize that the child's concepts or understandings determine the things he can study and learn about. Although researchers have investigated the process of concept formation, much remains to be learned. The results of research are not conclusive, and it is therefore difficult to describe the process, but certain characteristics are generally agreed upon to be applicable to the enhancement of visual perception.

The formation of art concepts begins in very early childhood. The young child is surrounded by a seemingly chaotic array of stimulating sensations, including sounds, textures, forms, colors, odors, and tastes. To deal with each would be impossible and unnecessary; very early in life the child begins to discriminate among all these sensations and pays attention only to those that have meaning for him. These discriminated sensations are percepts or sensory impressions to which a child has attached meaning, and are the result of direct, sensory contact with the environment. Concepts—the ideas or understandings that a child develops about things with which he has had experience and for which he has developed an awareness—are formed from his sensory impressions or percepts.

The art concepts formed by the child depend upon the experiences he has. As he touches the sides of the crib, his blanket, or his mother's skin, he perceives texture and begins to form concepts of texture: some surfaces are rough and some are smooth; some are hard and others are soft. Concepts of odor—some pleasant and others unpleasant—are formed as a result of olfactory sense impressions. As the child hears the sounds around him, he forms concepts of loud and soft, as well as concepts of the objects that make the sound. Light and color help him form many visual concepts: some objects are bright, others are dull, many are colored. Even before a child has words to describe them, he has formed many concepts related to the world of art. These serve as a link between the child and the environment and provide a basis from which he learns to cope with the world. As Harry Broudy [2] has

[2] Harry S. Broudy, B. Othanel Smith, and Joe R. Burnett, *Democracy and Excellence in American Secondary Education* (Chicago: Rand McNally and Co., 1964), pp. 130–31.

explained, concepts organize one's experience and thus determine how one sees the world; they serve the dual purpose of bringing the experience to the individual and of giving meaning to the experience.

The young child's art concepts are not the result of using one sense exclusively or one sense at a time; they are the result of multi-sensory experiences. The rattle, which most children in our society have as an early toy, will serve as an example. A child forms concepts of the rattle not only by touching it, but by tasting it, listening to it, looking at it, and even smelling it. And, although he may use one sense more often in some experiences, he learns to abstract what he has learned through one sense and to use it with another. Concepts of texture, for example, are formed as a result of a child's tactual experiences with his hands, fingers, and perhaps tongue. Such tactual experiences teach him that some objects are rough and others are smooth. Later he uses this concept visually; some objects look rough and others look smooth. Concepts of texture are formed tactually and are abstracted and used visually so that the child does not have to touch every surface to determine the textural qualities of the surface. This process of abstraction also takes place in other sensory experiences.

Multi-sensory Experiences

The kind of environment in which the young child grows and develops determines, in large measure, the kind of adult that child will become. Although there is still a great deal to learn about the best kind of environment for a young child, the research done to date indicates that the environment should include rich, stimulating experiences, materials to explore, encouragement for exploration, and guidance in learning. When these factors are present, there is a greater likelihood that the child will develop confidence in his ability, will enhance that ability, and will build a foundation for a lifetime pattern of living and learning. If there is little in the environment for the child to explore, the foundation of concept formation will be limited and he may not reach the potential that is within him. Millie Almy[3] has stressed the importance of stimulating experiences to help children advance from simple to complex levels of thinking. And J. McV. Hunt

[3] Millie Almy, "New Views on Intellectual Development: A Renaissance for Early Childhood Education," in *Intellectual Development: Another Look*, eds. A. Harry Passow and Robert L. Leeper (Washington, D.C.: Association for Supervision and Curriculum Development, 1964), pp. 12–26.

suggests that early experiences—the earlier the better—are the best safeguards against the retardation of children's ability to learn.[4]

The young child is surrounded by many toys and manipulative devices which can be used to help him develop concepts basic for changing aesthetic behavior. However, there is a tendency to remove these from him at an early age and to substitute the quieting devices of television and other forms of passive entertainment. There is also a tendency to surround the child with too many devices—blocks, plastic beads, stuffed animals—selected with little regard for their potential for helping him to learn. As Lois Barclay Murphy has pointed out, "The child may be overstimulated by too complex an environment, too many toys, too many attentions and distractions impinging on his senses."[5] The child in our society may have too much guidance so that his own explorations and discoveries are not needed, or too little guidance so that his experiences are not directed toward specific goals.

An understanding of what specific features of an environment will provide appropriate experiences for concept formation can be derived from two main sources: (1) research studies, and (2) observations of children.

Research studies. In surveying research, one finds studies which indicate the importance of early sensory stimulation and experiences for concept formation. Some of these studies come from research done with animals, such as those by Melzack and Scott[6] and Riesen,[7] and show the effects of early sensory deprivation on the behavior of animals. Others, for example the studies reported by Bugelski,[8] Hunt,[9] and

---

[4] J. McV. Hunt, "The Psychological Basis for Using Pre-School Enrichment as an Antidote for Cultural Deprivation," *Merrill-Palmer Quarterly of Behavior and Development,* 10:3 (1964), 209–48.

[5] Lois Barclay Murphy, *Feelings and Learning* (Washington, D.C.: Association for Childhood Education International, 1965), p. 27. Reprinted by permission of the Association.

[6] Ronald Melzack and T. H. Scott, "The Effects of Early Experience on the Response to Pain," *Journal of Comparative and Physiological Psychology,* 50 (1957), 155–61.

[7] Austin H. Riesen, "The Development of Visual Perception in Man and Chimpanzee," *Science,* 106 (1947), 107–08.

[8] B. R. Bugelski, *The Psychology of Learning* (New York: Henry Holt & Co., Inc., 1965).

[9] J. McV. Hunt, *Intelligence and Experience* (New York: The Ronald Press Co., 1961).

Figure 5

Hebb,[10] indicate that perception is learned behavior and that sensory deprivation interferes with learning. In addition, there are the data currently being collected to show what, if any, relationship exists between sensory deprivation and the disadvantaged child. Collectively, these studies point out the importance of early sensory stimulation and experiences for cognitive development. As David Russell has stated, sensations—awareness of environmental stimuli—are the "raw materials of thinking." [11]

Observations of children. Observing a young child will also shed light on the kinds of experiences which help him form concepts. When a child is born he enters a world of movement, or what might be called a kinesthetic world. Although the newborn child is helpless, he is not motionless and his first activities are ones of movement. These may be unorganized and uncontrolled, but they are signs of a child's reactions to his environment and the beginnings of his responses and adjustments to his world. The child's kinesthetic world does not consist only of self-initiated movements; much movement is provided by people around him. For example, it is a natural tendency for a mother to rock a child or to bounce him gently in her arms (Figure 5) because

[10] D. O. Hebb, "The Effects of Early Experience on Problem-solving at Maturity," *American Psychologist,* 2 (1947), 306–07.

[11] David H. Russell, *Children's Thinking* (Boston: Ginn and Co., 1956), p. 68.

of the soothing effect this has on him. These kinesthetic experiences of the infant become a part of his inactive knowledge to be drawn upon in later years.

Further observation shows that the child is doing more than moving; he is learning through his movements and through sensory exploration of the environment. Concrete experiences with actual objects afford the child an understanding of his world, a degree of mastery of it, and a foundation of learnings which he can abstract and use visually. The child in the crib explores his environment—the crib and the things that surround it. The child in Figure 6 is attracted by the mobile with its varying shapes, sizes, and colors. Objects that move and that can be explored constitute learning materials, even for the infant.

The child in Figure 7 is also attracted by parts of his environment. Although he probably cannot discriminate shapes, sizes, and textures, he is visually attracted to them, and·may be storing an awareness of them as a part of inactive knowledge.

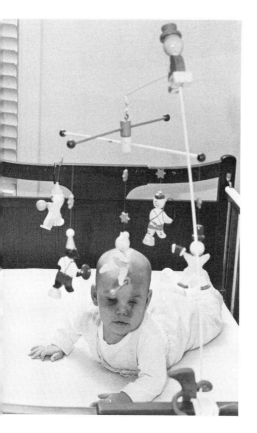

Figure 6
Six Month Old

Figure 7
Six Month Old

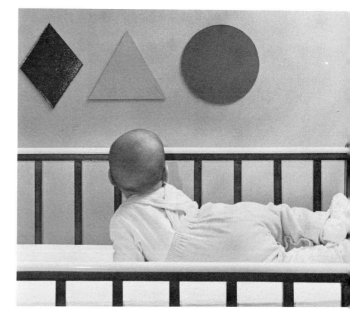

During the first year of life, the child makes tremendous progress. Random movements become better coordinated month after month until he is able to sit up alone, to crawl, and to stand. With each new activity and new movement, the child increases the possibilities for sensory exploration and learning and, when he learns to walk, is able to explore a wider range of his environment. He is full of curiosity and explores everything, going from one activity to another in fairly rapid succession.

Observations of the child as he develops reveal some of the materials which he explores and which serve as sources of learning for him. The sixteen month old child in Figure 8, active and curious, finds that water play is an enjoyable activity, as does the older child in Figure 9.

Figure 8
Sixteen Month Old

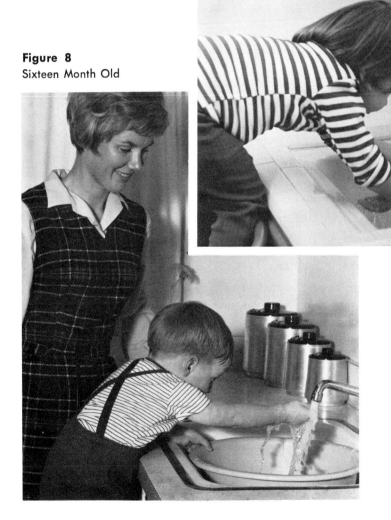

Figure 9
Two and a Half Year Old

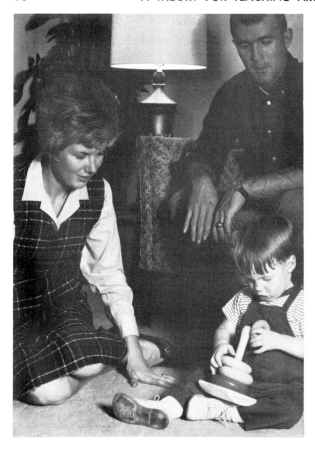

Figure 10
Sixteen Month Old

Play activities of this kind help children develop concepts about common features in the environment, such as texture and sound, and provide opportunities for kinesthetic responses.

Toys, such as blocks, textured squares, and pegs, are also a part of a stimulating environment for the child. As he manipulates the pegs, deciding which one must be used next, he is learning to discriminate sizes, shapes, and colors. The child in Figure 10 is learning many art concepts; although his understanding is simple, repeated exposures to objects of this kind will lead to more refined understanding. As blocks are manipulated and explored, there may be moments of intense concentration, such as that displayed by the child in Figure 11 as she decides which blocks belong together or what can be made from them. Tactual and visual discriminations are also being learned by the child in Figure 12 as he works with textured squares.

Figure 11
Two and a Half Year Old

Figure 12
Sixteen Month Old

Although the preceding illustrations show aspects of a prepared environment—an environment that has been created by thoughtful, conscientious parents—the young child also learns in the time he has to explore alone. A child learns, for example, that a brick wall is rough while a table top is smooth (Figures 13 and 14), and that some things smell pleasant (Figure 15).

Figure 14

Figure 13

Two and a Half Year Old

Figure 15

Figure 16
Sixteen Month Old

Figure 17
Two and a Half Year Old

The two and a half year old may accompany many of his activities with talk, for it is during this period that many children learn to communicate verbally. The ability to find out about the world through questions helps the child refine and enhance what he learns through his senses.

Many of the child's activities involve whole body responses; listening to music is one example. The child is an active listener, as shown in Figures 16 and 17, and the satisfaction of responding physically is coupled with the formation of concepts of loud and soft. As the child forms concepts of shape, size, color, texture, form, sounds, and odors, he also learns to apply these understandings to other, perhaps new, experiences. The child in Figure 18 is using many of the concepts he has formed earlier to solve a puzzle.

Figure 18
Sixteen Month Old

In all the experiences for concept formation just described, there has been a purpose. In one sense the purpose has been immediate—to involve the child in experiences designed to enable him to cope with the here-and-now world. In another sense the purpose is future-oriented; the experiences that the young child has will determine, in part, how he is prepared to cope with and apply what he has learned to different situations.

These learning experiences are examples of activities which help the child form concepts that are basic for learning experiences in art. The experiences that the child has before he enters school determine the background of concepts he takes with him, and, hence, may determine the success he has in school learning situations. As David Russell has stated:

> One agreement among all psychologists concerns the importance of concepts in the child's and adult's thinking. The clarity and completeness of a child's concepts are the best measure of his probable success in school learning because meaning is fundamental to such learning. The adult's concepts determine pretty well what he knows, what he believes, and thus in large part what he does.[12]

---

[12] Russell, *op. cit.*, p. 120.

As a child grows and develops, he needs fewer concrete, sensory experiences, although some of these are always needed. More abstract experiences serve for the further formation and enrichment of concepts. A child may read about persons and events or may experience events through hearing about them or watching them on television. Such activities provide him with other sources for forming and enriching art concepts. However, the effectiveness of these more abstract learnings depends upon the adequacy of the conceptual foundation which is formed in early childhood.

CONCEPT ENRICHMENT

Enlarging the Frame of Reference

The concepts formed by the child should not be regarded as fixed and final; they must be enriched so that the child will develop increasingly complex intellectual and aesthetic understandings and an enlarged frame of reference which can be used in interactions with the visual world. Enriching concepts can be accomplished by directed experiences designed to assist the child in this enrichment, such as those given in Part II. Not all children will need the same experiences, any more than all children need the same experiences in reading, mathematics, science, or social studies. Nor do all children need manipulative experiences at every grade level in school; media experiences, reading, and other common school experiences are used to help children enrich concepts, extend their frame of reference, and achieve enhanced visual perception. In all experiences, however, the enrichment of the concept is directed, eventually, toward works of art and environmental exemplars.

The frame of reference which is used in such interactions is an outcome of concept formation and enrichment. It is an assimilation of experiences—a synthesis of related concepts—which provides the child with a functional understanding of the concepts from the basic structure. The child's frame of reference determines the way he looks at works of art and nature, and the feelings and understandings he derives from them.

The enrichment of concepts, and the formation of concepts that have not been developed, may result from directed experiences, such as those recommended in Chapter 4. Pertinent to the present discussion, however, are the constants in concept formation and enrichment. One of these constants is the exemplar to which the child is exposed and which should become a part of his art environment. The other is the subject matter which the child uses in art activities.

Constants in Concept Formation and Enrichment

Exemplars.   Exemplars, the works of artists and designer-craftsmen that exemplify man's great contributions to our cultural heritage, are constants in a person's lifetime. For example, a Van Gogh painting or the reproduction of it remains constant, but the concepts the child forms and enriches, and the frame of reference developed from these concepts and used in interactions with the exemplar, will not be the same at the nursery school level and the intermediate level. As a result of various experiences, the child is forever interacting differently and, hopefully, on a higher level of aesthetic response. The work of art remains the same, but the child's experiences with it enrich his perceptions of it, and he is able to interact with the exemplar in a more sophisticated way and to show feelings and understandings.

Subject matter.   The subject matter which is used while the child is painting or engaged in other art media processes is also a constant in concept formation and enrichment. Technology increases the possibilities in subject matter, but once it is added to the environment, it becomes a constant. The concept of man illustrates how this constant is utilized by the child in concept enrichment. Very early in life the child forms a concept of man, and usually by the time he is three or four years old he has developed a symbol for man which he uses when he paints or draws. As a result of experiences which enrich this concept, the symbol changes. The subject matter—man—remains the same at all levels of development, but the child's experiences with the subject matter enrich his concept and this enrichment is reflected in the symbol. Figure 19 shows the constants in concept formation and enrichment through various stages of the child's development.

Figure 19

Constants in Concept Formation and Enrichment

Six year old

Seven year old

Eight year old

Nine year old

Ten year old

Eleven year old

Pablo Picasso, First Steps

Oil on canvas (1943, 51¼ × 38¾ inches)
(Yale University Art Gallery, Gift of Stephen Carlton Clark)

FURTHER READINGS

Allport, Floyd H. *Theories of Perception and the Concept of Structure.* New York: John Wiley & Sons, Inc., 1955.
Research and theories in the field of perception.

Armstrong, D. M. *Perception and the Physical World.* New York: The Humanities Press, 1961. Pp. 105–26.
The interrelationships of percepts and concepts.

Bloom, Benjamin. *Stability and Change in Human Characteristics.* New York: John Wiley & Sons, Inc., 1964.
The influence of rich experience on intellectual capacity and development.

Bruner, Jerome S. *The Process of Education.* Cambridge, Mass.: Harvard University Press, 1960.
The importance of structure in the learning process.

Hunt, J. McV. *Intelligence and Experience.* New York: The Ronald Press Co., 1961.
Effects of sensory stimulation on learning.

Kagan, Jerome, and Judith Lemkin. "Form, Color, and Size in Children's Conceptual Behavior," *Child Development*, 32 (March 1961), 25–28.

Phenix, Philip. "Key Concepts and the Crisis in Learning," *Teachers College Record* 58 (1956), 137–43.

Robison, Helen, and Bernard Spodek. *New Directions in the Kindergarten.* New York: Teachers College Press, Columbia University, 1965.
An analysis of new insights into children's learning potential which supports new content and procedures in kindergarten education.

Russell, David H. *Children's Thinking.* Boston: Ginn and Co., 1956.
Chapter 5, "Children's Concepts," Chapter 8, "Concept Formation."

Wann, Kenneth, *et al. Fostering Intellectual Development in Young Children.* New York: Teachers College Press, Columbia University, 1962.
Report of action research concerning the formation of concepts by young children. Emphasis on the importance of the intellectual development of young children.

4

Teaching Strategies
for Art Education

DIRECTED EXPERIENCES

When children enter nursery school or kindergarten they have already formed many concepts, and these are a foundation on which school learnings must be based. Upon this foundation of understandings and misunderstandings teachers must build the ability to read, to solve mathematical problems, to cope with society and contribute to it, and to develop aesthetic understandings. This is a large order for any teacher. Because of the innate differences in children, and more particularly because of the differences in children's experiences, there will be varying levels of conceptual development among groups of children and even within one child. Thus, the degree to which art concepts have been formed and enriched may not always be what the teacher desires or expects. Whatever the level of conceptual development, however, it constitutes the frame of reference into which new experiences and ideas are placed. The teacher's responsibility becomes one of selecting experiences that will raise the level of conceptualization.

In any subject taught in school, concept formation and enrichment depend upon directed experiences which are selected to achieve certain goals. Some subjects have developed a high degree of sophistication in structuring learning experiences to enable children to gain greater understandings as they progress through school. If the goal of enhancing the visual perception of children is accepted, it would seem that similar procedures are needed in the teaching of art. As Osborn suggests:

> We teach numerical skills, and verbal skills. Why not eye skills and hearing skills, touch skills, and skills of free and *full* physical motion? . . . And why not persist in teaching these skills year after year until children develop the capacity to see, to hear, to touch, until these capacities have, in fact, become so much a part of the sensibilities, thought and being of our young that they will remain with them through their entire lives and keenly affect their entire lives?[1]

To develop such seeing skills and more effective use of all the senses, and to enhance visual perception, directed experiences seem to be necessary. J. McV. Hunt suggests that experiences be guided and directed so that children may practice and develop their maturing abilities: "It is relatively clear that experience, defined as the organism's encounters with his environment, is continually building into the developing human organism a hierarchy of operations for processing information and for coping with circumstances."[2]

If experiences in art are selected and directed so that they contribute to an enhanced use of the visual sense, children should be able to continue to form and enrich concepts, enlarge their frames of reference, and become increasingly aware of and sensitive to the visual world. Directed experiences in art would provide a link between the world and abstract ways of representing it. Directed experiences in art do not mean formal, rigid activities in which all children are expected to learn certain principles. In commenting on the results of studies of children's experiences with varying qualities and varieties of artwork, Dale Harris stated:

> Together, these studies suggest that principles of aesthetic design do exist and can be detected readily by children, given some opportunity. It would seem, also, that the discussion of formal principles is unnecessary to learning discrimination though undoubtedly attention to such principles facilitates such learning.[3]

[1] Robert C. Osborn, "Art Gets the Tag End of Friday," *American Education* (Washington, D.C.: U. S. Office of Education, 1965), p. 6.

[2] J. McV. Hunt, *Intelligence and Experience* (New York: The Ronald Press Co., 1961), pp. 246–47.

[3] Dale Harris, "Aesthetic Awareness: A Psychologist's View," *Art Education*, 19:5 (May 1966), 22.

Multi-sensory Experiences for Young Children

Since young children have learned about their world through concrete sensory experiences, directed experiences for art should continue to capitalize on their natural inclination to explore the environment firsthand. As children manipulate cubes and balls of different sizes, shapes, and colors, they can discover concepts that are usable in art, mathematics, and science. But the manipulation cannot be without purpose or direction; teachers must know why certain experiences are being used and what their probable outcome will be.

The development of the use of the senses to enhance visual perception does not take place incidentally or accidentally. For example, nursery school and kindergarten children have probably already formed a concept of rough and smooth. Not all children will have the same concept, but they will have had tactual experiences which help them distinguish between objects that are rough and those that are smooth. Having children feel two textured squares, one extremely rough and the other smooth, would be an appropriate directed sensory experience for this level. Tactual experiences with these squares reinforce the existing concepts of rough and smooth; and since textural qualities are to be found in works of art, children develop a foundation of learnings which can be applied to this area. Children can then abstract from the tactual experience by visually locating objects in the room which have rough or smooth surfaces. Through this visual abstraction, they develop a frame of reference for locating rough and smooth qualities in an original painting, a reproduction, a piece of sculpture, or architecture.

In planning art programs, attention should be given to directed experiences of many kinds. It should not be assumed that desired learnings will occur without direction, or that one directed experience will accomplish the objective. The experience cited above, or similar ones, must be repeated in increasingly abstract and complex ways. After children have learned to discriminate between the extremes of rough and smooth, for example, they are ready to discriminate among degrees of roughness and smoothness. This again requires concrete experiences, followed by visual abstractions to be used in confrontations with works of artists and designer-craftsmen. The procedure described here for the tactile sense is basically the same for all sensory experiences. Elaborations of the procedure will be presented in a later section of this chapter.

Although it is important for young children to have multi-sensory learning experiences directed toward understanding works of art and nature, it is also important for them to have experiences which will enrich the symbols which they employ in their own artwork. Multi-sensory experiences are as usable for this objective as they are for others. Good teachers know that when children have the experience of rubbing their hands over the bark of a tree, the symbols which they employ for a tree will be ones which show the rough qualities of the bark.

Actually, such an experience not only helps children to develop enriched symbols, but also helps them develop frames of reference for a work of art, such as Van Gogh's *Pine Tree at Sunset*. A relationship between the knowledge of production and the knowledge of works of artists is established.

Directed Experiences for Older Children

Many of the experiences used with younger children can also be effective with older children. However, for children from about nine to twelve years of age, it is possible and desirable to use more sophisticated sensory and manipulative devices. Many of these can be derived from children's improved skills and abilities in the use of art media; as children improve their techniques and skills in the use of various media, their own art activities can be used as a source of directed learning experiences. And, since most children are capable of reading independently at these ages, learning experiences which draw directly on the knowledge to be gained from a study of artists and their works can be used.

Not all children, younger or older, will need the same experiences, but all will need directed learning experiences to insure the formation and enrichment of the art concepts found in the basic structure. Regardless of the age level or the background of experiences, teachers should structure learning experiences toward eventual interaction with the total environmental climate. The concepts and skills developed for reading are useless unless one reads; enriched concepts in art are useless unless these are directed toward the arts and nature.

ROLE OF THE MEDIA PROCESS

Many people believe that a child is hampered in his creative development if he learns about the basic structure of art. Evidence against this theory can be found in a comparison with other subjects. A child may be working with something as basic as magnetism in science, but the way he experiments, innovates, and learns about magnetism can encompass a form of creativity. A child who composes an original story uses words, which are basics, but through innovations and experimentations he produces a composition labeled "creative writing." Educators have long advocated Whitehead's "joy of discovery" theory and the use of creativity in acquiring knowledge. Good teachers know, however, that a child must be led into discoveries and encouraged in creativity, and that knowledge is not a drawback in this procedure. Using learnings drawn from the basic structure does not mean that a child will not innovate, discover, and create; rather, knowledge coupled with creativity will help him produce an enriched end-product in the creative process. For example, a child's discovery of color through a creative watercolor experience compels the good teacher to help him comprehend that he is applying color theory. This comprehension of color theory can then be used with a work of art and applied to appreciative skills.

At the other extreme are educators who would eliminate the media process completely and substitute a course in art history for elementary school children. This would seem to be a mistake. Samplings of art history may be given, but these should be used only for older children and even then should not replace creative activities. Well-planned, directed, and executed procedures for creative art activities contribute much to enriching concepts, enlarging the frame of reference, and directing this frame of reference toward comprehending and interacting sensitively with the work of others. As a child conducts experiments to develop a frame of reference for science, he learns the working process of adult scientists and should be better able to comprehend the processes and the end-product. Similarly, as a child works with art media he should learn the working processes of adult artists and comprehend the end-product with more understanding.

The enjoyment of art activities by children is something which should be maintained, but enjoyment is not enough. Enjoyment plus learning is the combination which should be sought. This combination can be attained if attention is given to helping children form and enrich art concepts.

THE CONCEPT–ENRICHMENT CONTINUUM

Art concepts are formed as a result of multi-sensory experiences, and are enriched through additional sensory and more abstract experiences. The enriched concepts enable children to develop extended frames of reference for viewing works of art. The continuous enrichment of art concepts leads to the continuous enhancement of visual perception (Figure 20).

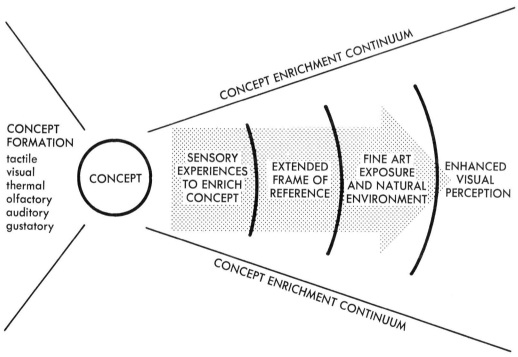

Figure 20
Concept Enrichment Continuum

Enhanced visual perception is learned, but the steps along the concept-enrichment continuum are not separate learning entities. Instead, as can be seen in the shaded part of Figure 21, the components are overlapping and interacting parts, all of which contribute to the enhancement of visual perception.

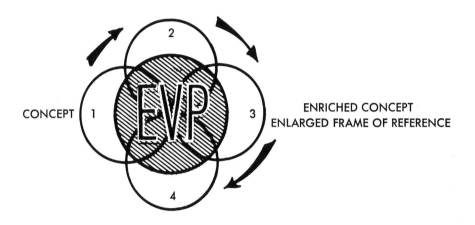

Figure 21
The Interaction of Parts into an Enhanced Visual Perception

EPISODIC AND SEQUENTIAL LEARNINGS

The formation and enrichment of art concepts may take place during informal encounters with the environment, and many of the understandings of children are the results of just such encounters. However, to insure what is learned, although we may never really be certain, experiences should be carefully planned so that children may be guided toward increasingly complex levels of conceptualization. The planning of such experiences involves: (1) the structuring of the experiences, or the *episodes* of learning, and (2) the arrangement of these episodes sequentially, from simple to complex.

Episodic Learnings

An episode is a learning experience which is introduced, experienced, and mastered. Each episode should be consistent with the over-all objective of enhancing visual perception, but each should have a specific objective of forming or enriching a particular art concept, such as, "To help children form or enrich their concept of color to include values and secondary color." The objective of each episode should be concise and realistically attainable by the children with whom the teacher is working.

Once the objective of a particular episode has been formulated, the teacher should make a careful and thoughtful selection of the materials and procedures to be used in helping children achieve it. The materials will, of course, vary in terms of the children with whom the teacher is working and their level of conceptual development. In many cases, the materials will include multi-sensory aids and/or art media, but in almost all cases the reproduction of a work of art, hereafter referred to as an *exemplar*, should be included.

The procedures for a given episode may be divided into two parts: those for motivation and instruction, and those to be used with the exemplar. The motivational activities are comparable to those for any subject: they elicit the depth of understanding and promote interest. For those episodes which consist, in whole or in part, of work with media, the motivational procedures presented in the following chapter will provide helpful guidelines. For other episodes, the motivational procedures will be ones consistent with the objectives.

Where exemplars are used, experiences with them must *follow* motivational activities. Exemplars should never be used before media processes. The child's problem-solving activities with media provide him with a frame of reference for responding to the exemplar.

Since an episode includes the mastery of the understanding to be developed, evaluation is an integral part of each episode. Evaluation actually begins before an episode is presented, for the effective teacher anticipates the reaction of the children to a particular experience and plans the lesson accordingly. Although it is possible to use formal evaluative techniques, much evaluation should be done informally throughout the episode. As the episode progresses, the teacher evaluates the on-going process so that variations in procedures may be developed. Evaluation should also be made at the completion of the lesson, possibly in the form of a written exercise, but more often in the form of discussions, observations, and talks with children. Children should be included in all phases of the evaluation so that they can learn to assess themselves and their products and contributions, the effectiveness of the lessons, and the contributions of others. Only by evaluation can the teacher and the children determine whether or not the purpose of the episode was accomplished, and the parts of it which were successful or unsuccessful. On the basis of all evaluation, suitable related activities can be designed to reinforce and extend understandings.

Evaluation should, of course, encompass more than the understandings to be developed in an episode; it should also consider aesthetic behavior. At the present time there is no effective measurement technique for aesthetic behavior since the aesthetic response, which is an integral part of this behavior, is highly personalized and not readily subject to refined ways of measurement. One cannot, for example, assess the enjoyment that a child gets from looking at a painting or a piece of sculpture. It is not always possible for the child to tell what is happening to him, nor does he always feel the need to tell this.

Although there are no precise measurements of aesthetic behavior, there are certain observable characteristics. Ones to which teachers should give attention are: (1) the degree to which the child becomes a "noticer" of his surroundings, (2) the degree to which the child is able to identify himself with the aesthetic, (3) the degree to which the child effects changes in his environment, (4) the degree to which the child's perceptions are heightened, (5) responses made in the classroom, and (6) the selections that the child makes as an art consumer and the responses he makes to his selections.

Series of episodes which are related to the accomplishment of the same or related objectives may be thought of as *episodic clusters*. Figure 22 depicts an episodic cluster with simple and complex episodes, all of which are related and all of which contribute to cognitive thinking in art. RT represents reflective thinking, a process important for learning in any area. In the teaching of art, personal interactions and emotional responses are encountered in the episode itself. These, plus the knowledge to be gained from the experience, indicate that children must have time to think, to mull over and digest what has happened as a result of the experience. Good teachers know this and allow for it. Perhaps, however, even more time should be devoted to this in school. The complexity of our society is such that even childen live on somewhat rigid schedules, and little time is allowed them to reflect on their

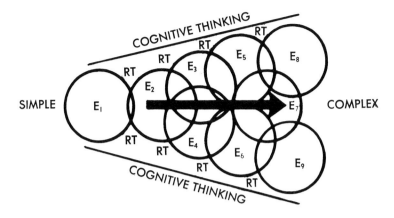

E_1 = Episode 1, E_2 = Episode 2, etc.
E_1 represents a simple learning episode; E_9 a complex learning episode
RT = Reflective Thinking

Figure 22
Episodic Cluster

experiences. It would seem, then, that an integral part of each episode and episodic cluster should be time—time for children to think during the episode and time to reflect on preceding ones before attempting to master the next.

Sequential Learnings

Episodes that are developed for art education should be arranged sequentially; that is, each should develop a basis for succeeding ones, creating a sequence from simple to complex in line with the complexity of the objectives and the psychology of growing minds. In developing sequential learnings, attention should be given to: (1) the level of conceptual development of the children, and (2) the episodes within an episodic cluster. In general, young children should be given rather simple episodes, with more complex learnings introduced as they progress through elementary school.

Sequential learnings are also found within episodic clusters. Each cluster is ordered from simple to complex, an order which shows the continuity and connection between the episodes. For example, an episodic cluster which includes the objectives of enriching concepts of line, closure of line into shape, shape into size, and repeated shapes into repeat patterns is one which moves from simple to complex. Just as episodes are developed sequentially to constitute a cluster, series of episodic clusters follow one another to constitute complex learnings. There must be continuity and connection within a cluster and between clusters or the learnings children acquire may be incomplete and fragmented. Children can master complex understandings if experiences are developed with regard to the necessary sequence.

The following outline gives each part of an episode. It has been found to be useful in preparing art learning experiences for children.

1 OBJECTIVE
   Concepts from the basic structure to be developed.

2 MATERIALS
   All materials, including the exemplars to be used in the episode.

3 VOCABULARY
   Terms appropriate and necessary to the episode which also contribute to the development of a knowledgeable art vocabulary.

4 INSTRUCTIONAL PROCEDURES
   a *Motivation:* Sensory and multi-sensory experiences; topic discussion. Procedures designed to give children experiences which will attain the objective and extend the frame of reference for the exemplar.
   b *Exemplar:* Frame of reference; use of exemplar. Procedures for introducing the exemplar and for giving children directed experiences with it. (The exemplar always follows the motivation.)

5 EXPECTED OUTCOME
   Judgments and discriminations to be developed as a result of the episode.

6 RELATED ACTIVITIES
   Visual exercises, books, poetry, films, records, activities related to other subjects, etc. Activities which reinforce and extend the understandings developed in the episode.

Every episode should be concerned with enriching concepts, enlarging frames of reference, and directing perceptions so that children can interact with intelligence and feeling to their visual world. Within each episode there should be a directed teaching procedure which helps children to learn and build on past learnings. Sometimes this directed procedure will include a quick review of a preceding episode to prepare children for the present one (Figure 23).

THE CONTINUUM OF ENHANCING VISUAL PERCEPTION

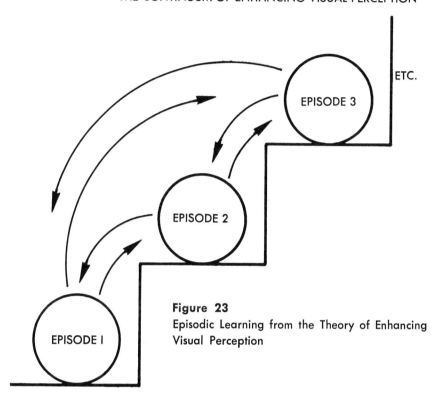

Figure 23
Episodic Learning from the Theory of Enhancing Visual Perception

FURTHER READINGS

Bruner, Jerome S. *The Process of Education.* Cambridge, Mass.: Harvard University Press, 1960.
  The importance of motivating for learning, and the readiness of children for learning at any age level.

Hunt, J. McV. *Intelligence and Experience.* New York: The Ronald Press Co., 1961.
  The importance of early learning experiences, and the need to govern encounters children have with the environment.

Standing, E. M. *The Montessori Method: A Revolution in Education.* Fresno, Calif.: The Academy Library Guild, 1962.
  Emphasis on a prepared environment for learning situations.

Wann, Kenneth, *et al. Fostering Intellectual Development in Young Children.* New York: Teachers College Press, Columbia University, 1962.
  The role of the teacher in guiding children toward the enrichment of concepts.

Children's Distinctive Characteristics and Art Expression

CHILDREN AND THEIR ART EXPRESSION

Before teachers can develop directed experiences to help children in the process of forming and enriching art concepts, they must understand the children with whom they will work.

It is particularly important that teachers understand children's art expression. A child's symbolic representation indicates his level of expression at the moment. Perhaps even more important, these art symbols give teachers a background for developing learning experiences to help children improve their knowledge of production through problem-solving activities. Understanding children and their art expression also provides teachers with a foundation for helping children see the relationship between their expressive intent and that of artists.

SIMILARITIES AND DIFFERENCES

It is generally acknowledged that children go through a sequential pattern of growth and development in art, just as they go through a sequential development in other areas. And, similarities will exist among children at any particular stage of this growth and development; in art, there will be similarities in the development of intellectual and aesthetic use of symbols. There will also be, of course, differences in the ways children go through sequential development. Identical levels of development in art expression will not be found in any specific age group or designated category; individual differences do occur, and these will be found in every classroom.

The differences in children's art expression are the results, in part, of inherent differences in children, but they are also the results of the kinds of experiences children have. These experiences determine what children perceive and the ways these perceptions are expressed. The self-expression of children with art media and the symbols they develop for this expression are visual evidence of their feelings, emotions, reactions, experiences, and attitudes. By understanding the sequential development in art, teachers can understand individual differences in expression and thus can help children achieve a higher level of expression.

THE CHILD'S KINESTHETIC WORLD AND HIS FIRST ART EXPRESSION

Toward the end of the child's second year of life, he begins his first art expression, an expression which is a kind of kinesthetic response to the environment. When the child is about two years old, he will make marks or scribbles on paper. These scribbles are a part of the child's kinesthetic experiences with his environment and are another evidence of his movements. At this period there is little if any motor control, and, as far as one can detect, no visual control. Figure 24 shows the child's first attempt at making marks on paper.

Figure 24
Two Year Old

Figure 25
Two Year Old

Figure 26
Three Year Old

The child of two or three makes great physical progress. Bodily activities are characteristic of the child at either of these ages, and he begins to show rather definite improvement in coordination. However, art activities such as cutting and pasting, which require good eye–hand coordination, will be difficult for the two and three year old.

As the two and three year old develops better physical coordination and improves his control over his movements, there is a noticeable change in his scribbling. The scribbling in Figure 25 shows evidence of some motor and visual control.

When a degree of motor and visual control has been reached, the child usually moves into a period of scribbling which seems to indicate his urge for variety, and he may, for a while, scribble in a circular fashion. Later he combines different types of scribbles which may, at least to the child, indicate his first attempt at representation. Although not always recognizable to the adult, these first attempts at representation are very real to the child, indicated by the fact that he later names them. Figure 26 has been entitled *My House* by a three year old. The transition from scribbles without motor or visual control to ones with control has parallels in the child's use of other art media. The child will first pound clay, then break it, and finally name it in the same way that he does with his scribbles.

When the child learns to talk, a significant event has occurred for both his intellectual development and his art expression. One way in which a child demonstrates his verbal fluency is in telling his parents about his scribbles and what they mean. The three or four year old will chatter endlessly about his work, and he should be encouraged to do this. Listening to a child talk about what he is doing is one of the most delightful experiences adults can have. This is also the time when the child is becoming wonderfully imaginative and expresses this in many ways; such expression should be encouraged. Imagination is important on any level, and although the child should not be confused more than he already is in distinguishing between reality and fantasy, his imaginative powers should not be destroyed, for it would rob us of a future architect, designer, composer, or writer, as well as an imaginative appreciator. The child needs experiences with other materials, such as the arranging of different tactile materials to make a collage (Figure 27). Selecting such materials gives the child a chance to use sensory exploration, to develop some powers of discrimination in the selection of different tactile materials for his own creative work, and to form a basis for enriching his own work and for understanding the work of others.

A child needs many opportunities to scribble, to do clay work, and to engage in other activities which capitalize on his movements and on his sensory exploration. He should have materials provided for just these purposes. He will scribble anyway, and it is far better to provide him with the materials for this—crayons and paper, paints, and finger paints—than to have him scribble on the walls.

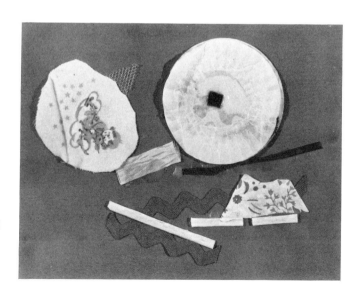

Figure 27
Four Year Old

THE EARLY PRIMARY CHILD

Between the ages of four and five, the child enters a period of slower growth but no less activity. The child begins to control and use his body more purposefully, and although he still does not have good eye–hand coordination, he is now able to cut, paste, and do more close work than he could at the preceding level. During this period the child knows more fully what he wants to do and has an idea of the activity before he starts. He wants to create something so that he can get a feeling of accomplishment, and the process of creating with art media is more important than the final product. This is a somewhat conforming age, although the child is still very much the individual. The sensory exploration of the environment continues, and the curious probing of the child shows that he wants to find out about everything. He explores, questions, and learns, and adults are often amazed at how much he does learn.

From the use of line in scribbling, the child moves naturally into geometric shapes and the use of representational symbols. He will use a series of geometric shapes which are of different sizes, and will use different shapes and sizes to symbolize man, house, tree, and animal. During this time the child will enhance these geometric shapes and sizes with color, although the color does not necessarily relate to the object. This has sometimes been called the "age of purple cows and pink elephants," for the child has not developed a color–object relationship: blue for sky, green or brown for ground. Figures 28 and 29 show the work of the five year old as he is forming his concept of geometric shapes, and it is at this time that the teacher can help him become conscious of size and shape.

Figure 28

Figure 29

Since the child at this time is primarily concerned with developing symbols from geometric shapes, he has not, as yet, formed a concept of order in space. Figure 30 shows the work of a five year old who is using geometric shapes to determine the symbol of his animal, barn, and fence, but who has not formed a concept of their arrangement in space. This is, of course, a progression from the use of abstract symbols alone, but when these shapes are isolated from the painting, they lose their meaning as representative symbols and become just geometric shapes again.

Figure 30

THE PRIMARY CHILD: ORDERLY
SYMBOL ARRANGEMENT

When the child is about six, physical growth is less rapid but the child continues to be physically active. He seems to involve his whole body in what he is doing, just as the younger child does. He likes to work with his hands and can do some things quite well, but eye–hand coordination is still difficult and precise movements may cause strain.

He does, however, cut, paste, and use simple tools with some skill. His eagerness to learn is best channeled into concrete situations so that he can have actual involvement and direct participation. At this age the child likes responsibility and is usually able to complete tasks if they are geared to his level.

Later in this period, when the child is about seven, one of his noticeable characteristics in art is that he likes to be first; he likes to get the best grade or paint the best picture because he is anxious to do well. He is sensitive to both adults and other children, a situation which may cause some conflict and confusion for him.

Still later, when the child is about eight, there is much improvement in eye–hand coordination and a better command of small muscles. During this period, the child sets standards for himself, and he needs many opportunities for success in meeting these standards. The child at this age is a collector, and although his collections are generally of all kinds of things, he begins to focus on planned ones. During the latter part of the primary level, he begins to relate himself to the past, the present, and the future. He becomes interested in things that happened a long time ago, although he will still be confused about the past. His expanding environment now includes other people and places, and he becomes very interested in them. There is evidence that the child is capable of self-evaluation, and that he realizes that some people do better than he does.

During the primary period, after the child has determined a representative symbol which meets his own standard, he often repeats the same symbol over and over. This is satisfying to him because he feels security and success with the symbol. However, teachers must be alert to prevent the symbol from becoming a stereotype. After the success of experiencing the symbol, the child seems to become conscious of order in space. Before this, he had neither the time nor the perceptual ability to arrange his objects on paper in what might be called an orderly or true-to-life fashion. As he becomes conscious of the gravitational experience of walking on something solid, he becomes conscious of the solid—the earth, the floor, the stairs—and indicates this by placing all his symbols on a line. Viktor Lowenfeld refers to this as the base-line concept and states that "the first origin of the base line is the kinesthetic experience of moving along a line." [1]

[1] Viktor Lowenfeld, *Creative and Mental Growth* (New York: The Macmillan Co., 1947), p. 46.

Figure 31
Five Year Old

Figure 32
Seven Year Old

Figure 31 shows the use of a base line by a five year old. Figure 32, which is by a seven year old, shows the child making a distinction between the base line and the water on which the boat moves.

At this level of development, the child has not yet discovered that there is a place where the sky meets the earth. This is not unusual when we consider that the child looks up to see the sky. He knows that the sky is up, for this is the way he perceives it. The same kind of perception can be seen in other features of child art: windows painted near the top of a house or a doorknob at the top of a door.

Along with the child's orderly arrangement of symbols in space are other innovations. If, for example, a child is asked to draw the top of the table, he solves the problem by simply lifting or elevating the top to let us know what is on it. Figure 33 illustrates this as well as the X-ray technique which the child uses to show both the inside and

Figure 33
Eight Year Old

Figure 34
Eight Year Old

outside of the house. Although the child is still using geometric shapes, he is now arranging them in a more interesting and orderly fashion and is an innate designer and composer. Figure 34 shows the innovations of a talented eight year old.

Quite often, a child will become so concerned with orderly arrangements of symbols that he will use several base lines, as illustrated in Figures 35 and 36. The base-line concepts shown are quite different, but they are both by eight year old children. Figure 36 shows another characteristic of child art at this level: a painting that would form a three-dimensional pattern if folded along the base line, but which is painted in a two-dimensional manner.

Figure 35
Eight Year Old

Figure 36
Eight Year Old

THE CHILD AT THE INTERMEDIATE LEVEL

At about the nine year old level, the child exhibits characteristics which show that he is capable of reasoning beyond the ability of younger children. The child wants and accepts responsibility and is dependable in carrying it out. He is willing to accept the criticism of others if he thinks that it is justified, but does not hesitate to stand up for his own point of view.

The influence of the group is very strong at this stage, and the child tends to follow the pattern of behavior established by his peer group. Critical of his own performance, he may be classified as a bit of a perfectionist. Since he relates to many other places and people, this is the time for hero worship and a desire to know more about his heroes. He is becoming more skillful with his hands and enjoys crafts and various media. Many of his ideas are original, and he takes pride in carrying them out.

Later, he becomes confused by conflicting standards. The child enters a period of disorganization which is a part of the pre-adolescent stage. During this time he may undergo critical emotional and physical changes, and needs helpful guidance for the use of energy and for developing self-confidence.

At this level, the child begins to analyze critically his own expression and to show in his expressions many discoveries about himself, his environment, and his society. This awareness of his culture tends to make a noticeable difference in his work, and he chooses subject matter that is related to human interests and activities, community and world events, and science and space explorations.

During this time the child moves the base line up to become a part of the horizon line. He also makes use of overlapping symbols as well as increased details on costuming and clothing. Figure 37 shows both of these developments in a nine year old child. One can also see that the child is no longer concerned with only geometric shapes, but now moves into the use of more realistic lines which tend to retain their meaning if they are isolated from the symbol. It can be seen that the child has become conscious of design and is using repeat pattern. Figures 38, 39, and 40 show the use of all-over pattern designed by the child at this level.

Figure 37
Nine Year Old

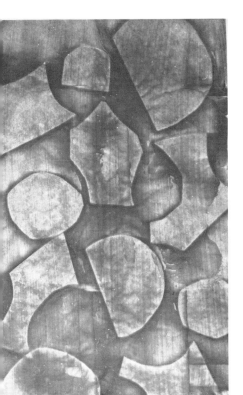

Figure 38
Nine Year Old

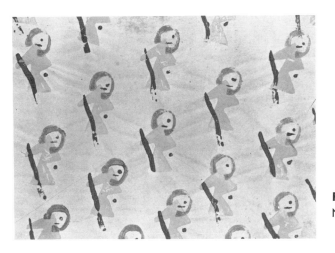

Figure 39
Nine Year Old

Figure 40
Ten Year Old

At this stage, the child is very critical of his own work; for this reason, various craft activities are used which will stand up under his own critical analysis. Figure 41 shows the use of paper scraps in a child's design; Figure 42 shows the use of various yarns with which the child has been able to design in an intellectual manner.

Figure 41
Ten Year Old

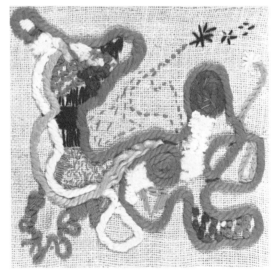

Figure 42
Eleven Year Old

Figure 43
Eleven Year Old

Figure 44
Ten Year Old

The ten or eleven year old also has an interest in animals and will innovate using lines, shapes, sizes, repeats, and overlapping symbols for them, as shown in Figures 43 and 44.

Individual differences in children's perceptions are easily observed in both their art expression and their behavior patterns. For example, some children become easily absorbed in details and demonstrate greater powers of concentration on details than others do. Other children are concerned less with details than with the over-all effect. One child acts as a spectator to his painting, while another seems to react as if he were in the center of the activity and not a spectator to the scene at all. Children perceive their world differently and express it differently.

Some children seem to be more interested in perspective, proper proportion, atmospheric conditions, and mixing colors; they approach their subject in an intellectual manner. The symbols employed are placed according to size, which constitutes for them perspective and a form of proportion. Figures 45 and 46 illustrate this representation of perception. Notice that the drawing and painting have been as if the child were a spectator to the scene.

Figure 45
Eleven Year Old

Figure 46
Twelve Year Old

Other children seem to be more interested in the activity, and are not necessarily interested in perspective or proper proportion. Such children frequently exaggerate the most important parts of their subject, and sometimes even revert to the use of base-line concepts. This is illustrated in Figure 47, which shows an interpretation of a bargain sale in which the child imagines himself to be in the center of activity. Notice, too, that the child has employed large, flat areas of color because he is not concerned with the use of broken color.

Figure 47
Eleven Year Old

This discussion does not imply that one form of perceptual expression is superior to the other. Children simply can and do express themselves in different ways. Children perceive differently, and what they paint or express is determined by what they perceive. This behavioral pattern—the way children approach and solve problems—can be noted in other subjects too.

The preceding illustrations provide some insight into children and their art expression. Such descriptions are useful, but are intended to serve mainly as an impetus for closer study of children's art. Prospective teachers should be exposed to many samples of children's art before they begin to teach, since this is the best way of comprehending children's art expression. When teachers understand the levels of development, guidance can be given to individual children so that they will be motivated to learn and to express their understandings.

THE MOTIVATIONAL PROCESS

Insightful teachers know that a child's symbolic expression is not fixed and final; it can be enriched and enhanced. Just as the natural development of the child is enhanced, so the art expression can be enhanced through motivational procedures. The level of achievement or the degree to which symbols are enriched will vary from child to child. Some children will have more enriched concepts, will acquire better skills with media, and will comprehend better the possibilities for media. However, opportunities for the enrichment of symbols should be provided to all children, whatever their level of development, and this enrichment should not be left to chance—any more than the nutrition of children is left to chance.

It was once thought that any interference with a child's expression in art activities would hamper creativity. Many teachers have accepted any form of expression or any symbol which the child used because it was the child's expression. However, the symbol that the child has developed for man, tree, house, or dog may be acceptable only for the moment. Only when the teacher knows that the child has enriched his symbol as much as he is capable of doing should the symbol be accepted. Figure 48 is an example of child art in which the symbols need to be enriched. The child has repeated the symbols for man and tree without variation, and has included little detail. In contrast to this is Figure 49, which shows an example of child art in which the symbol has been enriched. Since the symbol used by the child reflects

Figure 48
Seven Year Old

Figure 49
Seven Year Old

his concepts, symbol enrichment is a corollary of concept enrichment. Both require additional comprehension of art elements, art vocabulary, techniques, and manipulative skills which may be developed through motivational activities.

CREATING SITUATIONS FOR SYMBOL ENRICHMENT

A child is naturally curious and has a natural motivation to learn. The learnings acquired by the child before he enters school can be and are used in art activities, if the child is motivated to draw on this knowledge and to "trigger" it into active use. Art materials themselves may motivate the child in art activities, particularly if he has had no previous experience with them.

The newness of such encounters soon wears off, and other procedures must be used for the learning process if symbols are to be enriched. Teachers must learn to capitalize upon the child's curiosity and intrinsic motivation and direct these toward behavioral changes. Teachers must learn to create situations which will help the child draw on his reservoir of knowledge, learn new understandings, and, consequently, enrich his symbols.

MOTIVATION FOR SYMBOL
ENRICHMENT

In art education the motivational process brings forth concepts from the child's knowledge, makes them active, and enriches them so that they can be used in media activities and in interacting with works of art. Good motivation requires a lot of effort from a teacher. She must understand the child and have some information about his past experiences. She must also understand the procedures for making the knowledge of these past experiences active. For, just as the performing artist paints best that which he has experienced and knows, so the child paints best what he knows. The teacher can help the child to know more of what he has experienced by causing the concepts in his inactive knowledge to become active, and can help him enrich these concepts by providing additional experiences and knowledge. Finally, to direct this process toward changes in aesthetic behavior, the motivational process must include knowledge of the basic structure of art education. Without this, the motivational activities and stimulation may result in creative art activities which produce exciting art expression from a child but which do not necessarily enhance visual perception.

For the beginning teacher it seems pertinent to interject a word of caution. Since a child paints or draws best what he knows, he cannot be expected to paint or draw subject matter with which he has not had experiences. If a child has never seen, read about, or been shown pictures of palm trees or windmills, he will have a very meager store of knowledge to draw on for expression with art media. Meaningful expression is that which comes from the child's own experiences. However, the symbols used can be enriched by sound motivational activities.

For example, an object as simple as a tree can be used for enriching a symbol. Almost every child has a concept of a tree. The teacher can help each child enrich this concept by using the topic motivation "Tree," and by directing attention to differences in trees: height, width, color, shape, and environment. Tactile sensory experiences can also be employed to develop ideas about the textural qualities of trees. In this process the teacher helps the child gain a knowledge of art elements —line, texture, size, shape, form, and color, an art vocabulary, and an awareness of the environment. The result of the symbol-and-concept enrichment is seen in the child's art products. Motivational activities for media not only help the child enrich his symbols, but extend his frame of reference for exemplar, such as Van Gogh's *Pine Trees at Sunset.* Tree, of course, is only one of the symbols used by a child; many others could be cited, but the motivational process would be the same.

Guidelines for Motivation

No two teachers ever motivate in the same way; the ability to do this well seems to be a part of the inner spirit which enables one teacher to stand out among others. The technique of motivating children for creative experiences cannot be learned from reading or from a lecture, but there are guidelines which help teachers avoid common pitfalls.

GUIDELINES FOR
MEDIA PROCESS EPISODES

I. Objective

An art lesson should not be presented to children unless it is directed toward a specific objective. The objective should encompass knowledge, experiences, and concept enrichment which lead toward an extended frame of reference for a work of art. A specific objective should be in keeping with the level at which children are working and/or the level for which they are ready. This means that the objective should encompass episodes of learning and contribute to sequential episodic clusters.

II. Materials

The teacher should determine what materials are needed and have these in front of the children before they receive a topic motivation. A teacher may motivate well, but may lose what has been accomplished if children have to assemble materials after the topic motivation has been given. The selection of the materials is determined by the objective.

Before expecting children to work with art media, the teacher should be familiar with them herself. By working with media, a teacher can become aware of their possibilities and limitations, and some of the problems encountered with them, and can understand more fully problems that children might encounter. Such experiences for prospective teachers should be provided in an art education course.

III. Motivation

Depending upon the lesson and the material, experimentation or demonstration procedures are needed. If the materials are new to children, they should be given opportunities to discover what they can do with them. Children can be led into such discoveries by a demonstration in the use of the materials, by a discussion, or by a combination of both. The most successful procedures are those which combine techniques. For example, for nine year old children it may be advisable to demonstrate how watercolor can be controlled and to explain the limitations of the media.

When presenting the topic it is advisable to pinpoint it. Often teachers use a topic which is too broad in scope. "Springtime," for example, may trigger the knowledge of trees, wind, green, flowers, kite, rain, smells, buds, and baseball. Such a topic may only confuse children. It is often more successful to select one activity from this topic: "Flying a Kite," "Walking in the Rain," or "Walking in the Wind."

In presenting the topic the best procedure to use is the question-and-answer discussion. The questions should be leading ones so that children may draw from experiences.

IV. Reinforcement

Once the topic has been discussed and the children have been stimulated to work, the teacher will need to walk around the classroom and reinforce the topic for those children who need it. Sometimes this second motivation will need to be followed by a third and fourth. If the teacher cannot determine this need readily, the children will make it known through their symbols.

V. Teacher Evaluation

The end-products which children produce should enable the teacher to determine just where the majority of the children are, and what experiences (including sensory experiences) will help individuals in the class enrich their symbols. For example, in the primary grades children may make the arms of a person come out from the waist. A follow-up topic might well be "Throwing a Ball." The activity and discussion involved in such a topic help the children see that their arms come out of the shoulder socket and not the waist. This is no different from teaching life drawing on the college level, but it is approached on a level which children can comprehend. Evaluation of this kind is not the same as correcting the errors of children's drawings. It is simply an evaluative procedure which lets the teacher know what to do next and to determine whether or not perceptual learnings have taken place. These guidelines are related to topic motivations dealing primarily with painting and drawing when used as a part of picture making. In other areas, such as design, the procedures are more formalized and do not encompass a topic as such.

OBJECTIVE EVALUATION

To evaluate art products objectively in terms of each individual, three evaluative criteria should be considered: (1) the child's level of development, (2) the organization of visual elements, and (3) technique. The interaction of these in child art is fairly obvious. For example, the intermediate level child paints and organizes visual elements differently from the way he did in kindergarten because of his development, his increased understanding of art elements, and his improved technique. Consideration of these three criteria should assist the teacher in helping each child enrich his symbols and gain deeper satisfaction from art activities.

Although the child's work with media should be a creative experience that is satisfying to him, he should not be encouraged to be satisfied with mediocre results. A teacher may unknowingly encourage this when she praises, indiscriminately, every art product of the child, even when both the child and the teacher know that better work can be done. The lavish use of adjectives for all the child's artwork leaves few words to describe those products which meet the child's and the teacher's standards in terms of the objective evaluative criteria.

The knowledge of production gained by children in working with art media provides them with countless ways of expressing themselves. Year after year, as they have experiences with media, they should develop deeper understandings of the many possible uses of media, the problems encountered in the use of media, and the role of art as visual communication. The knowledge that children acquire through creative art activities is, therefore, an important source of understandings which can be applied to their own art products and to the work of artists and designer-craftsmen.

FURTHER READINGS

Eisner, Elliot W., and David W. Ecker. *Readings in Art Education*. Waltham, Mass.: Blaisdell Publishing Co., 1966. Pp. 171–75.
"Developmental Stages in Children's Drawings."

Eng, Helga. *The Psychology of Child and Youth Drawing*. New York: The Humanities Press, 1957.
A study of a single child's sequential drawing from age 9 to 24.

Lark-Horovitz, Betty, *et al*. *Understanding Children's Art for Better Teaching*. Columbus, Ohio: Charles E. Merrill Books, Inc., 1967.
Chapter 4, "Some Characteristics of Art Development."

Lowenfeld, Viktor. *Creative and Mental Growth*. New York: The Macmillan Co., 1957.
Chapters 3–7. Characteristics of children at various stages of development and their art expression.

McVitty, Lawrence. "An Experimental Study on Various Methods in Art Motivations at the Fifth-Grade Level." Unpublished doctoral dissertation, Pennsylvania State University, 1954.
A study of various ways to motivate children in art activities.

Maslow, A. H. "Creativity in Self-actualizing People," *Journal of Aesthetics and Art Criticism,* 19 (Fall 1960), 90.

6

Selecting
Exemplars

SOURCES OF EXEMPLARS

To direct the understandings that children acquire through work with art media and other activities toward intelligent, empathic interactions with the works of artists and designer-craftsmen, one must deal with the question of what exemplars to use in directed learning experiences. The use of exemplars is a very important part of the art program described in this text, and great care should be given to their selection so that they will be consistent with what children can and should learn at different levels. The selection should not be the responsibility of any one person, whether it is the classroom teacher or the art supervisor, since personal preference could become the chief criterion by which selections are made. Everyone has personal preferences in art, but using preference as the criterion could lead to emphasis on certain schools of art to the exclusion of others, thus limiting the experiences that children have.

In his cultural heritage there are numerous outstanding representations of man's artistic reaction to life—his problems, joys, fulfillments and frustrations, strife, social unrest, and aspirations. These representatives are not just products of the past; the experimentations and innovations in media, architecture, and industrial design of the present are also included. The number of works of art available for use in schools is overwhelming; it is from these that a limited number must be selected.

The magnitude of the problem of selecting works of art can be lessened if the sources from which they are to be drawn are delimited. Over the years repositories for some of man's greatest achievements in art have been developed in the form of museums and galleries. Because reproductions of works of art are easily obtained from these institutions, museums and galleries are a valuable source from which exemplars can be chosen. More important, however, these works of art represent the greatest among the total possibilities in art: they are, truly, exemplars of artistic achievements.

Not all works of art can be found in museums. Many are a part of the environmental climate, i.e., architecture, city planning, architectural sculpture, works of designer-craftsmen. Selection of exemplars must also be made from these sources so that children's experiences are not limited to those from museum collections.

THOSE WHO SELECT
EXEMPLARS

Museum Directors and Curators

Those who make acquisitions for permanent collections and who are responsible for preserving our art heritage are the directors or curators of museums and galleries. These people have attained their position because of their training and experience. Their study of the accumulation of knowledge of art and/or their experience in a specific area has given them the background for making judgments about works of art and for deciding which should be preserved and made available to all. Museum directors and curators constitute a referent group which has provided an available source of exemplars to be used in art education.

Few acquisitions for museums and galleries are made by one person; very often panels of authorities participate in making decisions. Those who make selections do not always agree, but it is often easier for panels of persons who have had comparable experience and training to reach a consensus about a work of art than it is for less knowledgeable people. Thus, when selections are made, they are likely to be exemplars which may be considered great.

Although the best of man's cultural heritage is often found in museums and galleries, many exemplars are found only in private collections that are not accessible to the public. Reproductions of these works are, of course, often available. The directors and curators can provide guidance concerning such exemplars, whether reproductions are being sought or acquisitions are being made for permanent museum collections.

Other Referent Groups

There are other knowledgeable people who use aesthetic judgments about architecture, sculpture, and the products of designer-craftsmen, and who decide what will be built or what will be exhibited. It is sometimes difficult for people to understand the choices that are made, but selections made by these referent groups are an indication of the future. The judgments made by them provide other sources of exemplars which are future-oriented and which will help prepare children for adult life.

Art Educators

Delimiting the sources for exemplars is helpful, but it still leaves a large number from which selections must be made for classroom use. Museum curators and directors and other referent groups are most interested in having an informed population and are willing to help in this selection, but they can provide only the large group from which individual selections for each school and each classroom must be made. For such individual selections assistance should be sought from those who know children and their needs, behavior, and reactions in school situations. Art educators can furnish this help, for they should be the ones best prepared and equipped to determine which among the available exemplars suit the needs and abilities of children at various stages of development and learning.

Before discussing selections from museums and other sources, two rather popular misconceptions should be clarified. These involve first the role of popular art, and second children's preferences in art.

POPULAR MISCONCEPTIONS

Popular Art

Popular art, or popular choices in art, consists of two main categories: works which appeal to many people and enjoy mass consumption, and works which appeal to the self-appointed elite. Representatives in both categories have one thing in common—they are usually the creative products of either recent or contemporary artists and designer-craftsmen who have utilized the visual art elements. In other respects, however, there are vast differences.

Popular art which appears to the majority is highly enjoyed, and one cannot deny that a form of appreciation or interaction exists since this art stimulates the senses through recall, familiarity, and experience association, and allows the viewer brief moments of escape. Popular art enjoys a place with the public comparable to that of popular music. As with music, its frequent exposure and availability account for a part of its popularity. Volume production permits the sale of reproductions at prices which can be afforded by many, so we often find examples in homes, offices, banks, and other places. Works which appeal to the majority of the people are frequently felt to be poor art. However, popular art has its own degrees of excellence, and there is evidence that the standard is rising.

The second category of popular art is one which gains importance daily in an affluent society as people increasingly seek more and different kinds of status symbols. The art encompassed in this category includes the work of relatively unknown artists and the lesser works of well-known and established people. The popularity of this art is a direct result of the equating of culture with affluency: the purchase of a Picasso print is not necessarily the result of a recognition of the aesthetic quality or the ability to interact aesthetically, but may be only a demonstration of a person's ability to afford the work.

There is a great deal to be learned from the purchase of both kinds of popular art. Man seems to have a psychological need to surround himself with pictures and other decorative objects, which may range from original prints, paintings, and reproductions to dime-store imitations of original ceramics. The increasing number of works of art available to all means that children are surrounded daily by one or both categories of popular art. It is questionable whether this situation should be duplicated in the classroom.   The learning environment and learning experiences in the classroom need not be, and often should not be, a replication of those outside the classroom.   In fact, in most cases, school time should be used for experiences that children will not get in other situations.

Children's Art Preferences

During the past fifty years educators and psychologists have conducted research and have accumulated substantial data on the art preferences of children.   For the most part these studies have used a variety of procedures but have been limited mainly to the subject-matter preferences in painting of children at various grade levels.   The findings of almost all these studies may be summarized as follows:

1   Children's preferences for pictures are largely determined by subject matter.
2   In general, children prefer pictures of familiar things to things that are unfamiliar.
3   Children prefer portraits of their own sex to those of the opposite sex, and portraits of children to those of adults.
4   Children's choices seem to be guided by the type of pictorial pattern they have tried and understood in their own work.
5   Children largely prefer traditional to modern painting.
6   Young children prefer simple pictures.
7   Children become increasingly aware of art qualities and pictorial detail as they become older.   Their choices become increasingly consistent with adult standards.
8   Any sex difference in preference for pictures stabilizes as children grow older.
9   Color preferences change from elementary to subdued colors as children grow in maturity.

While many of these studies are good examples of empirical research, a critical analysis reveals that they provide little sophisticated information about aesthetic response.   For the most part, the studies were concerned with children's spontaneous reactions based upon uncultivated taste and not upon knowledge, experience, or enhanced perception.   There is little indication given of the capacity of children to develop discriminating aesthetic judgments.   In addition, none of the studies was concerned with *why* children responded as they did. These studies simply let us know that children do respond, even when they are forced to respond to something which is foreign to them, something for which they have not developed a frame of reference.

Two of the studies of children's art preference dealt with instruction designed to develop some frame of reference.[1,2] The data from these suggest that a significant increase in the ability to analyze the aesthetic organization of a picture occurs after the children are instructed in the principles of art or after they have had a person knowledgeable in the area speak to them.

Clarification of the widespread misconception about the role of popular art and children's art preferences provides a further delimitation of the selection of exemplars for classroom use. It does not, however, provide a positive approach for determining the exemplars to be used with children. A positive approach can be found when one considers: (1) children's interest and level of art development, (2) exemplars which complement the total curriculum, and (3) exemplars which represent a visual history of art.

SELECTING EXEMPLARS FOR CLASSROOM USE

Children's Interest and Development Level

Children's interest and level of development in art expression can help in determining those exemplars to be used in classrooms. Although research into children's art preferences offers little help in understanding the way aesthetic behavior is developed, it does provide a clue for selections since it shows the relationship between the selections children make and their own natural and creative art expression. It tells us that children's choices seem to be guided by the type of pictorial pattern they have tried and understood in their own work.

A child can best comprehend works of the artist whose structure is analogous to his own because both have been confronted with solving

---

[1] Mildred Voss, "A Study of Conditions Affecting the Functioning of Art Appreciation Processes at the Child Level," *Psychological Monographs*, No. 48 (1936), pp. 1–40.

[2] D. P. Ausubel *et al.*, "Prestige Suggestions in Children's Art Preferences," *Journal of Genetic Psychology* (1956), pp. 83–96.

problems using the visual art elements. For this reason the child can identify with the works of the artist. Although the expressive intent of the child and that of the artist differ in level of sophistication, they should not be isolated from one another; and with a careful, sensitive selection of exemplars they need not be. Determining a child's level of art expression and then basing selection upon works which are analogous to the child's level can provide exemplars which will be understood by him and with which he can interact. Experiences with the exemplars can also help the child enrich his own symbols in creative activities.

An analysis of child art provides numerous analogies between the work of the child and that of the adult artist. Space does not permit a discussion of the many that are available, but several simple, direct, and obvious ones can be found in the following examples.

1   The child at one stage of his development copes with the problem of showing time sequence, just as the artist does (Figures 50 and 51).

Figure 50
Ten Year Old

Figure 51
Marcel Duchamp, *Nude Descending a Staircase,* Number 2, 1912

Figure 52
Ten Year Old

Figure 53
Ernest Lawson, *Sea Coast, Cape Cod,* 1915

Oil on canvas, 25⅛ × 30¼ inches

2 The child at one level of development solves problems in perspective which create space. So does the artist (Figures 52 and 53).

3 The child's early symbols are composed of geometric forms and shapes. The artist also innovates with geometric forms and shapes in creating symbols (Figures 54 and 55).

Figure 54
Five Year Old

Figure 55
Robert Motherwell, *The Voyage,* 1949

Oil and tempera on paper mounted on composition board, 48 × 94 inches

4   The child and the artist are often interested in creating new effects with art media (Figures 56 and 57).

Figure 56
Nine Year Old

Figure 57
Jackson Pollock, *Autumn Rhythm,* 1950

Oil on canvas, 105 × 207 inches

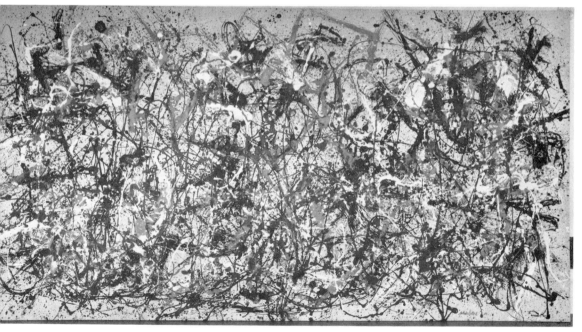

5   The child and the artist are often interested in depicting the atmosphere and feelings of seascapes (Figures 58 and 59).

Figure 58
Eleven Year Old

Figure 59
William Glackens,
Mahone Bay, 1911

Oil on canvas,
26¼ × 31⅛ inches

6   The child creates depth with paint without using subject matter. The artist has also been interested in such innovations (Figures 60 and 61).

Figure 60
Five Year Old

Figure 61
James Brooks, *Rasalus,* 1959

Oil on canvas, 66 × 79¾ inches

7 The child and the artist are often interested in portraiture, texture, and pattern (Figures 62 and 63).

Figure 62
en Year Old

Figure 63
Jan Vermeer, *The Girl with a Red Hat*

Oil on canvas, 9⅛ × 7⅛ feet

Comparisons can be made between what the professional has done and what the child is doing and learning, and these analogies can provide a source of criteria to be used in selecting exemplars which will assure us of making selections that are within the realm of children's interest and comprehension. This means, however, that more must be done than questioning a child or having him decide between this painting and that one; it means that careful observations of the child as he engages in creative art activities, and careful evaluations of his use of the visual art elements in his finished products, must be made.

There are other factors, in addition to children's interest and level of art development, which should be considered. The most important of these is the number of exemplars available and suitable for use at a particular level. Many different but related exemplars may serve the same purpose, but if the child has a frame of reference for one well-selected exemplar, he will be able to use this when he is confronted with others. A limited number of exemplars, consistent with what a child needs and can handle, is better than several hundred, since the frame of reference developed for the few can be used and expanded with other exemplars.

Children are interested in more than painting; they are interested in the products of other artists and designer-craftsmen. When children are involved in creating and solving problems in three-dimensional design, they can develop a frame of reference for interacting with exemplars of works of designer-craftsmen.

Complementing the Total Curriculum

Children seldom, if ever, should experience and learn about one subject in complete isolation from the others. Far too often, however, art has been taught as if it had no relationship to any other part of the curriculum. Even within the area of art, certain aspects have been treated apart from the others; exemplars, when used, have often been presented as something distinctly different from the media processes that children use. The preceding discussion has indicated some ways of overcoming this.

It is also possible to select exemplars which complement and contribute to the total curriculum, thus providing increased opportunities for learnings in art and in the other areas. With so many exemplars to choose from, it is regrettable that more reproductions are not included in textbooks to replace or supplement the commercial illustrations used so frequently. In social studies texts, for example, reproductions could really contribute to a child's understanding of his cultural heritage. Since reproductions are not often included in textbooks, however, the exemplars which are selected for art education should, whenever possible, contribute to and complement the other subjects, especially social studies, science, language arts, creative movement, and music.

It is not difficult to find such exemplars. Science is the study of man and his environment, yet reference is seldom made to those works of art which depict seasonal changes, the universe, plant life, or animal life. Social studies, with its emphasis on man's interactions with his environment, offers many possibilities for the use of exemplars: artistic contributions of other cultures, portraits of great men and women of the past and present, and artifacts which show the development of many objects used by man today. Language arts also provide rich opportunities: comparisons can be made between elements that are common both to poetry and to the visual arts, showing what each does that the other cannot. Not only should the exemplars used complement the topics studied in the other areas, but they should be selected and used to reinforce the nucleus of commonalities. Integration of this nature requires a skillful and sensitive teacher, for no one subject should be allowed to dominate the other. Integration presents another way for the child to extend his frame of reference for the exemplar: he sees the exemplar placed in relationship to man's natural and cultural development.

A Visual History of Art

In selecting exemplars, consideration should also be given to the history of art. Exemplars representative of different periods in art, from primitive man to contemporary times, should be included. Art historians and companies that sell reproductions can assist in making such selections. By the time children leave elementary school, they should have some concept of the history of art as it represents part of man's cultural heritage.

QUANTITY AND QUALITY OF EXEMPLARS

The number of exemplars that can be used depends, in large part, upon the amount of time spent in art education. As a rule, children are in school thirty-six weeks a year; approximately thirty-three weeks are actually spent in instructional situations, and very little of this time is devoted to art education. Because the art program suggested here requires that children have time to become familiar with an exemplar, to learn about it, and to reflect upon it, the number of exemplars which can be used during the year is limited.

If a different exemplar is used each week, children can have experiences with at least 230 exemplars by the time they leave elementary school. This is a somewhat limited number when the whole scope of man's cultural heritage is considered, but it is a total which surpasses the number now being used.

Numbers by themselves mean very little. With the procedures recommended in this text, however, numbers plus the understandings which children develop about the exemplars will give elementary school children more literacy in art than many adults now have. More important, children will have a foundation on which to extend their literacy in art because they have had opportunities to develop and enrich concepts related both to the exemplars used and to others which may be encountered in the future.

Since it is not possible to use originals of great works of art in the classroom, transparencies or full-scale color reproductions must be used. Of the two, reproductions are preferable because these can be exhibited at the children's eye level for long periods of time. The quality of reproductions has not been standardized; many good ones and many poor ones are available. It is important to have the finest quality possible, for poor reproductions make it difficult to help children become aware of the artist's use of the visual art elements. Comparisons of products from several companies demonstrate the varying qualities of reproductions. A study of several reproductions of Van Gogh's *Sunflowers*, for example, reveals that in some the original colors used by the artist are hardly recognizable. It would be highly desirable if the quality of reproductions could be determined by making comparisons with the original, but this is seldom possible. The next best thing that can be done, and a very good substitute, is to rely on the many reputable companies which provide reproductions. The advisory boards of such companies are composed of international curators and gallery directors who are responsible for the quality of color reproductions of their permanent collections and who make comparisons with the original, thus insuring good quality.

Reproductions of paintings are not the only exemplars which should be used. Visuals of architecture, ceramics, and sculpture are also a part of the learning materials with which children should have experiences. There are problems of reproduction, particularly of pieces of sculpture, which should be recognized. The visuals used in the episodes in Part II are of the quality recommended for classroom use.

All the exemplars used should meet the standards of those who are knowledgeable in art. Although the classroom teacher or the art teacher may be a performing artist, this does not mean that her work should be used as an exemplar. Children need to know how the performing artist works in printmaking, ceramics, and painting, and very often a demonstration of these techniques is helpful. However, such works should not be used as examples of man's artistic achievements. A good color slide or reproduction of an original selected by a museum for its permanent collection is preferred.

FURTHER READINGS

Broudy, Harry S. "Aesthetic Education in a Technological Society: The Other Excuses for Beauty," *The Journal of Aesthetic Education* (Spring 1966), 13–23.

Broudy, Harry S., *et al. Democracy and Excellence in American Secondary Education.* Chicago: Rand McNally and Co., 1964.
    Explanation of art exemplars and rationale for limited number of exemplars.

II

EXPERIENCES
WHICH ENHANCE
VISUAL PERCEPTION

7

Introduction to
the Use of Episodes

In the preceding chapters, suggestions have been given concerning (1) the knowledge of art considered appropriate for nursery and elementary school children, (2) the concepts selected from this knowledge to be formed and enriched by children, and (3) the ways in which art episodes may be structured to help children form and enrich art concepts. The content of these chapters lays the theoretical foundation for an art curriculum for children, but theory is effective only when it can be put into practice. This part of the book, which consists of selected episodes for early primary, primary, and intermediate levels in school, presents procedures for making the transition from theory to practice.

Before presenting these episodes, it seems pertinent to interject a word of caution about the art education program developed in this book. It is not intended to be classified as another course in "art appreciation" or "art history." Certainly it is to be expected that children will develop appreciative skills as a result of the procedures presented in the sample episodes, and that they will develop feelings and understandings for the works of art for which they have had learning experiences. But the notion that "appreciation" can be taught as a separate subject in which children learn to recognize and analyze works of art is not a tenable one. This approach, which has been often used in the past, makes no allowance for the obvious relationships between the expressive intent of children and that of artists, and limits the possibilities for developing empathic interactions with works of art.

Nor should the use of works of art lead one to imagine that this is an art history course developed for the elementary school, in which lectures about works of art are given to children. In an intellectual approach, such as the one proposed here, there is a real danger that the media processes will be abandoned completely and that lectures and study about art which have little meaning to children will be substituted. It seems necessary to stress this point since it is often found that teachers, in their desire to improve children's aesthetic education, resort to the approach used by the art historian on the college level. The art historian is primarily concerned with a critical analysis of works of art which involves recognition of them within an historical framework. The use of this adult approach on the elementary school level will present children with an exemplar for which they usually have no frame of reference, a situation readily acknowledged by the art historian. To overcome this inadequate background, stories about the work of art and the artist are read or told to the children so that they will understand the subject matter, the techniques used, and the intent of the artist. If, for example, the subject is an historical figure, such as George Washington, children may be told that he was an honest man (a characteristic attested by the fact that he admitted chopping down a cherry tree), that he was beloved by all his countrymen, and that he did things that were just, right, and good—all of which have been conveyed by the artist. This may have been the intent of the artist, and again, it may not have been. Often, the stories that are told about works of art do not show the original intent of the artist, or are simplified so much for children's comprehension that they foster misconcepts.

Such an approach is based on the assumption that children will be able to evaluate art if they learn something about art in an historical framework. This is a valid assumption, but one which applies only after children have had appropriate experiences that contribute to their understandings. Used on the secondary and college level this procedure works well because older students have had a chance to develop the background and tools for critical analysis. Almost all students at this level are fine arts majors with studio work in their background, or are astute and interested observers whose intellectual level enables them to develop the tools visually.

The critical analysis used by art historians should not be considered synonymous with aesthetic understandings; it is only a component which contributes to the whole of understanding. Aesthetic understandings, as used here, are ones which facilitate empathic interactions between the viewer and the exemplar. The level of empathic interaction achieved by the viewer, in this case the child, is dependent upon critical analysis only insofar as this contributes to the store of knowledge necessary for intelligent interaction. One may possess the intellectual capacity for critical analysis but lack the ability for empathic interaction. The enriched concepts necessary for such interaction with the works of artists, designer-craftsmen, and the natural environment are not those achieved through academic lectures leading toward critical analysis only. Before children are taught to analyze the visual art elements in painting and sculpture, they should be given experiences which enable them to enrich their concepts of these elements, to become noticers of them, and then to use them as a frame of reference for a study of art history, as such, at a higher level in school. In the art historian's approach the critical analysis is developed after the exposure to the exemplar. In the procedures recommended in this book, the frame of reference is developed before the exposure to the exemplar by bringing children, art, and art experiences together in a way that fosters understandings and feelings.

By the time children leave elementary school they should have some concept of the history of art as a part of man's heritage. The exemplars used, however, should be consistent with children's characteristics and needs and with the concepts to be developed from the basic structure; and the teaching procedures used with the exemplars should be ones that will help children look with curiosity, make discoveries, form comparisons, and lay a foundation for the use of appreciative skills.

CURRICULUM DEVELOPMENT

With some exceptions, the art curriculum now being used by many schools does not keep pace with today's children and with objectives for art education, or with curriculum development in other subjects. For the most part, the art curriculum is planned by classroom teachers who, through their demands upon the special art teacher, indicate what lessons they want taught or need help with: watercolor, specific landscapes, perspective, profile drawing, or seasonal decorations. The resulting curriculum is either so loosely organized that there can be little assurance that basic learnings are fostered, or so rigid that each class is doing the same activity at the same time with little recognition of the fact that young children may need more concrete experiences, while older ones can work in more sophisticated ways.

In bringing the art curriculum up to date, teachers should profit from what has been done in other subjects. In mathematics, for· example, the curriculum has in many instances been organized from early primary levels through secondary school; it has started with simple concrete experiences and has led into abstractions of these experiences, and has returned to concepts again and again so that children may constantly enrich and expand them. Children learn addition early in elementary school, but their concepts of addition are used in many different ways: subtraction, division, multiplication. They use these concepts throughout their lives in almost any mathematical problem they encounter. An art curriculum based on these same principles can be developed and is recommended.

Suggestions for Developing an Art Curriculum

1. The art concepts in the basic structure for teaching art can be the foundation for an art curriculum for nursery and elementary schools. With this structure to draw upon, it is possible to develop a curriculum which is in keeping with the total elementary school curriculum and the possibilities within art. The art concepts can be used by teachers at every level, and the episodic clusters developed around each of these concepts help children form and enrich them throughout their school experience.

2. The learning experiences developed for the formation and enrichment of art concepts should, of course, be appropriate to the various levels at which they are used. They need to be arranged sequentially according to the complexity of the concepts and the psychology of growing minds: learning experiences proceed from the simple to the complex.

3. A cyclical approach should be used with the content; that is, all the art concepts in the basic structure should be used at every level. Children will not, of course, be expected to have developed these concepts fully at any one level. For example, children will not learn all there is to know about color at the early primary level; they will experience and learn about primary colors and, perhaps, secondary colors, but values and intermediate colors will be introduced at higher levels.

4. In developing learning experiences which will help children enrich art concepts, the goals of art education presented in Chapter 1 should be constantly reviewed. Particular attention should be given to those objectives concerned with children and their expressive intent, and those concerned with helping children interact knowledgeably, sensitively, and empathically with the expressive intent of artists and designer-craftsmen. The frame of reference which children develop from experiences with media and other art activities help them to develop frames of reference for viewing their own work and that of others.

5. The art learning experiences developed should make use of the many ways of learning about art. These include:

a *Media activities*—those which help children to solve problems using the visual art elements and to enrich their symbols, and which contribute to their creative expression.

b *Multi-sensory experiences*—activities which include the use of sensory devices to enhance the visual experiences.

c *Discussion*—activities in which leading questions asked by the teacher elicit the depth of understanding of children and in which explanations contribute to understanding.

d *Activities for developing seeing skills*—those which help children to become noticers.

e *Museum trips*—culminating experiences which introduce children to original works of art and to the works of designer-craftsmen.

f *Other field trips*—trips to see the works of designer-craftsmen, such as architecture.

g *Activities with visual media*—those in which children are helped to see structure in nature or works of art through the use of media described in Chapter 11.

h *Reading activities*—those through which children can independently reinforce and deepen understandings about art and artists.

i *Activities related to other subjects*—those which draw on the interrelationships that exist between art and other subjects. Art concepts can be enriched through the use of other subjects and can, in turn, enhance these subjects.

Children can learn about art through all these activities. Quite often, children do not need to use the media activities for enriching art concepts. For example, seeing skills are sometimes best developed through the use of visual media; children may more easily become aware of line qualities in natural forms by studying structural design qualities in nature through the use of many and varied visual media. These seeing skills can then be used with art, architecture, and nature exemplars, and can also help children enrich their own symbols in media activities.

6. The exemplars which are to be used with children should receive considerable attention in developing an art curriculum. Suggestions given in Chapter 6 are helpful ones to follow.

7. An art curriculum can be structured into episodes of learning which are based on children, the many ways of learning about art, and art itself.

8. All episodes developed should center on the children and their interests and stages of development, but should also consider the adults we would like to have them become. The here-and-now world of children is very important to educators, but preparing them for a future world is of equal importance. The art learnings which children acquire in elementary school in a very real sense help to determine what their future learnings, and the future itself, will be.

9. Any curriculum which is developed should be consistent with the needs of a school system. The art curriculum used by the classroom or special art teacher should be specifically designed for a particular school and/or group of children. Although a district may develop a curriculum for use by its teachers, modifications may be needed for a given classroom. The basic understandings to be developed will be the same, but the episodes may be different because of differences in children and in environmental situations.

10. In developing a curriculum, the process, scope, and sequence of art education should be basic considerations.

On page 313 of this book we have included a scope and sequence outline which can be used to develop an art curriculum based on the theory presented in this text. The outline illustrates quite clearly the content of art that can be presented to children and the sequence for introducing the content. It also shows that an art curriculum developed from a basic structure need not be rigid and inflexible.

Sample Episodes
for an Art Curriculum

To illustrate how an art curriculum which incorporates all the suggestions given above can be developed, sample episodes are included in Chapters 7, 8, and 9 for the early primary, primary, and intermediate levels. These do not represent a complete curriculum; from these selected episodes others can be developed for use with children on various levels. There are certain requirements for the teacher in making effective use of these episodes. Many of these apply more to the classroom teacher than to the special art teacher, but all are important if the episodes are to be taught effectively. These include the preparation of the teacher and the use of the episodes.

Teacher preparation

1. Teachers should be visually literate. Although ideally visual literacy should be acquired during professional preparation, it is possible to acquire this through in-service education and independent study.

2. There should be a thorough understanding of the basic structure and its use in art education.

3. Experiences in the media processes to be used with children are a must for all teachers. These will alert teachers to problems which children may encounter in work with the media, and will help them understand the appropriateness of certain media for certain levels.

4. Teachers should understand procedures for stimulating and motivating children for symbol enrichment.

5. There should be an awareness of the relationships which exist between children's art expression, the basic structure, and the enhancement of visual perception.

6. Teachers should understand the need for the use of exemplars in art education, and should be thoroughly familiar with ones that are used.

7. It should be understood that the development of appreciative skills is not confined to painting or sculpture but is a part of other aspects of man's life which can be equally aesthetic, e.g., industrial design.

8. Teachers should be thoroughly familiar with the organization and the use of the episodes.

9. Teachers should understand that the use of sensory aids and the development of seeing skills are not solely the responsibility of the museum. Schools have a very important role to play in the aesthetic education of children.

10. Within each episode or episodic cluster is a section entitled "Teacher Background." These sections include understandings which the teacher should have to do an effective teaching job with the episodes. In many instances they indicate what experiences prospective teachers in art education classes should have.

Organization and use of episodes

1. When an episodic cluster is presented, the sequence of the episodes must be followed. The episodes have been developed from the simple to the complex; any variation in the order disrupts the continuity necessary for achieving the objectives.

2. The sequence of procedures within each episode must be followed. Each teacher will, of course, discover her own way of using the episodes and of adapting the procedures to fit her particular class, but each step in the procedures leads into the next and should be followed accordingly. Each episode has been constructed so that the frame of reference for the exemplar is developed *before* the exposure to it. In some cases, two or more sequential episodes (without exemplars) are needed to develop this frame of reference. The procedure should not be reversed; to do so would be to employ the teaching technique of the art historian—that is, working directly from the exemplar into a critical analysis of the work.

3. The instructional procedures for the teacher are written in considerable detail as guidelines. These procedures do not include all the learning activities possible, but only those considered to be most appropriate for achieving the objective of the episode. The questions suggested for discussion activities are given only to show the knowledge which is to be elicited or discovered; teachers will want to substitute their own or elaborate on those given. The tendency to tell children things which they can find out on their own should be resisted, but there are times when telling is expedient and useful. These have been indicated in the episodes as "Explain to the children . . . ." Teachers should always be alert to possibilities for using leading questions and procedures which will help children develop the desired understandings. Children need to discover, and good teachers lead them into discoveries.

4. Teachers will find that it is not always possible to complete one episode in one class session. Because of the differences in the learning rates of children, some episodes will have to be divided into two or more parts. If such a division is necessary, it should be made at a point which will not disrupt the continuity.

5. Reproductions of the exemplars are included in the episodes for illustrative purposes. Although it is possible to use these with an opaque projector, this is not recommended. Instead, reproductions of

the exemplars should be obtained so that they can be displayed in the classroom, as suggested in the episodes.

6. The vocabulary which has been given consists of terms that are appropriate and necessary to the episode. Vocabulary need not be restricted to these terms; children and teachers will add others that are suitable for a particular group. Terms that are introduced and/or used in one episode are not usually repeated in the vocabulary lists of succeeding episodes, but teachers should review words introduced earlier so that they become a part of the children's vocabulary and so that meanings can be expanded. The terms are to be used functionally; they are not to be merely memorized. The terms are important because they are the vehicles which carry the concepts.

7. It is recommended that teachers employ grouping procedures that are used in other subjects. However, in procedures with large groups of children, it is not always possible to help individual children and meet the objectives.

8. In the sample episodes presented, media processes are included only as one kind of learning activity which helps children enhance their visual perception. This has been done so that episodes which are unique, or used infrequently in schools, could be shown as a guide for developing similar ones. As indicated in the introductions to each of the following three chapters, teachers will see many places where media processes and different exemplars can and should be used between the episodes given.

FURTHER READINGS

The references listed below are suggested for teacher background for the episodes in Chapters 7 through 11.

Understanding Visual
Art Elements

Anderson, Donald M. *Elements of Design.* New York: Holt, Rinehart and Winston, Inc., 1961.

Wilson, Robert C. *An Alphabet of Visual Experience.* Scranton, Pa.: International Textbook Co., 1966.

Art Media Techniques
For Elementary Classrooms

Becker, Edith C. *Adventures with Scissors and Paper.* Scranton, Pa.: International Textbook Co., 1959.

La Mancusa, Katherine C. *Source Book for Art Teachers.* Scranton, Pa.: International Textbook Co., 1965.

Lord, Lois. *Collage and Construction.* Worcester, Mass.: Davis Publications, Inc., 1958.

Mattil, Edward. *Meaning in Crafts.* 2d ed. Englewood Cliffs, N. J.: Prentice-Hall, Inc., 1965.

Montgomery, Chandler. *Art for Teachers of Children.* Columbus, Ohio: Charles E. Merrill Publishing Co., 1968.

Moseley, Spencer, *et al. Crafts Design.* Belmont, Calif.: Wadsworth Publishing Co., Inc., 1962.

Pasadena Art Museum. *California Design Ten.* Pasadena: Pasadena Art Museum, 1968.

Pattemore, Arnel W. *Printmaking Activities for the Classroom.* Worcester, Mass.: Davis Publications, Inc., 1966.

Randall, Arne W., and Ruth E. Halvorsen. *Printing in the Classroom.* Worcester, Mass.: Davis Publications, Inc., 1963.

Rainey, Sarita R. *Weaving Without a Loom.* Worcester, Mass.: Davis Publications, Inc., 1966.

Exemplars and
Background Information

Janson, H. W., and Dora Jane Janson. *The Picture History of Painting.* New York: Harry N. Abrams, Inc., 1957.

Lowry, Bates. *The Visual Experience.* Englewood Cliffs, N. J.: Prentice-Hall, Inc., 1961. Pp. 124–215.

McCallum, Ian. *Architecture U.S.A.* New York: Reinhold Publishing Corp., 1959.

Pasadena Art Museum. *California Design Nine.* Pasadena: Pasadena Art Museum, 1965.

The Shorewood Art Reference Guide. Prepared under the direction of the editors of Shorewood Publishers, Inc. New York: Shorewood Reproductions, Inc., 1966.

Taylor, Joshua C. *Learning To Look.* Chicago: University of Chicago Press, 1965. Pp. 43–130.

8

Early
Primary Level

INTRODUCTION

The sample episodes included here for the early primary level represent an episodic cluster, that is, a series of episodes building upon each other in a sequential order. The selected episodes develop the concepts of the basic structure in a related and sequential pattern; the major art concepts of line and color become the foundation for the enrichment of concepts of shape, primary colors, size, texture, repeat pattern, and solid form. Each episode is also a part of the continuum for extending a child's frame of reference for interaction with exemplars.

No specific time during the early primary level is suggested for beginning these episodes, but they should be used only after the child has reached the stage of naming his scribbles and is approaching, or is already in, the stage of using geometric shapes for representative symbols in activities with media. To introduce these episodes at an earlier period in the development of the child might be frustrating to him. Before the child reaches this stage, he is still forming concepts through many and varied sensory experiences as described in the preceding chapters. Teachers who know their children and their children's artwork will know when to begin. In nursery schools, many children will be ready while others will not. Most kindergarten children are ready for the experiences in the episodes and are capable of comprehending the basic structure as it is presented on this level. Whenever the episodes are introduced to children at this level, certain considerations should be kept in mind, in addition to those given in Chapter 7:

1. The frame of reference which a child at the early primary level develops for the exemplar is only the beginning. As he discovers, experiences, and learns more at succeeding levels, his frame of reference is extended and he interacts differently and in a more sophisticated manner with the same exemplar.

2. It has been recommended that the experiences in the episodes be given to small groups of children. However, in many of our kindergartens there are as many as forty children in each classroom with only one teacher. Some kindergarten teachers have learned to group their children for instructional purposes, much as they do at other levels.

3. The omission of the art media activities in many of the episodes does not mean that such activities should not be given to children at this level. Encouraging the imagination and creativity of children is very important, and art activities which contribute to this should be used. These include experiences with tempera paint, crayon, clay, and materials for collage, all of which provide satisfaction for children before and after they have developed representative symbols. After they have begun to use symbols, such materials are useful in the enrichment of these through topic motivations. Since children at the beginning of the early primary level may still be in what has been called the "I and My" stage of development, topics which deal with children and their experiences can help them enrich their symbols. These topics might include: "My Parents," "My House," "My Pet," "I Am Running," "I Am Playing Ball," "I Am Playing House," "I Am Playing School," and other similar ones. Well-selected activities and motivation with media can also help children form and enrich concepts of line, color, size, shape, texture, and solid form. Episodes 7, 9, and 10 are examples of activities with art media which can be used to help children solve problems using the visual art elements so that they can comprehend the artist's use of these elements. The other episodes are examples of other ways young children can learn about art—the use of manipulative materials, visual media, and discussions, all of which can lead to discoveries.

4. Names of artists and exemplars have been included with other vocabulary. At this level it is not necessary for children to be able to identify either, but it has been found that when the names of the artist and his work are used in the episode (and they should be used), children learn them and learn to associate them with the work of art.

EPISODE 1

Objective: To introduce the concept of a reproduction
of a work of art as distinguished from an original

Teacher background

1 Understand the difference between an original painting or drawing and a reproduction.
2 Understand the difference between an original print and a print.
3 Know the difference between a photograph and a halftone.
4 Know the difference between a slide and a reproduction.

Materials

Reproduction: Pablo Picasso, *The Studio* (or any reproduction in which the composition is one of geometric shapes and lines)
Children's books which contain photographs of animals found in a zoo
Photographs of the children in the room

Vocabulary

picture	original painting
photograph	Pablo Picasso (or whichever artist is used)
real	*The Studio* (or whatever reproduction is used)
original	museum
artist	

Instructional procedures

Motivation and instruction: Sensory, multi-sensory experiences; topic discussion

1 Introduce the episode by showing photographs of the children in the room. Ask children to identify those shown in the photographs and to tell what kind of pictures these are. Ask questions which will have children explain why photographs are taken. Try to elicit the response that, since the children cannot be in many places at once, a photograph is a way of sharing them with parents, aunts, and grandparents.
2 Show photographs of the animals from a picture book. Ask the children to describe the differences between the photograph and the real animals. If they have not seen the real animals, ask them whether or not they think they would recognize them if they saw them and to explain why they could.

3 Ask children to tell where they have seen such animals or where they might go to see them. When children suggest the zoo as the place where they might see them, have them explain why the animals are kept there, and try to elicit the response that they are housed there for protection and so that many people can see them.

Exemplar:

1 Introduce the exemplar shown in Figure 64. Explain that this is a photograph of the real painting, but that it is called a reproduction of the real painting, not a photograph. Explain that if they had a photograph of one of their own paintings, it too would be called a reproduction. Review the reasons for having photographs made (e.g., so that the real object can be shared with others) and help children understand that the reproduction of a painting is a way of sharing it with many people.

2 Introduce the terms *original* and *original painting*. Have children make comparisons between a real person or animal and its photograph and an original painting and its reproduction. Ask if they would be able to recognize the original from having seen the reproduction and to explain why. Develop the idea that the original is important enough to be shared and enjoyed with many people, not just the person who owns it or those who can go to the museum where it is kept.

Figure 64
Pablo Picasso, *The Studio*, 1927–28
Oil on canvas, 59 × 91 inches

3   Introduce the terms *museum* and *gallery*. Compare these with a zoo. Explain that although an animal is kept in a zoo, its photograph can be shared with many; a painting is kept in a museum, but a reproduction of it can be found in many places, including the classroom.

Expected outcome

Children should be able to explain:

1   The term *reproduction* as it is related to a work of art.
2   Where original paintings can be found.

Related activities

(Visual exercises, books, poetry, related activities in other subjects)

1   Children may collect photographs of real objects: fruit, vegetables, animals. When possible, compare these with the real objects.
2   Discuss the differences between real objects and photographs of them in terms of size, shape and color.

EPISODE 2

Objective: To enrich the concept of line to include
straight and curved lines *

Teacher background

1   Understand the similarities and differences between mathematics concepts and art concepts.
2   Know that lines are to be used for the development of art concepts.
3   Know the different kinds of lines.
4   Understand the development of learnings from simple to complex.
5   Understand the stages of development of children and know which stage each child has reached in the use of lines.

Materials

Chalk and chalkboard or newsprint and black crayon

Two sets of 4 × 4″ pieces of construction paper with curved and straight lines in different positions

* This and the following episode are very simple ones to show that curved and straight lines are used to make shapes. These two episodes may be combined, if children are ready; otherwise, they should be presented separately.

Vocabulary [1]

curved lines
straight lines

Instructional procedures

Motivation and instruction: Sensory, multi-sensory experiences; topic discussion

1 Using the chalkboard or newsprint, illustrate a curved line by drawing a half circle. Use the same procedure and draw straight lines: one vertical and one horizontal (see Figure 65). *Do not make shapes from the lines.*

Figure 65

2 From this concrete visual experience, move immediately into the abstraction of it by having children locate curved and straight lines in the room, such as the edge of the table.
3 Make a game with the 4 × 4″ pieces of construction paper which have curved or straight lines on them. Have the corresponding pieces placed on the bulletin board. Have a child select one piece of paper and find its match on the bulletin board and tell whether it is a curved or straight line.

Exemplar:

No exemplar is to be used for this episode. Instead, the children's paintings and drawings can be used so that kinds of lines can be identified.

Expected outcome

Children should be able to discriminate between curved and straight lines.

---

[1] Children at this level often invent words and enjoy improvising terms. As long as this does not become so extreme that the concept becomes confusing, it may be allowed and even encouraged.

Related activities

(Visual exercises, books, poetry, related activities in other subjects)
1 Whenever possible, have children locate different kinds of lines in the room and in their clothing.
2 During rhythmic activities children may be encouraged to show different kinds of line by using body movements.

EPISODE 3

Objective: To introduce concepts of shape derived from closure of line and to enrich concepts of color

Teacher background

1 Know that shapes can be developed from closure of lines.
2 Understand how shapes can be enhanced by color.
3 Develop sensitivity to shapes in the classroom.

Materials

One of each of the following flat shapes: [2]

round blue	round yellow	round red
square blue	square yellow	square red

Flannel board large enough to hold all shapes

Vocabulary

primary colors	shape
red	round shape
yellow	square shape
blue	

Instructional procedures

Motivation and instruction: Sensory, multi-sensory experiences; topic discussion

---

[2] These must be large enough for children to see them on the flannel board. Recommended size: round—6″ in diameter; square—6″. (See Figure 66, page 106.)

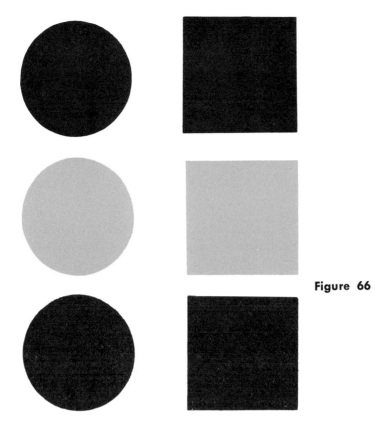

Figure 66

1 Introduce the episode by having children locate curved and straight lines in the room.

2 Using the chalkboard, show that if a half circle is closed, it makes a round shape. Use the same procedure to show that a square can be made from straight lines.

3 Place a round blue shape on the flannel board. Discuss the shape and its color.

4 Have a child find a square blue shape and place it on the flannel board.

5 Repeat this procedure with the remaining shapes so that children know the meaning of shape and can discriminate the primary colors and name them. Use the term *primary colors*.

6 Follow these concrete experiences with an abstraction of them by having children locate in the room: red, yellow, and blue colors, and round and square shapes. It is helpful to have jars of liquid tempera paint in primary colors, and round and square shapes in primary colors, placed at various spots in the room.

7 Display the shapes listed under "Materials" on the flannel board or on a bulletin board.

Exemplar: No exemplar is to be used in this episode.

Expected outcome

Children should be able to:
1 Discriminate between round and square shapes.
2 Identify red, yellow, and blue, and classify these as primary colors.

Related activities

(Visual exercises, books, poetry, related activities in other subjects)
1 Have children find round and square shapes and the primary colors in magazines provided by the teacher.
2 Have children collect pictures of round and square shapes in primary colors at home and bring them to school for discussion time.
3 Read *I Like Red* by Robert Bright.

EPISODE 4

Objective: To introduce concept of size derived from shape and to form the related concept of a repeat pattern

Teacher background

1 Know the visual art elements.
2 Know what makes a repeat pattern.
3 Understand the relationship between nature, art, and the environment.
4 Have experience in using repeat pattern.
5 Understand the relationship between the teacher's use of repeat pattern and the artist's use of it.
6 Know non-objective and abstract painting.
7 Recognize that rhythm can be developed in paintings with lines, repeated lines, shapes, and repeated shapes, and can be accentuated with color.

Materials

One of each of the following shapes, as shown in Figure 67 (see Figure 193, page 278):

6″ blue square	3″ blue square	flannel board
6″ red square	3″ red square	
6″ yellow square	3″ yellow square	

Figure 67

Reproductions: Piet Mondrian, *Broadway Boogie-Woogie*
Josef Albers, *Homage to the Square: "Insert"*

Vocabulary

red	Mondrian	big	} comparative terms
yellow	*Broadway Boogie-Woogie*	little	
blue	Josef Albers	large	} comparative terms
primary colors		small	

Instructional procedures

Motivation and instruction: Sensory, multi-sensory experiences; topic discussion

1 Introduce the episode by having all the squares on the flannel board in random fashion—with sizes and colors mixed. *Do not have the squares turned so that they seem to be diamond shaped.* Have children tell what kinds of shapes and what colors they see on the board.

2 Have the children match the squares according to color. Ask them to explain the differences in the sizes of the squares. Use this exercise several times, and vary it by having the children match all the big squares and all the little squares.

3 When children have shown that they can discriminate visually between the big and the little squares, introduce the concept of repeat pattern by putting all six small squares across the flannel board. Explain to them that these shapes follow one another, and that this is called a *pattern*—a pattern requires the repeated use of shape.

4 Let the children make patterns with the big squares and the little squares.

5 Have children visually abstract from these experiences by locating objects which are repeated in the room: windows, lights, desks, floor tiles, etc.

6 After children have located many objects that are repeated, use the flannel board and the square shapes and place one of the small shapes inside a big one to show that little shapes can also appear inside big shapes. Let the children demonstrate this themselves with the rest of the shapes. Repeat this as many times as is necessary for the children to understand.

7 Now have the children find objects in the room which have smaller shapes inside larger shapes: drawers in cupboards, window panes in frames, etc.

Exemplar:

1 Introduce the reproduction of Mondrian's *Broadway Boogie-Woogie* (Figure 68) by explaining to the children that an artist has also used big and little, blue, red, and yellow square shapes. Have the children locate the squares, colors, repeated squares, and repeat pattern.

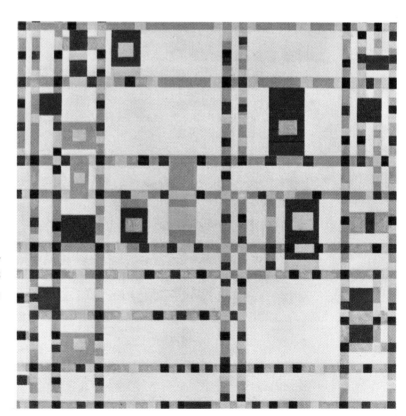

Figure 68
Piet Mondrian, *Broadway Boogie-Woogie,* 1942–43

Oil on canvas, 50 × 50 inches

Figure 69

Josef Albers, *Homage to the Square: "Insert,"* 1959

Oil, 48 × 48 inches

2 Introduce the reproduction of Josef Albers' *Homage to the Square: "Insert"* (Figure 69) by asking the children to tell what this artist has done and how his work is different from what Mondrian did. Have the children locate the squares.

3 Encourage the children to talk about the way the reproductions make them feel, particularly *Broadway Boogie-Woogie.* The title itself should prompt lively discussions.

4 Discuss the different ways that the artists have used squares.

5 Display both reproductions in the room at the children's eye level.

Expected outcome

Children should be able to:

1 Discriminate square shapes of different sizes and colors.

2 Find shapes, colors, and repeat patterns in the exemplars.

3 Explain how different artists have used shapes and colors for different expressive intents.

Related activities

(Visual exercises, books, poetry, related activities in other subjects)

1 Have children bring pictures from magazines which show big and little square shapes and primary colors.
2 Have children locate other repeat patterns, e.g., square tiles on the floor, tiles on the walls, etc.
3 During free-time activities, have the shapes and flannel board available so that children can match the shapes according to color and size, and can make repeat patterns.

EPISODE 5

Objective: To introduce the concept of texture

Teacher background

1 Be able to distinguish between different degrees of texture.
2 Understand the creation of texture from line, closure of line into shape, and repeated shapes.
3 Understand that texture has physical properties which are repeated three-dimensional shapes.
4 Understand how three-dimensional texture is abstracted into the visual.
5 Know where textures are to be found.

Materials

Sandpaper squares of varying degrees of roughness (see Figure 190, page 275).
Assortment of different fabrics: satin, velvet, corduroy
An original oil painting which has texture (if one is available)
Reproductions: Vincent Van Gogh, *A Peasant of the Camargue*
                Vincent Van Gogh, *The Starry Night*

Vocabulary

rough	repeated shapes
rougher	texture
smooth	Vincent Van Gogh

Vocabulary

smoother	peasant
hard	*The Starry Night*
soft	stars
repeated lines	moon
shapes	

Instructional procedures

Motivation and instruction: Sensory, multi-sensory experiences; topic discussion

1   Have the children look at the sandpaper squares. Ask them to tell which ones look rougher, and to explain why.

2   Let the children feel the sandpaper squares and ask them to decide which ones are rougher. Ask them to tell how rough things feel. It should be noted that children at this age often confuse rough and hard, so the teacher should also ask questions which will help children discriminate between the two.

3   Now have the children look at something smooth, such as a desk top, and ask them to describe the way it looks as compared with the sandpaper.

4   Have the children feel the top of a desk and again describe the way it feels. If children do not use the word *smooth*, introduce the term as a way of describing the desk top.

5   Have the children feel the various fabrics and tell which ones feel rough and which feel smooth. Have them arrange the fabrics in order of roughness and smoothness so that the terms *rougher* and *smoother* can be used.

6   Have children locate objects in the room which look rough or smooth. Ask them why objects look rough or smooth.

Exemplar:

1   Introduce the exemplar shown in Figure 70 by asking the children what they notice in it. Answers should include: dots, repeat patterns, lines on face.

2   Ask the children why the artist used these dots, lines, and repeat patterns. Ask them to describe how the painting might feel if they touched it.

3   Let the children feel the reproduction so that they will discover that, although it looks rough, it feels smooth.

4   Let the children touch the original oil painting and ask them to describe how it feels. Ask them what was done to make this feel rougher than the reproductions.

Figure 70
Vincent Van Gogh, *A Peasant of the Camargue*

Drawing, 19¼ × 15 inches

5 Introduce the exemplar shown in Figure 71 by asking the children to describe the texture shown. Is it rough or smooth? Ask them to tell how the artist has made the painting look rough. Why has he made it look rough?

6 Encourage the children to describe how the exemplar makes them feel.

7 Display both reproductions at the children's eye level.

Figure 71
Vincent Van Gogh, *The Starry Night,* 1889

Oil on canvas, 29 × 36¼ inches

Expected outcome

Children should be able to:

1 Discriminate, tactually and visually, objects that are rough and smooth.
2 Explain that artists create texture by using dots, lines, and repeat patterns.
3 Tell why artists create texture in their works.

Related activities

(Visual exercises, books, poetry, related activities in other subjects)

1 Continue the tactual and visual experiences of having children discriminate degrees of roughness in objects. Use the original tactile squares, but include other objects which can be handled by children.
2 Have the children bring in magazine pictures that look rough but are smooth.
3 Have a "touch bag" in which there are rough and smooth objects. Ask children to find objects in the bag that are rough or smooth, or to find the roughest object, etc.

EPISODE 6

Objective: To enrich the concept of shape to
include rectangle and triangle

Teacher background

1 Understand that shapes are constantly being employed by artists.
2 Know that shapes are to be found in architecture and in the total environment.
3 Know the uses of the opaque projector (see Figure 182 and pages 266–67).

Materials

3 large square shapes: red, blue, yellow
3 large round shapes: red, blue, yellow
3 large rectangular shapes: red, blue, yellow
3 large triangular shapes: red, blue, yellow
Smaller shapes of all the above in primary colors
Flannel board
Opaque projector
(See Figure 72; see also Figure 193, page 278)

Figure 72

Exemplars of interiors: Herman Miller Furniture Company
Reproduction: Lyonel Feininger, *City Moon*

Vocabulary

rectangle   city
triangle   buildings

Instructional procedures

Motivation and instruction: Sensory, multi-sensory experiences; topic discussion

1 Introduce the episode by placing square, round, rectangular, and triangular shapes on the flannel board. Ask the children to identify the shapes they have already studied. Ask them whether or not they notice any new shapes on the board and to identify them. If the children are not able to identify the shapes by name, introduce the terms *rectangle* and *triangle*.

2 Use the 6″ red square and show the children how two shapes called rectangles can be made by cutting the square in half. Place a red square shape and the two rectangles on the flannel board, and ask the children to describe the similarities and differences between the two. Place the remaining rectangles on the board.

3 Place a large triangle on the board and ask the children to tell how it is different from the other shapes. Help them to discover that the triangle is formed from three straight lines. Place the three large triangles on the board.

4 Place the small and large rectangles and triangles on the board and have the children tell which ones are larger or smaller. Have the children match the shapes according to size or color.

5 Have the children use the triangles and rectangles to make repeat patterns on the flannel board.

6 Ask the children to locate rectangles in the room. When they identify windows, ask them why windows can be called repeat patterns. Ask them to describe what shapes they can see through the windows that could be called rectangular. Have them look through the windows and identify the rectangular shapes they see.

Exemplar:

1 Using the opaque projector, introduce the exemplar from Herman Miller, Inc. (Figure 73). Ask the children to find an object in the exemplar that looks like a rectangle, a triangle, a square, or a circle. Repeat this until the children have included the rooms themselves as well as the objects in them.

Figure 73

Figure 74
Lyonel Feininger, *City Moon,*
1945

Oil, 28½ × 21⅜ inches

2 Introduce the exemplar shown in Figure 74 by asking the children to tell what they think the artist is showing. Ask them to tell how the artist has used straight lines and rectangles.

3 Ask the children why they think the artist called this *City Moon.*

Expected outcome

Children should be able to:

1 Discriminate visually circles, squares, rectangles, and triangles of various sizes.

2 Locate these shapes in rooms and in exemplars.

3 Explain why artists have used shapes in certain ways. (The reasons given should be highly individualistic; there is no right or wrong.)

Related activities

(Visual exercises, books, poetry, related activities in other subjects)

1 Have a touch bag containing flat round, square, rectangular, and triangular shapes of different sizes. Let the teacher or the children decide which shape is to be selected, and have a child select it from the bag without looking. Many variations of this procedure can be developed.

2 During discussion time, have children discuss objects and rooms in their homes according to different shapes.

3 Play the "Shape Game." Have a child select a shape and whisper it to the teacher. Let the other children question the child to find out the shape (e.g., does it have three sides?). The child who guesses the shape is "it."

EPISODE 7

*Objective: To enrich the concepts of texture, shape, and size ***

Teacher background

1   Have experience making collages from a variety of materials of different textures, colors, shapes, and sizes.
2   Understand the tactual differences between collages and reproductions of collages.
3   Be able to help children understand the difference between a real collage and a reproduction.

Materials

12 × 18″ white construction paper—1 piece for each child
Texture box which contains an assortment of precut shapes (round, square, rectangular, triangular) in a variety of sizes and textures: terrycloth, sandpaper, satin, ribbon, netting, buttons, etc.
Elmer's glue
Reproduction: Georges Braque, *The Courrier*

Vocabulary

Braque
collage

Instructional procedures

Motivation and instruction: Sensory, multi-sensory experiences; topic discussion
1   Introduce the episode by using the materials from the preceding episodes to review shape, size, and texture.
2   Show the texture box to the children and display some of the materials in it. Explain to the children that they are going to work with many different shapes, sizes, and textures selected from the texture

---

* This and the two following episodes are art media activities designed to help children solve problems of expressive intent using shapes, size, and texture. These problem-solving experiences are used to help children develop a frame of reference for the exemplar and the expressive intent of the artist. Any one of these episodes may require several repeated experiences.

box. Stimulate the children to select different shapes, sizes, and textures by giving them an opportunity to explore the materials and to use tactual and visual discriminations.

3 Provide children with construction paper, paste, and materials to make a collage. While they are working, reinforce their learnings about size, shape, and texture, and motivate them to use variety in each.

4 When the collages are finished, display the work of all the children. Discuss with the children what they have done with size, shape, and texture.

Exemplar:

1 Introduce the exemplar shown in Figure 75 by asking the children why they made a collage instead of a painting. Show the reproduction of *The Courrier* and tell the children that this is a reproduction of a collage. Ask them why the artist did a collage instead of a painting. Ask them to find different sizes, shapes, and textures which have been used in *The Courrier*.

2 Display the reproduction in the room at the children's eye level.

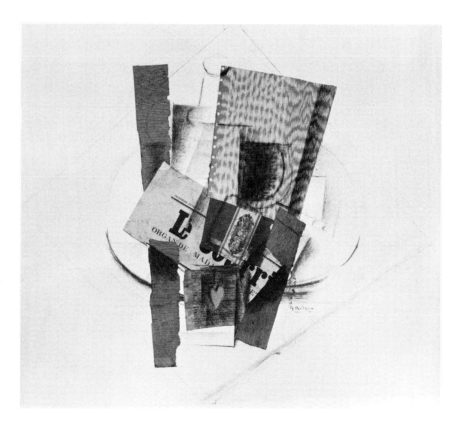

Figure 75
Georges Braque, *The Courrier*, 1913

Expected outcome

Children should be able to:

1 Use the elements of shape, size, and texture in making a collage.
2 Explain the meaning of the word *collage*.
3 Describe the artist's use of shape, size, and texture in a collage.
4 Tell why a collage is made instead of using some other activity.

Related activities

(Visual exercises, books, poetry, related activities in other subjects)

1 Have the children take a walk around the schoolyard and locate tactually and visually textures found in buildings, trees, and other objects. When they return, write an experience story about the walk and the textures they found.
2 Have a touch bag containing materials of different textures. Let the children have experiences in identifying the materials and/or textures by feeling them, and then verify their tactual discriminations by looking at the objects.

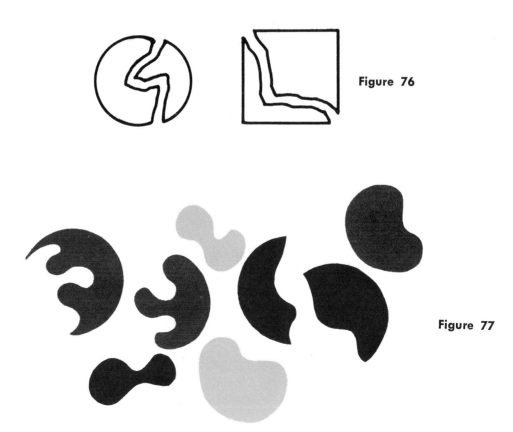

Figure 76

Figure 77

EPISODE 8

Objective: To enrich the concepts of shape and size and of the ways that artists have used them

Teacher background

1 Understand the variety of shapes, color, and sizes employed by artists in their symbols.
2 Understand that children are using geometric shapes in developing their symbols in painting, drawing, and collage work.

Materials

Precut shapes (circles, squares, rectangles, triangles) of different sizes made from red, yellow, blue, black, and white construction paper
Bulletin board
Scissors
Displays of children's paintings in which they have used different shapes
Reproductions: Joan Miro, *Carnival of Harlequin*
　　　　　　　　Ralston Crawford, *New Orleans #5*
　　　　　　　　Wayne Thiebaud, *Salads, Sandwiches and Desserts*

Vocabulary

Different kinds of shapes (or whatever description is best understood by the children)

Miro	desserts
carnival	sweet
salads	Ralston Crawford
sandwiches	Wayne Thiebaud

Instructional procedures

Motivation and instruction: Sensory, multi-sensory experiences; topic discussion

1 Use some of the materials from preceding episodes to review briefly the shapes children have already learned.
2 Explain to the children that there are many other kinds of shapes, and that some of these can be made from the shapes they already know. Demonstrate this to children by cutting free-form shapes from squares, circles, triangles, and rectangles. Place these on the bulletin board. Ask the children to tell what these new shapes look like. There should be a variety of shapes, such as in Figure 76 (see also Figure 77 and Figure 193, page 278).

3 Have children locate different kinds of shapes in the room. It is helpful to have a variety of shapes placed around the room. Explain to the children that, although they have talked about these shapes, there is not as yet a name for them. Encourage children to name the shapes. Introduce the term *different kinds of shapes* to include all these shapes.

4 Ask children to find something in the room that does not have a shape. When they have discovered that everything in the room has a shape, ask them to describe the shapes of pie, potato chips, crackers. Ask them to find different kinds of shapes in repeat patterns in their clothing.

Exemplar:

1 Before introducing the exemplars, direct the children's attention to the display of their paintings, and discuss the different kinds of shapes that they have used. Introduce the exemplar shown in Figure 78 by asking the children to name the shapes that the artist has used.

2 Introduce the exemplar shown in Figure 79 by having the children find the shapes used by the artist. Ask the children to compare the two works in terms of the shapes used and why they were used. Display the reproduction along with the other.

Figure 78
Ralston Crawford, *New Orleans #5,* 1953–54

Oil on canvas, 50½ × 36½ inches

Figure 79
Joan Miro, *Carnival of Harlequin,* 1924–25

Oil on canvas, 26 × 36⅝ inches

Figure 80
Wayne Thiebaud, *Salads, Sandwiches and Desserts*

Oil, 55 × 72 inches

3 Have children recall the shapes of foods which they discussed earlier. Introduce the exemplar shown in Figure 80 by asking the children where they might find food arranged like this. Ask them to tell how the painting makes them feel. In this discussion, bring out the point that artists paint things that they see and know. Display the reproduction with the others.

4 Encourage children to compare the exemplars.

Expected outcome

Children should be able to:
1 Visually discriminate common geometric shapes of different sizes.
2 Explain that different kinds of shapes can be derived from these common ones.
3 Tell that all objects have shape.
4 Tell that artists use shapes of all kinds.

Related activities

(Visual exercises, books, poetry, related activities in other subjects)
1 Refer to the displayed exemplars whenever possible. Let children continue their exploration to find the various kinds of shapes used and to compare their sizes.
2 Read *Shapes* by Miriam Schlein to the children.
3 Read *How Big Is Big?* by Herman and Nina Schneider to the children.
4 Play the record *Noisy and Quiet—Big and Little* (Camden, 1070). Discuss this with the children. They may want to hear it many times.

EPISODE 9

Objective: To introduce the concept of solid form

Teacher background

1 Have experience with clay in making a finished product, such as a model of an animal.
2 Have experience in viewing clay work from various angles.
3 Be able to distinguish between visual and tactual experiences in determining solid form as opposed to flat shape.
4 Know works of contemporary sculptors.
5 Understand that sculptors have been inspired by nature.
6 Know the techniques and materials used by sculptors.
7 Be acquainted with three-dimensional works of art.

Materials

Prepared moist clay
Newspapers for desk tops
Halftones: Barbara Hepworth, *Small Form Resting*
         Douglas Moryl, *Walnut and Aluminum Creatures*

Vocabulary

hot	solid form
cold	rock
warm	marble
hard	walnut
sculptor	

Instructional procedures

Motivation and instruction: Sensory, multi-sensory experiences; topic discussion

Part I.

1 Prepare for a clay activity:
     a Stimulate children to talk about animals they know, particularly their pets.
     b Stimulate them to model animals in clay.

c While they are working, motivate them to discover the limitations of clay—i.e., they may find that they cannot make an animal with long thin legs.

d Help children understand the possibilities of clay. Ask: Can you make animals rough? Can you make them smooth? What characteristics of animals can you show?

Part II.

1 Display the clay models.

2 Discuss the animals in terms of solid form. Help children see that the animals can be viewed from many angles.

3 Ask children to describe what their animals would look like if they made a photograph of them. Help them to distinguish between the solid forms and photographs of solid forms.

Exemplar:

1 Introduce the exemplar in Figure 81 by explaining that it is a picture of a solid form created by an artist. Although it appears flat, it is a solid form like the ones they have made. Review the reason for making a photograph of the form: it is owned by a museum but the photograph of it can be shared with many people.

2 Ask the children to tell what the solid form might be made from. Explain that this was made from walnut wood. Explain that the sculptor has used the walnut wood to make unusual animals. Ask the children to tell how it would feel to touch the real solid form: rough, smooth, hard, soft. Display the exemplar at the children's eye level.

Figure 81
Douglas Moryl, *Walnut and Aluminum Creatures*

3 Introduce the next exemplar by asking the children to name the things they use for their artwork. Explain that the sculptor, who works with solid form, also uses different materials. Pass around a rock so that children can feel it. Display the exemplar shown in Figure 82 and explain that this sculptor has used a material that is hard like the rock, a material called marble. Ask the children to describe what the sculpture looks like. Ask them how it would feel: hard, soft, rough, smooth, hot, cold. Display the halftone at the children's eye level.

Figure 82
Barbara Hepworth,
Small Form Resting,
1945

Marble, 9 × 12¼ × 10½ inches

4 Ask the children to tell the differences between the two exemplars and the materials used in terms of rough, smooth, cold, warm, hard, soft.

5 Ask why an artist would work with wood and marble rather than paint.

Expected outcome

Children should be able to:

1. Discriminate between a flat shape and a solid form.
2. Locate shapes that are flat and objects that are solid.

Related activities

(Visual exercises, books, poetry, related activities in other subjects)

1   Direct the children's attention to objects that are solid forms, such as rocks, logs, balls, oranges, lemons, eggs, etc. Relate these to the exemplars used in this episode.

2   Have children collect solid objects and corresponding photographs of them from magazines.

3   Read *Are You Square?* by Ethel Kessler.

4   Have a touch bag containing many different solid objects which are familiar to the children. Have them identify them by feeling. Vary this by putting only a few objects in the bag and let the children identify them by feeling. Have the children close their eyes; remove one object and then let one child identify the missing object by feeling the other objects. Repeat this so that all children get a chance.

EPISODE 10

Objective: To enrich the concepts of sound and texture

Teacher background

1   Know the effect of auditory stimulation on painting.

2   Be familiar with various records which can be used for auditory stimulation.

3   Have experience with tempera painting.

4   Know ways of creating texture with paint.

5   Understand the different ways that artists have portrayed animals.

Materials

Tempera paint
Brushes
Paper
Record player
Record: *Sounds of Animals* (Folkway Service and Record Co., 6124)
Reproductions: Edward Hicks, *The Peaceable Kingdom*
                 Henri Rousseau, *The Sleeping Gypsy*
                 Francisco de Goya, *Don Manuel Osorio de Zuniga*

Vocabulary

rough	lion
rougher	turtle
roughest	hamster
smooth	tiger
smoother	elephant
smoothest	Indian
The Peaceable Kingdom	Rousseau
The Sleeping Gypsy	Goya
Hicks	

(other words which may be used in connection with the reproductions)

Instructional procedures

Motivation and instruction: Sensory, multi-sensory experiences; topic discussion

1 Pass out the materials needed for tempera painting.

2 Introduce the episode by having children get very quiet and listen to all the sounds in the room. Ask them to tell the different sounds they heard. Discuss sounds they hear at home, particularly the sounds of their pets or animals in the neighborhood.

3 Introduce the record to the children by explaining that they are going to hear some sounds of animals in a zoo.

4 Play the record and then have the children identify the sounds which they heard. After a brief discussion, let the children paint the animals they heard in the record. Replay the record while the children are painting.

5 While the children are painting, motivate individuals according to their needs—for the texture of animal fur, etc.

6 After the paintings have dried, display them in the room. Figure 83 shows the kind of painting that can be expected from such auditory motivation. Other kinds of motivation for such an activity include having children touch boards covered with various kinds of fur.

Figure 83
Six Year Old

Figure 84

Edward Hicks, *The Peace-able Kingdom*

Oil on canvas, 17½ × 23¾ inches

Exemplar:

1 Before introducing the exemplars, ask the children to talk about their paintings in terms of the animal sounds they heard and the animals they painted. Discuss the kinds of animal fur they painted with regard to textures that are rough, rougher, roughest, and smooth, smoother, smoothest.

2 Introduce the reproduction shown in Figure 84 to the children and ask them to identify the animals that the artist painted. Ask them to describe different sounds these animals might make. Discuss the different kinds of tactual qualities in the fur. Ask the children to tell how the reproduction makes them feel, and lead the discussion into the idea that not all animals are vicious and that this exemplar shows a peaceable kingdom of animals. Ask the children to find other things in the painting: water, Indians, and different textures in the trees. Display the exemplar at the children's eye level.

3 Introduce the exemplar shown in Figure 85 and ask the children to tell how this exemplar is different from the other one. Have the children explain the way this exemplar makes them feel, and lead the discussion into how it feels to have a dog lick one's face: warm, cold, wet, sticky, etc. Ask them to find the shapes in the reproduction, and the repeated lines which appear in the costume of the sleeping gypsy. Display the exemplar with the first one.

Figure 85

Henri Rousseau, *The Sleeping Gypsy,* 1897

Oil on canvas, 51 × 79 inches

Figure 86

Francisco de Goya, *Don Manuel Osorio de Zuniga* (Boy with Bird)

Oil, 50 × 40 inches

4 Introduce the exemplar shown in Figure 86 by explaining to the children that another artist has been interested in painting animals and that this is a painting of a little boy who lived long ago and his pets. Ask the children to describe the various textures which are to be found in the animal's fur, the texture and color of the boy's suit, the repeated lines in the bird cage, and the way that the artist has used line in the cord attached to the pigeon's leg. Display the exemplar with the others. Explain that these reproductions of original paintings were done by artists who lived a long time ago.

5 Ask the children to compare the exemplars and to decide which one they might like to have in their homes.

Expected outcome

Children should be able to:

1 Identify sounds around them and sounds of animals.
2 Explain how artists have used texture and line.
3 Explain that artists paint animals differently, just as the children painted them differently.
4 Understand that the paintings were done a long time ago. (Children at this age do not have a well-developed concept of time, but efforts should be made to help them become aware of the past.)

Related activities

(Visual exercises, books, poetry, related activities in other subjects)

1 Read *Let's Imagine Sounds* by Janet Wolff.
2 Read *A Trip to the Zoo* by Brian Phillips.

ANALYSIS OF THE EPISODES

In analyzing the episodic cluster just presented, one can see how the basic structure for art can be used at the early primary level. The major concepts of line and color are used as a basis for helping children form and enrich concepts of texture, size, shape, solid form, and primary colors. These concepts assist children in forming and enriching concepts of and for representative symbols used in the media process, and lay a foundation for learnings in design and art history. The last episode, for example, has the first reference to the exemplar in historical perspective—a painting made a long time ago. Vocabulary, of course, has been stressed throughout, and the terms developed will contribute to a conscious approach to design on the primary and intermediate levels.

Teachers who have used these episodes know that almost any exemplar could have been used to insure all the learnings in this cluster. However, young children need to be exposed to well-selected exemplars of fine art and architecture if they are to develop aesthetically and intellectually. The elementary classroom is no place for works that are mundane and banal. Those used in the episodes demonstrate what can be used and comprehended by children. Others from galleries and museums could be used just as well, as long as they are consistent with what the children are learning and in keeping with their own growth in those symbols which are common to them.

The cluster represents only a sample of what is possible at this level; additional episodes and episodic clusters can and should be used. Teachers with insight, initiative, and ingenuity will be able to develop many from the samples given here. Episodes for the early primary level lay the foundation for continued learnings in art education.

FURTHER READINGS

Suggested readings for this chapter are given on pages 97 and 98.

9

Primary Level

INTRODUCTION

The episodes presented in this chapter are not intended to form an episodic cluster comparable to that for the early primary level; they are samples selected from several episodic clusters for the primary level. One will not find, for example, that each episode builds upon the preceding one, although there is continuity and relationship among the samples given. As these episodes are studied, one can see where others should be included between the samples. In studying these episodes, several points should be considered.

1. These are unusual episodes in that they are designed primarily to help children become "noticers," that is, to develop appreciative skills for interacting with exemplars in an intellectual, aesthetic, and empathic way. Some episodes are designed solely for the development of seeing skills.

2. The episodes selected for this chapter are examples of the various kinds which can be developed for this level to introduce children to schools of art, the functional use of art, and the relationship of art to other subjects, as well as to help them enrich art concepts.

3. Episodes which deal exclusively with the media processes have not been included. However, these can also help children become noticers. The media processes that have been used were selected for

their value in helping children acquire appreciative skills and solve problems using the visual art elements—thus establishing a relationship between children's work and the work of the artist. These activities help children enrich art concepts and enhance their own creativity through increased understanding.

4. Other media activities should be developed for the primary level. These should include numerous painting activities—tempera and possibly watercolor; drawing activities—crayon, charcoal, colored chalk; printmaking activities—cardboard, spoon, gadget, and string printing, and possibly linoleum cutting; other craft activities—collage, cut paper, clay, papier-mâché. Motivation for media activities should make use of procedures which will contribute to symbol enrichment. Topic motivations which can assist in this include "We" topics and others within the realm of the children's own experiences. Motivational procedures and media activities should help make children conscious of the visual art elements and their use in design.

5. Some of the episodes require certain procedures to be used with the visual media, as described in Chapter 13. Reference should be made to this chapter as needed.

6. In many cases, it will be impossible for one episode to be completed in one class session. Teachers must be aware of the progress made by the children and should know when to break the episode into two or more parts. For example, when a media process is included in the instructional procedures, it is probably better to present the process in the first part of the episode so that the paint can dry or a display can be made, and so that there will be a good starting place or a point of review and departure for the next part of the episode on the following day, or whenever the episode is continued.

7. These episodes are, of course, more complex than those presented for the early primary level. Remedial teaching will be required for those children who have not had the learning experiences encompassed in the earlier episodes. In most cases this will mean using the episodes designed for younger children, with modifications made for the increased maturity of the primary children. In other cases it will mean using selected experiences from the episodes for the early primary level as introductory learning activities for the episodes on the primary level. If children are to be successful in attaining the objectives for the primary level, they must have the necessary foundation.

EPISODE 1

*Objective: To enrich children's concepts of color, size,
and shape and to introduce concepts of
values and secondary colors*

Teacher background

1   Understand color pigment theory and that secondary colors are made from primary colors.
2   Know how to use the overhead projector (see pages 262–66).
3   Know value scales from dark to light, including black, white, and all primary colors.
4   Understand the relationship of values to pigment color theory. ment color theory.

Materials

Overhead projector and screen
Selected theatrical jells or selected colored acetates
Tempera paints—primary colors plus black and white
Brushes
Porous paper
Reproduction: Marc Chagall, *I and the Village*

Vocabulary

secondary colors	value
green	light
orange	dark
purple	Marc Chagall

names of other colors used in episode (pink, maroon, etc.)

Instructional procedures

Motivation and instruction: Sensory, multi-sensory experiences; topic discussion

1   Introduce the episode by reviewing what the children have learned about color, size, and shape. Use recommended materials from the early primary level for this review: different sizes of circles, squares, triangles, and rectangles of primary colors.

2 Discuss with the children the differences to be found in each of the primary colors. Use the overhead projector and selected theatrical jells to demonstrate that red may be lighter or darker in color but that it is still called red. Continue the demonstration with yellow and blue. Explain that there is a range from light to dark in each color and that this is called *value*.

3 Follow this demonstration by having children find different values of the primary colors in objects in the room and in their clothing. Different values of primary colors should be placed in various spots in the room.

4 After children have had experiences which help them to understand value, discuss how other colors can be made from the primary colors. Use the overhead projector and selected theatrical jells, and overlap yellow with blue to make green, red with blue to make purple, and red with yellow to make orange. (*Note:* Careful selection of theatrical jells or colored acetates is most important because only selected primaries will produce orange and purple. Some commercial companies have colored acetates for this purpose.) Discuss the colors which have been made from the primary colors and introduce the term *secondary colors* for these. Explain that secondary colors also have different values.

5 Prepare for a tempera painting experience.

  a Distribute materials; use only primary colors and black and white.

  b Stimulate children to discover what happens when primary colors are mixed with each other: red with yellow, yellow with blue, etc. Children should experiment to create colors using pigments just as they created colors using theatrical jells.

  c Have children mix black with the primary colors; then mix white with the colors to learn the values of the primaries.

  d Motivate children to paint different shapes of primary and secondary colors and different values.

6 Display paintings. Ask the children to tell about the different shapes and colors they have used.

Exemplar:

1 Introduce the exemplar shown in Figure 87 by asking children to find colors they have learned about which have been used by the artist: green, light green, dark green; red, light red or pink, dark red; etc. Continue until the children have identified all the colors they have studied. Discuss the lines and shapes used by the artist. Ask the children to describe the reproduction in terms of the activities shown. Ask them to explain why the artist has shown his village this way. Explain that the original painting may be as old as one of their grandparents.

2 Display the exemplar at the children's eye level.

Figure 87
Marc Chagall, *I and
the Village*, 1911

Oil on canvas,
75⅝ × 59⅝ inches

Expected outcome

Children should be able to:
1 Identify primary colors and the secondary colors derived from them.
2 Explain the property of value ranging from light to dark that each
   color has.
3 Locate all these in exemplars.

Related activities

(Visual exercises, books, poetry, related activities in other subjects)
1 Discuss with the children how colors make them feel: happy, sad,
   sweet, pleasant, unpleasant, etc.
2 Read *Let's Imagine Colors* by Janet Wolff.
3 Read *What Color Is Your World?* by Bob Gill.

EPISODE 2

*Objective: To introduce the concept of structural
qualities found in nature*

Teacher background

1 Understand structural qualities in nature.
2 Know how to make 2 × 2″ transparent slides using minute particles
   from nature (see Figure 175, page 259).
3 Understand science concepts of sound.
4 Understand line and texture in nature.
5 Understand analogies between line and texture in nature and in
   paintings.
6 Be able to form judgments and discriminations about texture and
   sound as they occur in nature and in music.

Materials

2 × 2″ slide projector and screen
2 × 2″ photo mounts
Clear acetate, precut to fit 2 × 2″ mounts
Small piece of leaf lettuce
Very thin slice of cucumber
Tomato skin
Minute particles from plants: pistils, stamen, etc. (dandelions are excel-
   lent for this)
Make slides with the above materials according to the directions given
   in Chapter 13 (see Figure 175, page 259).
Reproduction: Jimmy Ernst, *Sounds Across the River*

Vocabulary

structure   nature
design   Jimmy Ernst

Instructional procedures

Motivation and instruction: Sensory, multi-sensory experiences; topic discussion

1 Show a teacher-made transparent slide of lettuce. Ask the children to locate and describe the many kinds of lines they see. Ask them to describe the shapes made when lines cross each other. (Show the slide as large as possible.)

2 Move from the concrete visual experience into an abstraction of it by having children locate lines in the palms of their hands. Direct their attention to lines that cross. Ask them to tell about similarities between these lines and the ones seen in lettuce.

3 Ask children to identify other foods which have lines. Show the next slide, a cross-section of the cucumber. Talk about the lines in the cucumber slice. Then show the slide of the tomato skin so that children can discover that its texture is composed of many repeat patterns which come from repeated shapes.

4 Show the slides of minute particles from plants so that children can see the textural qualities invisible to the naked eye.

5 After children have seen these slides, discuss the various lines, patterns, and shapes which can be found in nature, including food. Introduce the terms *structure* and *design in nature.*

Exemplar:

1 Display the exemplar shown in Figure 88 and ask the children to describe shapes and lines that look familiar. Direct their attention to various patterns and shapes created by crossing lines. Compare these with the slides presented earlier.

Figure 88
Jimmy Ernst, *Sounds Across the River,* 1958

Oil, 51⅞ × 59⅞ inches

2   Ask the children to describe the sounds they might hear from this painting. Have them describe the sounds in terms of loud, soft, high, and low, and to explain why the artist called this *Sounds Across the River.*

3   Display the reproduction at the children's eye level.

Expected outcome

Children should know:

1   The design qualities that exist in nature, including those that are not visible to the naked eye.

2   That the artist uses different kinds of shape, texture, and design.

3   That shape, texture, and design can be found in common objects around us.

Related activities

(Visual exercises, books, poetry, related activities in other subjects)

1   If possible, science lessons on sound can be used.

2   Children can cut oranges, lemons, apples, and other foods in sections to study their structures.

3   Records of sounds, such as *Sounds of Camp, Sounds of Insects,* and *Sounds of Satellites* (Folkway Records), can be used to help children discriminate different sounds.

4   Read *Nature as Designer* by Bertel Bager.

5   With teacher guidance, children should make their own transparent slides.

EPISODE 3

Objective: To introduce the concept of "still life" representation and to enrich concepts of shape, solid form, and texture

Teacher background

1   Know what "still life" is.

2   Be acquainted with some artists who have painted still lifes.

3   Be aware of how light strikes solid objects.

4   Understand composition used by artists.

5   Know how multi-sensory experiences can be used to enhance the visual.

Figure 89
Paul Cézanne, *The Basket of Apples*

Oil on canvas, 24⅞ × 31 inches

Materials

Reproduction: Paul Cézanne, *The Basket of Apples*

Vocabulary

descriptive words of different shapes   still life
painter   Cézanne

Instructional procedures

Motivation and instruction: Sensory, multi-sensory experiences; topic discussion

1 Introduce the episode by discussing the objects in the room in terms of shape, solid form, texture, and degrees of roughness and smoothness.

2 Have children categorize things in the room that do or do not move by themselves. Demonstrate this with apples, if necessary.

Exemplar:

1 Direct the children's attention to the exemplar shown in Figure 89. Explain that the artist was interested in painting objects which do not move. Introduce the term *still life* to the children by explaining

that it is a painting of objects that do not move. Ask children to describe the objects painted by the artist and to explain how they differ from real objects. Explain that the artist has shown solid forms on a flat surface. Ask children to describe the taste and texture of apples they have eaten.

Expected outcome

Children should:

1 Know the term *still life* as applied to paintings.
2 Be able to distinguish among the various textures, shapes, and forms used by the artist.
3 Be able to explain differences in textures and taste of one kind of food, such as apples.

Related activities

(Visual exercises, books, poetry, related activities in other subjects)

1 Children may cut pictures of oranges, apples, and other fruits from magazines. These pictures should be of different sizes and textures. They may be arranged on 12 × 18" colored construction paper to make a still life collage.

EPISODE 4

Objective: To extend children's frames of reference for exemplars through experiences with art media

Teacher background

1 Have experience with tempera painting to understand the properties and limitations of tempera and to help children with problems in using it.
2 Understand motivational procedures for symbol enrichment before and during the art activity.
3 Know that auditory stimulation can enrich symbols for this topic.
4 See relationships between the expressive intent of children and that of artists.
5 Understand ways of helping children understand their use of visual art elements.
6 Understand the environmental atmosphere of a circus and how this relates to the artist's use of visual art elements.

Materials

Tempera paint
Brushes
Paper
Record player
Record: *Sounds of Carnival, Merry-Go-Round* (Folkways Record and Service Co., 6126)
Reproductions: Walt Kuhn, *The Blue Clown*
                Henri de Toulouse-Lautrec, *The Ring Master*
                Pablo Picasso, *Family of Saltimbanques*

Vocabulary

The Blue Clown	Toulouse-Lautrec
The Ring Master	circus
Walt Kuhn	

Instructional procedures

Motivation and instruction: Sensory, multi-sensory experiences; topic discussion

1 Prepare for a tempera painting activity.

    a Distribute the materials necessary for tempera painting.

    b Stimulate the children to discuss the different people and animals in a circus. Ask questions which will lead the children into a discussion of the clown: what he wears, how he acts, and how he makes them feel. Do not limit the discussion to clowns, but encourage the children to discuss others, such as ringmasters and animals.

    c Stimulate the children to paint their favorite person in a circus. While they are painting, play the record *Sounds of Carnival, Merry-Go-Round* for auditory stimulation.

    d Motivate each child to enrich his symbols by mentioning lines, shapes, sizes, colors, textures, and repeat patterns which he has already noticed in other objects.

    e When the children's paintings have dried, display them in the room. Ask the children to describe the person they painted. What did they show about this person? Although individual levels of development will differ, some of the paintings may look like the one in Figure 90.

Figure 90
Six and a Half Year Old

Exemplar:

1 Introduce the exemplar shown in Figure 91 by asking questions about the painting: Where do you think this clown is? How has the artist let us know that he was painting a clown? What is the clown doing? How does the clown look—is he happy, sad, proud, etc.? Direct the children's attention to the shapes to be found in the jacket, the textures used by the artist, and the degrees of roughness in the texture. Have children compare the textures in their paintings with those created by the artist. Display the reproduction at the children's eye level and move directly to the next exemplar.

2 Introduce the exemplar shown in Figure 92 by explaining that different artists painted clowns in many different ways and that this one shows a family of circus entertainers. Help the children to discover the repeat pattern to be found in the costume as well as the different textures to be found in the paint. Display the reproduction at the children's eye level, and move directly to the next exemplar.

Figure 91
Walt Kuhn, *The Blue Clown*, 1931
Oil on canvas, 30 × 25 inches

Figure 92
Pablo Picasso, *Family of Saltimbanques*
Oil on canvas, 83¾ × 90⅜ inches

Figure 93
Henri de Toulouse-Lautrec, *The Ring Master*, 1888

Oil on canvas, 38¾ × 63½ inches

3 Show the exemplar in Figure 93. Ask the children what this artist is showing. Direct the children's attention to the kinds of lines used by the artist: the broad curved line repeated to form the circus arena and the seats for the spectators, the repeated lines on the ringmaster's clothing made with paint strokes. Display the reproduction at the children's eye level.

4 After the three reproductions have been displayed in the room, have children compare them in terms of the subject matter and visual art elements. Help children with their time concepts by explaining that *The Ring Master* and *Family of Saltimbanques* were painted a long time ago, but that *The Blue Clown* is not nearly as old.

Expected outcome

Children should be able to:

1 Use their inactive knowledge of circus experiences and enrich their active knowledge through the use of media and exemplars.

2 Find similarities and differences among the three reproductions.

3 Associate some sounds from the record with the reproductions as well as with their own paintings.

Related activities

(Visual exercises, books, poetry, related activities in other subjects)

1 Read *What's in a Line?* by Leonard Kessler.

2 Play the record *Circus Time* (Simon Records, 6). Discuss with the children the activities that the music stimulates them to "see."

3 Keep the children's paintings to use later for evaluative purposes.

EPISODE 5

*Objective: To introduce concepts of surface
texture created by architects*

Teacher background

1 Be aware of practicing contemporary architects and their works.
2 Know that architects use all the visual art elements, especially repeat patterns in surface textures.
3 Be able to see the architect's use of visual art elements.
4 Understand that the use of a building, in part, determines its design.
5 Know how to help children translate visual experiences into understandings about their own environment.
6 Know the uses of the overhead projector (see pages 262–66).

Materials

Overhead projector and screen (see page 263).
Rectangular shapes of window screen, hail screen
Two strips of corrugated cardboard large enough for demonstration purposes
Halftones: Seagram's Building, New York, by Mies van der Rohe and
          Philip Johnson
          Federal Building, Kansas City, Missouri

Vocabulary

architect   Federal Building
building textures   Seagram's Building
Mies van der Rohe   plans
Philip Johnson   designs

Instructional procedures

Motivation and instruction: Sensory, multi-sensory experiences; topic discussion

1 Discuss the materials used for building schools and houses: brick, stone, wood, etc. Ask the children to describe the various textures of the materials and the repeat patterns they make. Introduce the word *architect* by explaining that he is a person who plans schools and other buildings and decides what materials will be used. Compare him with artists studied in preceding episodes.

2 Using the overhead projector, show the rectangular shape of a piece of window screen. Discuss the shapes that are created when lines cross each other. Ask the children to describe the shapes: rectangular, square.

3 While the children are discussing the shapes, place the hail screen beside the window screen on the projector to show the children that the repeat patterns may be small (window screen) or large (hail screen).

Exemplar:

1 Introduce the exemplar in Figure 94 by asking children if they see any repeat patterns like the ones on the screen. Have them point out such patterns. Ask the children to recall any buildings in their neighborhood which have almost identical repeat patterns.

2 Using the two strips of corrugated cardboard, demonstrate how different textural qualities are created when the two strips are not matched. Show the halftone in Figure 95 and ask the children to find similarities between the cardboard and the building.

3 Display both halftones at the children's eye level.

4 Have the children describe the activities which might go on in the two buildings. Relate these to occupations of their fathers or other people they know.

Figure 94
Mies van der Rohe and Philip
Johnson, Seagram's Building

Figure 95
Federal Building, Kansas City, Missouri

Expected outcome

1 Children should be able to see the relationships between the shapes, textures, and repeat patterns they know and their application to buildings designed by architects.

Related activities

(Visual exercises, books, poetry, related activities in other subjects)

1 Invite a local architect to talk to the class about how buildings are planned.
2 Read *My Skyscraper City* by Penny Hammond and Katrina Thomas.
3 Collect picture postcards of buildings in the community: federal building or post office, office buildings, etc. Make a bulletin board display of these cards. Have children find lines, textures, and shapes in the buildings. Discussions of buildings may also work well during social studies time, since children at this level often study communities, including cities.

EPISODE 6

Objective: To introduce concepts of relief sculpture and frottage

Teacher background

1 Know the origin of frottage.
2 Have experience in creating frottage.
3 Understand techniques used in frottage.
4 Know contemporary uses of relief sculpture.
5 Understand how designer-craftsmen make functional objects aesthetically pleasing.
6 Understand the relationship between the visual art elements and relief sculpture.
7 Know the uses of the opaque projector (see pages 266–67).

Materials

9 × 12″ pieces of cardboard
Elmer's glue
Precut pieces of cardboard in a variety of shapes
Newsprint
Black marking crayon
Halftone: Mabel Hutchinson, *Art Gallery Doors*

Vocabulary

frottage

rubbings

relief

relief sculpture

gallery

Mabel Hutchinson

Instructional procedures

Motivation and instruction: Sensory, multi-sensory experiences; topic discussion

1 Introduce the episode by demonstrating how various shapes can be arranged on a piece of cardboard and then glued in place.

2 Have the children select a variety of sizes and shapes from the precut pieces of cardboard and arrange these pieces on the 9 × 12″ cardboard until they have a variety of sizes and shapes with spaces left between each one. After they have experimented with placement, have them glue the pieces in place. When they have completed their arrangements, put the work away until the next day. The glue should be allowed to dry completely.

3 Use the arrangements which the children have made and explain that each is called a *relief,* which means that some pieces are raised. Have the children rub their hands over the arrangements and experience tactually the sensation of a relief—that the glued pieces are higher than the piece of cardboard underneath.

4 Provide the children with newsprint and black marking crayons. Demonstrate how the impression of the shapes they make can be picked up by placing the newsprint over the arrangement and rubbing crayon over the newsprint. Explain that this technique is called *frottage,* which means rubbing a surface and recording the texture and size of the shapes underneath.

5 Have the children find objects in the room which have relief qualities.

6 Let each child use a penny to make rubbings or frottages.

7 Ask the children to explain their frottages in terms of shapes and the lines around the shapes.

Exemplar:

[1]1 Introduce the exemplar in Figure 96 by having the children hypothesize about the way that the artist made this relief sculpture. Explain that an artist sometimes works with pieces of wood, arranges the shapes in an interesting pattern, then glues, screws, or nails them to a flat piece of wood—as the children did with pieces of cardboard.

---

[1] If a halftone of this exemplar is not available, an opaque projector can be used to show the figure above.

Figure 96
Mabel Hutchinson, Art Gallery Doors

Handcrafted

2 Explain that this is relief sculpture which will be used as a door. Ask the children to explain why the artist has made the doors this way. Explain that artists are always designing things we use and that we use their relief sculpture in architecture and homes. We also use the works of artists on the walls of our homes or other buildings: we hang reproductions of works of art.

3 Ask the children to identify artists (groups, not specific ones) who have designed something that they use. Explain that the artist who did the doors in Figure 96 intended that they be used in an art gallery. Ask children to describe other buildings where these doors might be used.

4 Have children find the shapes, sizes, and textures they have learned about in the exemplar. Direct their attention to the way that the doorknob blends in with the other shapes.

Expected outcome

Children should:

1 Know that impressions can be recorded by rubbings and that these are called frottages.

2 Be able to discriminate among various sizes, shapes, and textures.

3 Know that art has a function in their daily lives.

Related activities

(Visual exercises, books, poetry, related activities in other subjects)

1 Have children find relief qualities in different kinds of furniture.

2 Read *Full of Wonder* by Ann Kirn.

3   Direct children to look at doors on public buildings, churches, etc., and have them describe these to the other children to see whether or not the rest of the class can guess what building it is.

4   Have children write a story about what is behind the doors shown in Figure 96.

EPISODE 7

Objective: To introduce the concept of ceramics and to enrich children's concepts of texture

Teacher background

1   Have experience with clay in making simple pots using either the pinch or coil method.

2   Know how ceramists work.

3   Be able to relate problem solving in the visual art elements to ceramists' problem-solving experiences.

4   Know the uses of the opaque projector (see pages 266–67).

Materials

Halftones of ceramic exemplars: J. Sheldon Carey, *Ceramic Pottery*
Marilyn Kay Austin, *Three Planters*

Prepared moist clay
Newspapers to cover desk tops
Orange or lemon
Magnifying glass

Vocabulary

texture   J. Sheldon Carey
ceramics   Marilyn Austin
ceramists

Instructional procedures

Motivation and instruction: Sensory, multi-sensory experiences; topic discussion

1   Prepare for an art activity with clay.
    a   Pass out one small ball of clay to each child.
    b   Have children wedge the clay—pound it to remove air pockets.

c Demonstrate how to make a round ball of clay.

d Have children form clay into a round ball similar to an orange.

e Demonstrate the use of the thumb in making a hole in the clay.

f Have children make a hole in the ball of clay (see Figure 97).

Figure 97

g Place the clay on the desk to flatten the bottom so that it will stand.

h Have children work the clay so that the walls will be the same thickness.

i Stimulate children to make different hollow shapes or pots from the basic beginning.

j Demonstrate ways of making designs on the pots with pencil, spoon handle, and other implements.

k Stimulate the children to make repeat patterns on the pots.

[2]l Allow the clay to dry. If a kiln is available, the pots should be bisque-fired in the kiln. If a kiln is not available, paint the pots with tempera and cover with a coat of clear varnish or shellac.

Exemplar:

1 While the clay is drying introduce the exemplar shown in Figure 98 [3] by explaining that an artist called a ceramist creates all kinds of pots which can hold water, flowers, or plants, and that the ceramist is concerned with both form and texture. The pots will have degrees

---

[2] See (1) under "Exemplar."

[3] If halftones of this and the following exemplars are not available, an opaque projector can be used to show the figures.

Figure 98
J. Sheldon Carey, *Three Ceramic Pots*

Figure 99
Marilyn Kay Austin,
Three Planters

of roughness, as shown in Figure 98. Ask the children to describe the different sizes and textures of the pots. Explain that the texture on the ceramic pots has been created from repeated shapes much like those that can be found by looking at an orange or a lemon. Have them look at an orange or lemon through a magnifying glass. Have the children compare the textures that they have created with those in the exemplar. Explain that many art galleries and museums have ceramics in their collections, as well as paintings.

2 Introduce the next exemplar by explaining to the children that some ceramics are produced by manufacturers and can be bought just as we buy cups, cereal bowls, and glasses. These ceramics were once created by a ceramist, such as the pottery shown in Figure 99. Discuss the differences between these pieces and the ones in Figure 98. Discuss the intended use of the pottery in Figure 99, and lead the discussion into planters which the children have seen in buildings or outside buildings and homes.

3 Explain that ceramic pottery need not always be used for practical purposes, and that some pots are used just for decorative purposes because we like to look at them. Have children describe objects which they like to have around just to look at.

Expected outcome

Children should:

1 Know that some ceramics are intended for functional use as containers for water, flowers, and plants, while others are decorative.
2 Know the meaning of the words *ceramics* and *ceramist.*
3 Know how to create texture on their own clay work.
4 Understand that texture is created by repeat patterns.

Related activities

(Visual exercises, books, poetry, related activities in other subjects)

1 Have children find different ceramic examples in magazines such as *Craft Horizons.*
2 If there is a ceramist in the community, ask him to give a demonstration of how ceramic pots are thrown on a potter's wheel. A field trip for this purpose will not only give children firsthand experience, but will also provide materials for experience stories and group discussions.

EPISODE 8

Objective: To enrich children's concepts of sculpture

Teacher background

1 Know the various materials used by sculptors.
2 Know that the different materials require the use of different tools.
3 Be able to demonstrate simple sculptural techniques.
4 Understand that various materials can be used to create different textures and different thermal sensory experiences.
5 Understand the historical background of sculpture.

Materials

Small block of soft wood (soft pine) and cutting instrument (wood-cutting tool or linocutter)

Medium-size rock or marble

Halftones: Ernst Barlach, *Standing Woman with Folded Arms*
Sculpture—Sumerian, *Figure of a Nobleman*

Vocabulary

sculptor

sculpture

hammer

chisel

sculpture tools

gouge

Mari gypsum

Barlach

Instructional procedures

Motivation and instruction: Sensory, multi-sensory experiences; topic discussion

1   Ask the children to recall clay work in which they made solid forms of people or pets.

2   Ask the children what other ways there are of showing people in solid form. Explain that an artist called a sculptor carves from both wood and stone to develop a symbol for a person.

3   Demonstrate how the small block of wood can be carved by making several gouges in the wood with a sharp instrument (wood-cutting tool or linocutter). Explain that some woods are much harder than others and that special tools and wood hammers are sometimes needed by the sculptor.

Exemplar:

1   Introduce the exemplar in Figure 100 by explaining that the sculptor who did this work gouged from a very hard piece of wood. Ask children to locate the over-all texture created by the sculptor's tools. Ask them to describe how it might feel to touch it. Direct their attention to the various lines in the sculpture. Introduce the word *sculpture* by explaining that it is the work of the sculptor and has solid form.

Figure 100

Ernst   Barlach,   *Standing Woman with Folded Arms,* 1922

Wood, 40 inches high × 8¾ × 10¼ inches

2 Direct the children's attention to the many repeat patterns which create texture in the sculpture. Ask them to locate the visual art elements used by the sculptor. Ask why he used wood instead of some other material.

3 Explain that when a sculpture is made from material that is harder than wood, such as rock or stone, different tools have to be used. Ask the children to name some of the tools they might have to use on stone. Demonstrate that rock or stone cannot be cut with the instruments used for the wood.

4 Display the exemplar at the children's eye level.

5 Introduce the exemplar shown in Figure 101 by explaining that this shows a piece of sculpture made from a very hard piece of stone called Mari gypsum. Have the children locate lines and shapes in the stone, and the different textures created by the sculptor. Ask them to describe how the stone would feel if they could touch it: cold, slick, rough, etc. Encourage the children to discover lines and shapes, such as the line of the eyebrows. Display the halftone at the children's eye level.

6 Have the children compare the two pieces in terms of shapes, repeat patterns, textures, and materials. Explain that the sculptor who did the nobleman lived a very long time ago and that the piece of sculpture is very old—much older than anyone they know. The sculpture of the woman is not nearly as old as the other.

Figure 101
Figure of a Nobleman,
Sumerian, c. 2500 B.C.

4 inches high

Expected outcome

Children should:

1 Be able to discriminate between stone and wood sculpture.
2 Be aware that the sculptor may use materials other than clay.
3 Know that wood and stone require different tools for gouging and cutting.
4 Know that artists use different materials because their expressive intent is different.

Related activities

(Visual exercises, books, poetry, related activities in other subjects)

1 If possible, have children locate and describe pieces of sculpture in parks, recreation centers, churches, and other public buildings. Discuss the material that has been used: wood, stone, or metal.
2 If a sculptor lives in the community, invite him to talk with the children and to show the tools with which he works.
3 Provide children with art books suitable for their age level which have photographs of pieces of sculpture. Encourage the children to talk about the pieces in terms of the materials and the sensory impression they might get from feeling them.
4 Prepare children for a visit to an art gallery or museum where they can see sculpture (see pages 247–53).

EPISODE 9

Objective: To enrich children's concepts of light and color

Teacher background

1 Be able to relate science concepts of light to art concepts.
2 Understand that both scientists and artists have been interested in light.
3 Know the Impressionist School of painting.
4 Understand the nucleus of commonalities.

Materials

Reproductions: Claude Monet, *The Zuiderkerk (South Church) at Amsterdam: Looking up Groenburgwal*
Claude Monet, *Morning on the Seine*

Vocabulary

light   Monet
impressions   white light
impressionist   reflected light

Instructional procedures

Motivation and instruction: Sensory, multi-sensory experiences; topic discussion

1   Introduce the episode by reviewing with the children what they have learned about primary and secondary colors and value. Conduct science experiments in light and color.

2   Take the children outside and let them discover the shadows they cast. If the weather and season permit, have them notice how the sun, when it shines on leaves, can create colors such as light green, dark green, light yellow, dark yellow, and perhaps even blue and purple. When the sun is out, one can see many different colors, not just green. Discuss the way these colors are also reflected in water if the trees are near still water.

Exemplar:

1   Introduce the exemplar shown in Figure 102 by asking the children if they think the scene really looks this way. Explain that this is a reproduction of a painting by an artist who was very much interested in light and color, and that he has painted his "impression" of the way sunshine creates different lights and colors at different times of the day—just as they have painted their impressions of people, pets, and trees. Because of the artist's interest in light and color and his desire to give his impression of them, he is called an "impressionistic" painter. Display the reproduction at the children's eye level.

Figure 102
Claude Monet, *The Zuider-kerk* [South Church] *at Amsterdam: Looking Up Groenburgwal,* 1872

Oil on canvas, 21½ × 25¾ inches

Figure 103
Claude Monet, *Morning on the Seine,* 1897

Oil on canvas, 34½ × 35½ inches

2 Introduce the exemplar shown in Figure 103 by explaining that the same artist was interested in painting his impressions of light and color in different scenes. Discuss the different scenes in the two paintings, but help children to discover that the qualities of light and color depend on the time of the day: colors are different in the morning from what they are at noon or in late afternoon.

Expected outcome

Children should:

1 Be able to discriminate between light and color created by the sun in the morning, at noon, and in the afternoon.
2 Know that the artist showed his impressions of light and color change in his paintings.

Related activities

(Visual exercises, books, poetry, related activities in other subjects)

1 Whenever possible, direct the children's attention to the way the sun creates different colors outside and even inside the room at different times of the day.
2 Have children compare what they see with the reproductions.
3 Read *Let's Imagine Colors* by Janet Wolff.
4 Read *What Makes a Shadow?* by Clyde Bulla.

EPISODE 10

*Objective: To extend children's concepts of visual art elements
into a frame of reference for industrial design products*

Teacher background

1 Know that industrial designers are designer-craftsmen.
2 Know that all objects in everyday use were once designed by industrial designers although they may be mass produced.
3 Understand the industrial designer's use of all visual art elements.
4 Be able to see how industrial designers have used visual art elements.
5 Understand the contributions made by industrial designers to everyday living.
6 Be able to help children understand changes which functional objects have undergone.
7 Understand the components of personal preference in choosing functional objects.

Materials

Halftones: Ball Clock
            Grandfather Clock
            Contemporary Floor Clock
            Wall Clock with Sculptured Dial
Opaque projector and screen (if the halftones in this book are used)

Vocabulary

designer	All the words for the
planner	visual art elements learned
everyday objects	in preceding episodes

Instructional procedures

Motivation and instruction: Sensory, multi-sensory experiences; topic discussion

1 Introduce the episode by discussing the different kinds of work people do, and the names we use for people who do a special kind of work: doctor, lawyer, plumber, trucker, policeman, engineer, etc. Guide the discussion to include artist, ceramist, architect, and sculptor.

2   Continue the discussion by talking about those people whose special kind of work includes planning the things we use every day, such as tables, chairs, paint boxes, spoons, knives, etc., and who are called *designers*. Explain that the designer also produced an original work of art and that his work is reproduced: the chairs in their room were once designed as an original and have been reproduced. Compare these objects with the reproductions of the paintings with which children have already had experiences.

3   Ask the children to name other objects in the room which might have been designed by a designer. Explain that these were designed by *industrial designers*.

Exemplar:

1   Introduce the exemplar shown in Figure 104 by explaining that the designer is conscious of line, shape, size, texture, solid form, and color, and that he uses all of these in the clocks shown in the figure. Let the children find the different sizes of round shapes used by the designer. Ask them to tell about the use of the smallest round shapes. Have the children count the round shapes and relate them to the numerals they are familiar with on clocks.

2   Introduce the exemplar shown in Figure 105 by explaining that years ago clocks that stood on the floor were designed and that these were called grandfather clocks. Some of these old clocks are still to be found in homes, and when they are very old, they are called antiques. Let the children talk about grandfather clocks which they may have seen, and discuss the numerals on them.

3   Introduce the exemplar shown in Figure 106 by explaining that the designer sometimes uses designs that are very old and from these develops new designs which are in keeping with the way we live today and the way we will live in the future. Talk about the missing numerals.

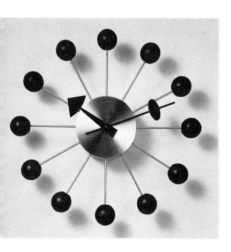

Figure 104
Ball Clock

Figure 105
Grandfather Clock

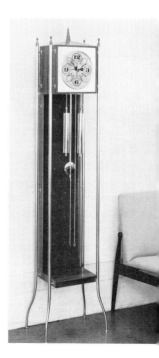

Figure 106
Contemporary
Floor Clock

Figure 107
White Case and
Sculptured Dial

4 Introduce the clock shown in Figure 107 by letting children compare it with the others. Explain that this shows another application of relief sculpture. Let them find the various shapes used by the designer. Discuss what has been used instead of numerals on this clock.

5 Discuss the differences among all the various clocks shown: some sit on the floor, some are used on the wall, some have numerals, some represent the old and others represent the new. Lead into the point that although clocks are different they have a functional purpose. Ask children which clock they would select if they could have one. Ask the children which clock they would select for an office, a spaceship, a home, a school hall, etc. Have them explain their selections.

Expected outcome

Children should:

1 Be aware that a designer designs or plans objects which are used every day in their homes and school.

2 Know that there can be many different designs for one everyday object, such as a clock, and that these designs will make different use of size, shape, texture, and other visual elements.

3 Be able to form a preference for one of the clocks and to decide on the appropriateness of different clocks for different places.

Related activities

(Visual exercises, books, poetry, related activities in other subjects)

1 Help children become "noticers" of the design of other objects by asking questions about them.

2 Collect pictures of new designs made from old: tables, chairs, lamps, etc.

ANALYSIS OF THE EPISODES

It can be seen that the episodes presented in this chapter are based on the concepts formed and enriched in the episodic cluster for the early primary level. It can also be seen that, although this chapter deals with the same concepts given for younger children, it presents them in a more complex way so that they can be further enriched and used in ways appropriate for children at this level. Teachers will find that some children are unable to grasp the concepts as readily as others, and that these children will need more time and, perhaps, additional experiences. Individual differences should be allowed for in art education as well as in other subjects.

By comparing the objectives of the episodes in this chapter with those for the early primary level and with the basic structure, it is possible to see how the concepts for art are returned to again and again, and are directed toward developing frames of reference for different exemplars. At the primary level of elementary school, children should be helped to reach higher levels of conceptualization through many sequential art learnings. These learnings should encompass experiences with color, design, and art history (chiefly through comparisons and encounters with schools of art, such as the Impressionist School), and should include an expanded vocabulary of art terms.

These episodes have been developed to help children become more acute observers and to increase the possibilities of what they can see by increasing what they know. The emphasis on seeing skills—begun at the early primary level, expanded at the primary level, and continued at the intermediate level—is an important part of art education in the elementary school. The exemplars which are used to help children become more aware also serve to increase understanding and to extend frames of reference for encounters with works of art in the future.

FURTHER READINGS

Suggested readings for this chapter are given on pages 97 and 98.

10

Intermediate Level:
Artists and
Designer-Craftsmen

INTRODUCTION

In this and the next chapter selected learning episodes are presented to be used with children at the intermediate level in elementary schools. Specific episodes have been selected from the many which can be presented at this level to show continued use of the basic structure in developing objectives and instructional procedures designed to enhance visual perception. The episodes presented in these chapters are based on learning experiences which children should have had at the early primary and primary levels. If children have not had these experiences or have not developed the understandings necessary for the episodes in these chapters, remedial work should be given using episodes from the early primary and primary levels.

One episodic cluster is included in this chapter. The first three episodes constitute this cluster. The remainder, excerpts from various clusters, need to be used along with other episodes. It is hoped that this cluster and sample episodes will serve as a guide for teachers in developing others. Some of the episodes given, especially those involving the media processes, will have to be divided into parts. There are logical places where divisions can be made without disrupting the sequence and the continuity of learning experiences. If the episodes are divided into two or more parts, it is suggested that the learning experiences which have been completed be reviewed with the children before beginning the next part.

The media activities included in these episodes have been designed to contribute to extended frames of reference for the exemplars used and for others to which children will be exposed. It is suggested that episodes encompassing only media activities be given along with episodes similar to those presented in this chapter. These activities should include all the ones introduced on the early primary and primary levels, with particular emphasis on activities which involve work with three-dimensional products. Work with media should help children to become conscious of the visual art elements as they are used in expressive intent and as they relate to exemplars. The experiences presented for the intermediate level help children to develop seeing skills and to draw on what is learned in the media activities to enhance these skills.

As teachers know, at the intermediate level children have reached a stage of critical reasoning and questioning, and are very much concerned with their environment, both physical and social. They are interested not only in their immediate environment, but in the real and imagined environment of space technology. Because of this interest and of the needs implied by it, an episodic cluster which encompasses environmental exemplars is presented on this level. Taste, the product of refined judgments and discriminations, does not just happen, any more than enhanced visual perception just happens. This, along with other qualities, is developed from exposures, interactions, and learnings which have their beginnings in the elementary school.

Although the episodes of learning included in this book have been designed for use in the elementary school, aesthetic education should not be considered finished here. Hopefully, the learnings acquired will be built upon at the secondary level. Learning to look, to see, and to interact must be emphasized from childhood through adulthood.

EPISODE 1

*Objective: To enrich children's concepts of
intermediate colors and values **

Teacher background

1   Understand light color theories and pigment color theories.

2   Understand how one color is affected by placement with other colors.

3   Know that artists have experimented with color, have used light in painting, and have created different effects and moods with these.

4   Know artists' use of color theories coupled with developed methods for such painting techniques as pointillism.

5   Know where children are in their developmental patterns and how they can be helped to understand color theories and the use of techniques so that symbols can be enriched in art expression.

6   Know the uses of the overhead projector (see pages 262–66).

Materials

Overhead projector and screen (see page 263)

Theatrical jells or selected acetates in red, yellow, and blue, precut in various geometric shapes and sizes [1]

Additional theatrical jells to demonstrate value

Tempera paint in primary colors, plus black and white

A variety of brushes

A variety of paper

Vocabulary

intermediate colors	blue-green	light
yellow-green	blue-purple	dark
yellow-orange	red-orange	warm
red-purple		cool

---

* This and the two following episodes form an episodic cluster on color built on previous episodes dealing with color from the early primary and primary levels.

[1] Some excellent commercial transparencies are available for this demonstration in color. The overhead projector and transparencies are recommended because it is difficult for children to mix opaque pigments in exact quantities.

Instructional procedures

Motivation and instruction: Sensory, multi-sensory experiences; topic discussion

1   Introduce the episode by reviewing with the children what they have already learned about colors, including primary colors, secondary colors, and values. As a part of the review, use the overhead projector to demonstrate how secondary colors are made from primary colors (see Chapter 8). Discuss with the children how other colors (ones which they have already used in their paintings) can be made by mixing equal quantities of primary and secondary colors.

2   Use the overhead projector to demonstrate what happens when yellow, a primary color, is placed over green, a secondary color. Explain that this color is called yellow-green and that it is an intermediate color. An intermediate color is derived by combining equal quantities of a primary and a secondary color. Continue with the concrete visual experience until all six intermediate colors have been produced and can be identified by the class as being intermediate colors.

3   Review *value*, the range from light to dark that all colors have. Use the additional theatrical jells or colored acetates so that children can discover values which are to be found in all colors.

4   Move immediately into the visual abstraction of the concrete experience by having children locate objects in the room which have these properties of color. They should identify colors of clothing as well as objects in the room. It will be helpful to display a bulletin board on which some of these colors are used, and to display a reproduction in which the artist has used these colors.

5   After this visual experience, prepare for a media activity:

   a   Have the children mix intermediate colors by using primary colors, plus black and white.

   b   After this experimentation with color, stimulate children for a painting activity. Topics such as "We Are Walking in the Street," "We Are Walking in the Country," or other topics derived from their experiences may be used.

   c   While children are painting, motivate individuals as needed for enriched concepts of texture, size, shapes, symbols, and design.

   d   Display the finished paintings. Ask the children how colors have been used to portray feelings in their paintings. Lead into a discussion of colors which are warm or cool. Help children understand that colors are sometimes described as warm or cool because of the way they make us feel. Use illustrations from nature; e.g., a lake sometimes looks blue and the water is cool. Lead the discussion into ways that the children have used color to create texture, shapes, and lines which enrich their symbols.

Exemplar: No exemplar is included with this episode, but teachers have found it helpful to use reproductions which show different seasons and which show how the artists have used color to portray different moods and feelings, such as:

Pieter Bruegel: *Children's Games, Hunters in the Snow*
Marc Chagall: *I and the Village, Snowing*

Expected outcome

Children should:

1 Be able to distinguish among primary, secondary, and intermediate colors.
2 Know how secondary and intermediate colors are derived as a result of mixing paint.
3 Be able to discriminate among colors found in objects and clothing, and to identify them as red-orange, etc.
4 Know the difference between warm and cool colors.
5 Be intellectually and empathically aware of their use of color and how all visual art elements are involved.

Related activities

(Visual exercises, books, poetry, related activities in other subjects)

1 Read about colors in science books or other books, such as *Let's Imagine Colors* by Janet Wolff.
2 Have children experiment with colored acetates using the overhead projector. These should produce secondary and intermediate colors.
3 If exemplars are used, have children read about the artists and their use of color.
4 Use science experiments for light and color.

EPISODE 2

Objective: To introduce concepts of color relationships

Teacher background

See background for Episode 1.

Materials

Use colored construction paper to cut the following:

8″ squares in a variety of colors except red

Materials

4″ squares—red
2″ squares in a variety of colors except red
Reproductions: Josef Albers, *Homage to the Square: "Insert"*
                       Nicholas Krushenik, *Red, Yellow, Blue, and Orange*

Vocabulary

optical illusion   Josef Albers
Op Art   *Homage to the Square: "Insert"*
arrangements   Nicholas Krushenik
color relationships   *Red, Yellow, Blue, and Orange*

Instructional procedures

Motivation and instruction: Sensory, multi-sensory experiences; topic discussion

1 Prepare a bulletin board using different colored 8″ squares. Leave at least a 4″ margin around each square. Direct the children's attention to the bulletin board and ask them if the colors look different when placed with other colors.

2 Direct the children's attention to the 4″ red squares which are now going to be placed inside the 8″ squares of various colors so they will notice how the red changes color when it is placed in the center of another color. Quickly pin all the small red squares inside the larger ones.

3 Have the children describe how colors have changed because of other colors. Explain that when colors are placed near one another, they change. After this visual experience, pin the 2″ squares inside the 4″ squares (without regard to color) and discuss the way colors have again changed—how colors affect one another. Red looks different when it is surrounded by other colors.

4 After this visual experience, discuss how some colors work better together than others. Have children experiment with the squares, selecting and discriminating with regard to color relationships.

Exemplar:

1 Introduce the exemplar shown in Figure 69, page 110, and discuss the fascination that artists have had with color and the experimentations they have done with paints for different color effects. Explain that artists have been interested in using color with geometric shapes (see Figure 108). Help the children understand that the painting is similar to the experiment with the squares of different colors and sizes. Display the reproduction at the children's eye level. (This figure

Figure 108
Josef Albers, *Hom-age to the Square: "Insert"*

Oil on composition board, 43½ × 43½ inches

has been repeated to show that an exemplar can be used at different levels and that children can develop a more sophisticated way of interacting with the exemplar as a result of more learning experiences.)

2 Introduce the exemplar shown in Figure 109 by discussing this artist's concern for creating a different kind of illusion. Ask the children to find the different shapes derived from rectangles, and to explain how these have been arranged in different ways to give the illusion of movement. Have them describe the illusion created and the feelings they experience as they look at the canvas. Introduce the term *optical illusion* and discuss how things look—Are things always as they look? Introduce the term *Op Art* and explain that this exemplar is an example of Op Art. Ask the children to recall additional examples that they might have seen on television, commercial packaging, advertisements, etc.

Figure 109
Nicholas Krushenik, *Red, Yellow, Blue and Orange*, 1965

Synthetic polymer paint on canvas, 84 × 71¼ inches

3 Display both exemplars and have children compare the two in terms of shape, size, and color as they have been used to create space. Ask the children to select the one they prefer and to explain their preference.

Expected outcome

Children should:
1 Have developed concepts of color relationships.
2 Understand how color relationships are used by the artists along with relationships of shapes.
3 Have extended their frames of reference for Josef Albers' painting.[2]

Related activities

(Visual exercises, books, poetry, related activities in other subjects)
1 Whenever possible, direct the children's attention to Op Art as it is used on billboards, packaging, television, and advertising.
2 Have children experiment further with color relationships. Provide them with a variety of shapes cut from different colors of construction paper and stimulate them to arrange these into pleasing color relationships and compositions.
3 Encourage children to read about the artists.
4 Provide art magazines that show different artists' work in optical illusion.

EPISODE 3

Objective: To introduce the concept of pointillism and its relationship to color

Teacher background

See background for Episode 1.

Materials

Crayons or tempera paint

---

[2] This exemplar was introduced on the early primary level. The conceptual frame of reference here is more extended than that for the early primary level, which included shapes. At the intermediate level this should also include color relationships.

White drawing paper

Reproduction: Georges Seurat, *Sunday Afternoon on the Island of La Grande Jatte*

Vocabulary

dots	Georges Seurat
points	*Sunday Afternoon on the Island of La*
pointillism	*Grande Jatte*

Instructional procedures

Motivation and instruction: Sensory, multi-sensory experiences; topic discussion

1   Demonstrate how the eyes can blend color from a series of marks and dots of color. Review what has been learned about using dots to create texture.

2   Prepare for an art activity:

   a   Provide the children with paper approximately $4\frac{1}{2} \times 5\frac{1}{2}''$ and let them experiment by using different dots or points of color. The first experiments should be with primary colors so that the children can learn that the eyes can reproduce secondary colors from the placement of the primary colors; i.e., red dots placed among yellow dots will produce orange.

   b   Continue these experiments using primary, secondary, and intermediate colors.

   c   After children have had time to experiment and learn about the blending of dots of color, pass out $6 \times 8''$ pieces of paper and introduce a topic motivation for a composition using dots of color only. Topics may include running, jumping, or other activities within the children's experiences. Motivate children to understand the relationships between texture and color which they are creating.

   d   Display all the compositions at the children's eye level, and discuss how the eyes blend dots and produce other colors. Introduce the term *pointillism*. Ask the children to explain how they have used pointillism to create different colors and atmosphere.

Exemplar:

1   Introduce the exemplar shown in Figure 110 by asking the following questions: How did this artist solve problems in the use of visual art elements by using dots only? Why did the artist use dots instead of flat color? How did he contrast curved lines with horizontal and vertical lines? Where is the sun in this exemplar?

2   Display the reproduction at the children's eye level.

Figure 110
Georges Seurat, *Sunday Afternoon on the Island of La Grande Jatte,* 1884–86

Oil on canvas, 81 × 120⅜ inches

Expected outcome

Children should:
1 Understand pointillism.
2 Know that color need not always be applied in a flat manner.
3 Understand that artists have been interested in experimenting with color.
4 Understand that they have solved problems with color in ways similar to those used by artists.

Related activities

(Visual exercises, books, poetry, related activities in other subjects)
1 Use the science experiment in which a spotlight is shone on a round form and casts shadows.
2 Have children study other artists' uses of pointillism.
3 Encourage children to read about Georges Seurat.

EPISODE 4

Objective: To enrich children's concepts of visual art elements to include design concepts used by artists and designer-craftsmen *

Teacher background

1 Understand that all art concepts are used in design.
2 Understand the difference between applied design and design woven into fabrics.
3 Develop sensitivity to different textures, patterns, and arrangements.
4 Have experience in working with yarns and fabrics, including stitchery techniques, ways of making different stitches with yarns, and ways of applying yarn on fabric with glue.
5 Have experience in simple weaving processes.
6 Know the history of man and his art so that other events can be associated with the exemplars used and so that art can be related to the total of man's history.
7 Understand the functional and emotional needs for tapestries and other works of art.
8 Know the uses of the overhead projector (see pages 262–66).
9 Know the uses of the opaque projector (see Figure 182, page 267).

Materials

Overhead projector and screen (see page 263).
Small piece of burlap
Pieces of burlap of different shapes and sizes
Elmer's glue and/or needles
Variety of yarns and fabrics
Opaque projector and screen, if halftones from this book or other art books are used (see Figure 182, page 267)
Reproductions: Henri Matisse, *Woman on Rose Divan*
Ernst Ludwig Kirchner, *Wildboden*

---

* This and the remaining episodes in the chapter are not part of an episodic cluster but are samples of episodes which can be used to develop frames of reference for the works of artists and designer-craftsmen. These are episodes that will require several sessions to complete, and teachers should look for places where they can be logically split.

Materials

Halftones: *Coptic Textile*
Lucia Suffel, *Small Flower Tapestry*
Martha Menke Underwood, *Flowers and Butterflies*

Vocabulary

fabric	Coptic
burlap	textile
weaving	Henri Matisse
yarn	*Woman on Rose Divan*
weaver	Ernst Ludwig Kirchner
warp	*Wildboden*
woof	Lucia Suffel
stitchery	Martha Menke Underwood
tapestry	contemporary

Instructional procedures

Motivation and instruction: Sensory, multi-sensory experiences; topic discussion

[3] 1   Ask the children to describe or explain the way cloth is made. Explain that cloth is woven and that weaving is done by passing yarn over and under yarns which run in another direction. Introduce the terms *warp* and *woof*. Using a small piece of burlap and the overhead projector, show that burlap is composed of tiny shapes created by the warp and woof, and that these also create texture.

2   Move into the visual abstraction of the concrete experience by directing the children's attention to their own clothing and helping them to notice that some clothing is rough (sweaters) and other clothing smooth (blouses and shirts).

3   Direct the children's attention to fabrics they are wearing which have various repeat patterns called designs. Ask them to explain how design can enhance fabrics.

4   Prepare an art activity with yarn and burlap:

   a   Have the children select small pieces of burlap on which to experiment.

---

[3] Before this episode is used, children should have had experiences with simple weaving in which texture, color, and pattern have been stressed.

b If needles are used, demonstrate several stitches for children to try, and stimulate them to try different kinds of stitches.

[4] c If glue is used, demonstrate procedures for applying it. Have children draw directly on the burlap with Elmer's glue and stick the yarn to the glue.

d After the children have developed some technique by experimenting with yarn, have them select larger pieces of burlap for their work.

e Discuss the possibilities of yarn and burlap. Review the visual art elements which children have found in cross-sections of objects in nature: line, color, size, shape, and texture.

f Stimulate children to plan their design for the burlap. Figure 111 shows the work of a talented ten year old girl who used burlap, needle, and yarn. Some children may want to combine both yarn and fabric in their design.

g While children are working, motivate them to think in terms of size, shape, color, line, texture, and placement. Several class sessions may be devoted to this activity or children may work on it when they have finished other work.

h When the work is completed, display all the pieces in the room. Ask children to describe their work in terms of arrangement, lines, shapes, sizes, colors, and textures which they have created.

---

[4] Teachers have found that stitchery is very time consuming, so glue may be substituted.

Figure 111
Ten Year Old, Creative Stitchery

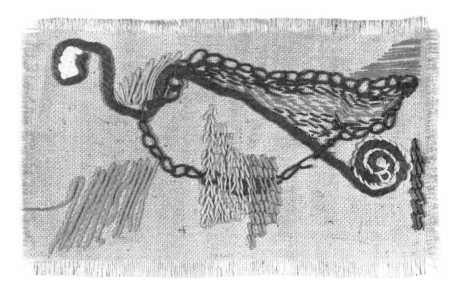

Figure 112
Martha Menke Underwood,
Flowers and Butterflies

Exemplar:

1   Introduce the exemplar in Figure 112 by showing the children that this
    artist has also worked with yarns and fabrics. Ask them what seems
    to have inspired the artist. Help the children understand the various
    ways that the artist has used yarns and fabrics to create different tex-
    tures, sizes, and shapes.

2   Before introducing the next exemplar, explain to the children that
    there is another type of woven fabric which is different from the kinds
    of fabric and design just worked with. It is made with many different
    kinds of yarn and is very heavy, and the design is woven directly into
    the material and not applied to it as the children have done. Explain
    that this particular type of design with yarns is called a *tapestry* and
    that tapestries have been woven for many centuries. Introduce the
    exemplar shown in Figure 113 and explain that this is a very old
    tapestry which was woven in the fifth century A.D. Ask the children
    how they can tell that this is an old tapestry. If topics have been
    studied in social studies which are related to this time in history, such
    as the Roman Empire, discuss other aspects of life in that period so
    that time relationships can be established. Ask children to find the
    different shapes which are repeated to form an over-all design and
    shapes which are repeated in the border.

Figure 113
Coptic Textile, 5th Century A.D.

Tapestry-weave wool and linen, 56½ × 79 inches

3 Introduce the exemplars shown in Figures 114 and 115 by discussing how objects in nature have influenced the artist and the ways he has recorded his impressions, just as the children have been influenced by objects in nature and have recorded their impressions through their symbols for trees, shrubs, etc. Explain that artists record their impressions in many ways using different materials. Ask the children to compare the exemplar in Figure 114 with the tapestry in Figure 115

Figure 115
Lucia Suffel, *Small Flower Tapestry*
Handcrafted

re 114
t Ludwig Kirchner, *Wildboden*, 1923
53 × 39 inches

Figure 116

Henri Matisse, *Woman on Rose Divan*, 1921

Oil, 14⅞ × 18 inches

in terms of materials used, use of visual art elements, and difference in ways of showing impressions of objects in nature. Introduce the term *contemporary* and help children understand that this means works done today.

4 Introduce the exemplar shown in Figure 116 by explaining that tapestries are sometimes as heavy as carpets and are usually displayed as wall hangings in homes, public buildings, and museums. Explain that since tapestries are displayed this way, an artist might paint a tapestry if it is a part of the scene he wants to depict, as Matisse has done in the exemplar shown in Figure 116. Help the children to notice the various designs and patterns which the artist has painted.

5 Display the reproductions and halftones at the children's eye level, and help them to see the relationship which exists between the artist who paints in oil and the artist who works with yarns and fabrics. Compare all exemplars in terms of materials used, dates, use of visual art elements, and impressions recorded.

Expected outcome

Children should:

1 Know that artists are inspired by objects in nature.

2 Know that artists record their impressions in different ways.

3 Have learned that design can be applied to or woven into material.

4 Have formulated some concepts about the time each exemplar was created so that they will have a basis for future learnings in art history.

Related activities

(Visual exercises, books, poetry, related activities in other subjects)

1 Have children look for tapestries which may be found in their environment. Discuss what they have observed, places where these are found, and comparisons with exemplars.
2 Stimulate children to read about Matisse.
3 Stimulate children to read books which will help reinforce the objective of this episode, such as *Create with Yarn* by Ethel Jane Beilter, *Adventures in Stitches* by Mariska Karasz, *Weaving without a Loom* by Sarita R. Rainey.
4 Do research and make reports on tapestries and how they have been used.

EPISODE 5

Objective: To extend children's frames of reference
for the visual art elements and their use
in jewelry making and silversmithing

Teacher background

1 Understand the techniques for making transparent visuals from nature (see Figure 175, page 259).
2 Understand jewelry making and techniques used by silversmiths.
3 Develop a degree of sensitivity for well-designed and well-crafted jewelry and other products.
4 Understand man's need for and use of jewelry throughout history.
5 Understand the uses of coins, both for decoration and for economic purposes.
6 Understand the historical development of function and design of works of art in this episode.

Materials

2 × 2″ slide projector and screen
2 × 2″ transparencies (3 or 4) which show design qualities to be found in nature: dandelion puffs, minute thistles, leaves, etc. (see Figure 175, page 259)

Materials

Halftones: *Necklace with Eleven Pendants*
Paul de Lamerie, *Cup and Cover*
Claudia Williams, *14K Gold Pendant*, handcrafted
Porter Blanchard, *Pewter Coffee Service*, handwrought

Opaque projector and screen (if halftones from this book or other art books are used)

Vocabulary

silver	handcrafted
gold	Claudia Williams
pewter	Porter Blanchard
handwrought	Paul de Lamerie

Instructional procedures

Motivation and instruction: Sensory, multi-sensory experiences; topic discussion

1   Introduce the episode by reviewing with the children what they have already learned about designers: their use of the visual art elements; their inspiration, which often comes from objects in nature; and the variety of materials which they use, such as yarns and fabrics for creative stitchery and various kinds of yarn for weaving.

2   Ask children to tell about other materials that designers can use. Direct their attention to jewelry they are wearing and to the designs on it. Explain that many designers have used gold, silver, and pewter for designing objects. Ask children to name objects in addition to jewelry for which gold, silver, and pewter can be used.

3   When coins have been mentioned, ask them to explain the various uses of coins: Have they been used for purposes other than exchange?

4   Draw on understandings developed in social studies to show that man has decorated himself for centuries with many objects, including jewelry. Groups which may be cited include Indians, people today, and people in other lands.

Exemplar:

1   Introduce the exemplar shown in Figure 117 by asking the children to tell what has been used to make this necklace and why coins were used. Ask them to describe the designs composed of lines which form shapes used in repeat patterns. Explain that this necklace was designed by a designer-craftsman and was made by hand. Introduce the term *handcrafted*. Discuss decorative uses of coins which the children may have seen. If the children have studied ancient times

in social studies, they may relate their understandings of history to the time that the necklace was made. If they do not have the background for this historical perspective, they should be helped to understand that the necklace is much older than some event they are familiar with, such as the discovery of America. Display the exemplar at the children's eye level.

2   Before introducing the next exemplar, use the 2 × 2 slide projector to show the slides of designs in nature, and discuss with the children the textures, lines, shapes, and repeat patterns which can be found in nature.

3   Introduce the exemplar shown in Figure 118 by asking children to describe the relationship between the pendant and the closeups of nature shown in the slides in terms of texture, size, shape, and line. Explain that this is a contemporary necklace called a pendant. Help children to understand that necklaces have been worn for centuries and that as cultures change, so do the products of the designer-craftsmen. Have children compare the Roman necklace with the contemporary one in terms of use, visual art elements, reflection of the culture in which it was made.

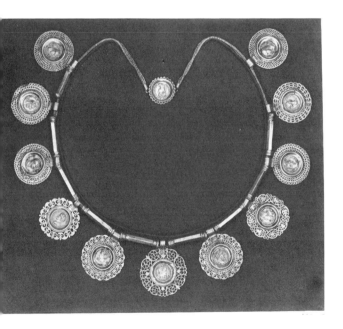

Figure 117
Necklace with Eleven Pendants, Roman,
3d Century A.D.

Gold, from the Egyptian coast near Alexandria

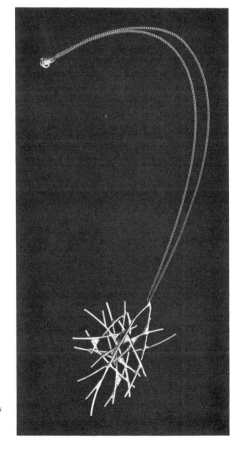

Figure 118
Claudia Williams, *Pendant*

14 K gold, handcrafted

Figure 119
Paul de Lamerie, *Cup and Cover*, 1737

Silver, made in London; 14½ inches high × 6½ inches diameter

4 Introduce the exemplar shown in Figure 119 by discussing other objects used in daily life which can be made from gold and silver. Ask questions which will lead children into suggesting functional containers (pitchers, coffeepots, teapots) that are made from these metals. Draw on the children's understandings from social studies so that they can discuss man's need for such containers throughout history. Ask children to describe the enhancement of a functional container, such as the one shown in Figure 119, by the designer-craftsmen. Discuss the designer's use of the visual art elements: line, repeated lines, shapes, sizes, textures, and repeat patterns. Help children understand that the surface decoration does not destroy the basic shape of the large cup and cover. By discussing events with which the children are familiar, such as the American Revolution, help them develop an historical frame of reference for this object. Display the exemplar at the children's eye level.

5 Introduce the exemplar shown in Figure 120 by having children compare it with the preceding one in terms of design. Ask them to tell what has been emphasized in this exemplar in comparison with the preceding one. Help the children understand that this designer-craftsman has emphasized the shape of the container and has not used surface decoration. Ask which of the two containers is older: How can we tell when something is antique? Help children understand that both simple and ornate designs can be found in the past and in the present, and that authorities can help us determine whether or not something is really antique. Introduce the term *handwrought* and explain that pewter, which has been used for the

Figure 120
Porter Blanchard,
Pewter Coffee Service

Handwrought

container in Figure 120, has been hammered into shape with special tools. Explain that pewter is a metal containing a lot of tin and copper and is easily hammered into shape, but that it is not nearly as precious as silver or as shiny. Discuss the many objects made of pewter. Explain that these were all designed originally by designer-craftsmen, but that many which are not handwrought can be purchased in stores. Have children compare the two containers and describe them in terms of how they would feel: rough, smooth, slick, cold, etc. Discuss the reasons for covering the handles with another material, as seen in Figure 120.

6 Encourage the children to visit local stores which carry silver, pewter, and stainless steel objects. Explain that the stores may look something like the one shown in Figure 121, which shows a display of silver, pewter, and stainless steel objects in a variety of shapes, sizes, designs, and intended uses.

Figure 121

Expected outcome

Children should:

1   Be able to discriminate the visual art elements used by designer-craftsmen working in silver, gold, and pewter.
2   Understand that simple or elaborate designs can be very old or contemporary.
3   Understand that products which have a functional use have not changed, but that the shapes may change.
4   Understand man's use of gold, silver, and pewter in designing jewelry and functional containers, both in the past and in the present.
5   Understand why changes in design are made.

Related activities

(Visual exercises, books, poetry, related activities in other subjects)

1   Have children do research and report on: Pewter from Colonial Times to the Present, Handcrafting Objects, Changes in Jewelry, Uses of Coins, etc.
2   Collect pictures which show how jewelry and silversmithing have changed.

EPISODE 6

*Objective: To enrich children's concepts of two-
and three-dimensional works of art and
their similarities and differences*

Teacher background

1   Understand motif as used in various ways by artists in two- and three-dimensional works of art.
2   Understand the differences between two- and three-dimensional works of art and their related functions in daily life.
3   Understand the historical background of ceramics.
4   Have experience with the use of repeat patterns created by lines in two- and three-dimensional work.
5   Know the uses of the opaque projector (see Figure 182, page 267).

Materials

Clay ceramic pieces made by the children

Opaque projector and screen (see Figure 182, page 267)
Halftone: *Corinthian Vase*
Reproduction: Paul Klee, *Around the Fish*

Vocabulary

two-dimensional   Corinthian
three-dimensional   Paul Klee
form   *Around the Fish*
terra cotta

Instructional procedures

Motivation and instruction: Sensory, multi-sensory experiences; topic discussion

⁵ 1 Use the clay ceramic pieces made by the children to introduce this
     episode. Discuss the characteristics of these objects: they can be held
     in the hand or placed on a table and seen from all angles. Explain
     that objects which have these characteristics are called three-dimensional.
     Contrast the three-dimensional pieces with a piece of paper
     placed flat on the table so that the children can see the difference
     between three-dimensional and two-dimensional pieces.

2 Direct the children's attention to objects in the room, and have them
   classify them as two-dimensional or three-dimensional. For example,
   papers which are lying flat should be identified as two-dimensional,
   while vases and pencil holders should be classified as three-dimensional.
   Help the children understand that three-dimensional objects
   can be hollow on the inside and can be used as pencil holders or containers
   for water, ink, milk, etc.

3 Review the paintings which the children have had in other episodes
   and help them understand that these are two-dimensional because
   they are painted on flat canvas and can be seen from one angle only—
   the front.

Exemplar:

1 Introduce the exemplars shown in Figures 122 and 123 by having children
   cite similarities and differences between the painter and the
   ceramist: they both use the visual elements of art and may express
   themselves in similar ways, but they use different materials. Ask
   children to describe Paul Klee's use of shapes to make repeat patterns
   and to create texture on the fish. Display the reproduction at the
   children's eye level and compare it with the halftone of the Corinthian

---

⁵ Children must have made ceramics or modelled objects out of clay before
this episode is used.

Figure 122
Paul Klee, *Around the Fish,*
1926

Oil on canvas, 18⅜ × 25⅛
inches

vase shown in Figure 123. (Use the opaque projector if the halftone from this book or another art book is used; see Figure 182, page 267.) Have children compare the similarities of the two exemplars in terms of pattern, line, and texture. Explain that terra cotta tells us that the vase is reddish or red-yellow in color and that it is made of clay. Discuss the age of the vase in relation to periods of history with which the children are familiar. Have them describe possible uses of this container.

Figure 123
Corinthian Vase,
7th Century B.C.

Terra cotta, 28⅞ in-
ches high × 20 in-
ches diameter

Expected outcome

Children should:

1 Be able to discriminate between two- and three-dimensional objects: two-dimensional objects such as paintings, are on a flat surface; three-dimensional objects can be held and/or walked around and seen from many angles.

2 See the similarities between the patterns used in paintings and ceramics.

3 Know that both painters and ceramists use the visual art elements although they work with different materials and different dimensions.

Related activities

(Visual exercises, books, poetry, related activities in other subjects)

1 Teachers may find it helpful to devise a test using different objects to determine whether or not children can recognize the difference between two- and three-dimensional works of art. It may also be helpful to develop a test in which children identify the relationships that can be found in fabric designs, paintings, etc.

2 Stimulate the children to read about Paul Klee.

3 There are many excellent books related to this objective for children to read, such as *Forms and Patterns in Nature* by Wolf Strache, and *Ceramics from Clay to Kiln* by Harvey Weiss.

EPISODE 7

Objective: To enrich children's concepts of line, shape, and form and to extend their frames of reference for stabiles and mobiles

Teacher background

1 Have experience in making a stabile and a mobile.

2 Work with balsa wood so that problems encountered by children will be understood and children can be helped.

3 Understand color repetition so that children can be helped to repeat colors.

4 Know the differences between a stabile and a mobile as works of art.

5 Understand the patterns created by light as it hits certain objects.

6 Know the historical development of a stabile as a decorative work of art to satisfy man's emotional needs.

7 Know the uses of the opaque projector (see Figure 182, page 267).

Materials

¼" balsa wood sticks

Corrugated cardboard bases (at least 4 × 4")

Pins

Scissors

Austrian tissue paper

Colored construction paper

Halftones: Constantin Brancusi, *Bird in Space*
           Alexander Calder, *Lobster Trap and Fish Tail*

Opaque projector and screen, if halftones from this book or other art books are used (see Figure 182, page 267)

Vocabulary

stabile

mobile

Constantin Brancusi

Bird in Space

Alexander Calder

Lobster Trap and Fish Tail

Instructional procedures

Motivation and instruction: Sensory, multi-sensory experiences; topic discussion

1 Introduce the episode by discussing the space which is all around us. Ask questions which will lead children to suggest that space is occupied by objects that move (people) and objects that do not move. Have the children locate three-dimensional objects which occupy space but which do not move: vases, books, flower pots, etc.

2 Prepare for an art activity:

    a Explain that three-dimensional constructions can be made which are different from the objects children have mentioned or have studied. Discuss the construction of *stabiles* (objects which do not move) from balsa wood, glue, and paper. Explain that a stick can represent a line and that a line can be erected in space. Show the children how a short piece (about 9") of balsa wood can be made to stand alone in space by cementing it at a slight angle to the cardboard base.

    b After this demonstration, have the children select different lengths of balsa wood and cardboard bases. Teachers have found that cutting a variety of lengths beforehand saves time and eliminates the use of razor blades in the classroom. Have the children make a small hole in the base and erect one length in space by cementing the balsa wood in the hole.

c When this has been done, stimulate the children to decide how other pieces of wood could be attached to the first one by using pins and cement. Have them use the other lengths of balsa wood that they have selected and attach them.

d While children are working, motivate them to consider lines which close and form shapes and different sizes, and the relationships between these in their constructions.

e After this has been finished, demonstrate the use of tissue paper or construction paper on the stabile to form solid shapes in space. Explain that color is used only to emphasize a shape.

f Have the children use tissue paper and construction paper to form solid shapes on their stabiles. Motivate them to study their lines, shapes, and sizes. Emphasize color repeats and relationships. Help the children to relate the concepts of balance (which they have developed in science through a study of simple machines) to their construction.

g When the children have finished, evaluate the constructions in space with the children in terms of lines which form shapes of different sizes, color repeats, and balance. Some of the work may look like that shown in Figure 124.

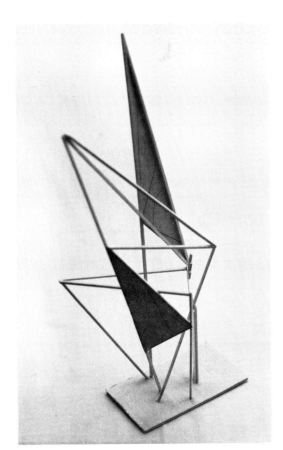

Figure 124
Ten Year Old

Figure 125
Constantin Brancusi, *Bird in Space*, 1919

Bronze, 54 inches high

Exemplar:

1 Introduce the exemplar shown in Figure 125 (use an opaque projector if a halftone from an art book is used) by explaining that the
artist has also been interested in creating stabiles and has used a
variety of materials for them. The stabile shown in Figure 125 is
made from bronze and is called *Bird in Space*. Help the children find
out the height of the stabile by using a yardstick or some visual scale.
Explain that stabiles are considered to be three-dimensional works of
art and are usually used as decorative pieces. Discuss the artist's
interpretation of a bird in space. Have the children express how the
stabile makes them feel.

2 Introduce the exemplar shown in Figure 126 by explaining that
artists have not always been satisfied with creating immobile objects
and that some artists create objects in space which move, called
mobiles. Such a mobile is shown in Figure 126. Explain that this
construction is entirely different from the stabile because it moves
with the currents of air. If the class has had experience in constructing mobiles, discuss how these mobiles also moved with currents
of air.

Figure 126

Alexander Calder, *Lobster Trap and Fish Tail*

Steel wire and sheet aluminum, 8½ feet high

3 Ask the children to describe the way a mobile would create shadows on the wall if a spotlight were focused on it. Help them to recall their study of shadows—how the trees make shadows on the earth when the sun is shining or how a house plant creates shadows on the wall or ceiling when a light is shining on it. Discuss the moving shadows which could be created by a mobile and the different sizes and shapes in the mobile. Discuss the mobile in terms of its title and the subject matter which inspired the artist.

4 Explain to the children the importance of balance for mobiles; if they are off balance they cannot move freely with the currents of air. Explain that the artist is a master at creating balance both visually and mechanically. Have the children express how a slow-moving object like this mobile might make them feel: restful, lazy, etc.

Expected outcome

Children should:

1 Be able to see the relationship between their stabiles and the stabile created by the artist.
2 Know the difference between a stabile and a mobile.
3 Be aware of lines that create shapes of different sizes.
4 Understand light, shadow, and balance of mobiles and stabiles.

Related activities

(Visual exercises, books, poetry, related activities in other subjects)

1 If the children have not created mobiles, they should have an opportunity to do so. Provide them with a variety of materials in different shapes and sizes. Emphasize variety, movement, balance, and technique.

2 Stimulate children to read such books as *How To Make Shapes in Space* by Toni Hughes.

EPISODE 8

Objective: To enrich children's concepts of line and to extend their frames of reference for artists' drawings

Teacher background

1 Have experience with art media used in self-portraits: paint, chalk, pen and ink, stick and ink.

2 Understand various ways that textures are created with art media.

3 Know the historical background of portraiture.

4 Understand the historical framework of the exemplars used.

Materials

Choice of one: pen and ink, felt marking pen, black crayon, colored chalk, watercolor, or tempera

12 × 18″ white drawing paper

Reproductions: Albrecht Dürer, *Four Heads*
Constantin Brancusi, *Head of a Girl*

Vocabulary

pen brush
charcoal
scribble
cross-hatch
stipple
Albrecht Dürer
Four Heads

Constantin Brancusi
Head of a Girl
portrait
self-portrait
profile
monogram

Instructional procedures

Motivation and instruction: Sensory, multi-sensory experiences; topic discussion

1 Prepare for a drawing activity:
   a Discuss the meanings of *portrait* and *self-portrait*.
   b Have children select materials for drawings. They may use crayons, pen and ink, etc.
   c Stimulate children to describe texture of skin and hair, color of skin and hair, shapes of parts of face. Use mirrors if necessary. Compare texture of hair, eyebrows, and eyelashes with the texture of skin.
   d Have children describe how they are alike and how they are different by looking at each other.
   e Review lines children know: cross-hatch, stipple, straight, curved, etc.
   f Discuss the ways of making a self-portrait: profie or front view.
   g Have children make a self-portrait. As they are working, motivate them to use different lines for texture when needed.
   h When the drawings are completed, display them at the children's eye level. Discuss the different techniques that have been used with lines.

Exemplar:

1 Introduce the exemplar shown in Figure 127 by having children look at the self-portraits which were done in profile. Ask whether or not people can be recognized by their profiles. Explain that profiles can be made of the entire figure, not just the head. Direct the children's attention to the exemplar. Ask them to describe the different kinds of lines which the artist has made with pen and ink and to compare these with lines they have used. Help children to see, for example,

Figure 127
Albrecht Dürer, *Four Heads,* 1513 or 1515

Pen and ink, 8¼ × 7⅞ inches

the different lines that have been used to represent hair. Direct their attention to how the artist has made some eyelids look heavier than others by his use of pen and ink. Have them notice the differences in eyelids, eyebrows, and eyes in Figure 127, and to compare these with differences in individuals in the room.

2 Ask the children to explain how the artist has made one head look closer than the others. Reinforce this by having them look outside to see how some objects look closer than others. Help them understand that the closer objects may not be as large as the ones farther away by comparing the first head with the fourth one in Figure 127.

3 Explain that an artist usually signs his work, just as they put their names on their drawings, but that this artist, Albrecht Dürer, used only his initials. These can be found in the upper right-hand corner. Introduce the word *monogram* by explaining that this means the use of the initials of a person's name in a design. Discuss the possible monograms that each child could design for himself.

4 Help the children develop an historical frame of reference for the exemplar by explaining that it was done in 1513 or 1515, shortly after Columbus discovered America.

5 Introduce the exemplar shown in Figure 128 by discussing different drawing tools that artists use. Explain that in the reproduction shown in Figure 128 the artist used pencil. Have the children compare this reproduction with the one in Figure 127, in which the artist has drawn the head of a girl in full or front view. Discuss the artist's use of line: he has not tried to use just one perfect line, but has used many to form the shape of the head and the neck. Help the children notice the artist's use of repeated thick and thin lines to represent hair.

Figure 128
Constantin Brancusi, *Head of a Girl,* 1905

Pencil, 23 × 15⅜ inches

6   Display both reproductions at the children's eye level and have them discuss the similarities and differences in terms of the way the artist has expressed himself and the different tools and materials he has used for this expression. Have them compare the dates of the two drawings.

Expected outcome

Children should:

1   Know the difference between profile and front view.
2   Know that objects can be drawn to look as if they are nearer than others, although the objects farther away may be much larger.
3   Know the kinds of materials with which an artist can work, and the different ways in which he can work.
4   Have added to their understanding of time by contrasting the dates of the two drawings.

Related activities

(Visual exercises, books, poetry, related activities in other subjects)

1   Provide the children with opportunities to experiment with designing their own monograms.
2   Provide children with opportunities to use different media in their drawings: charcoal, colored chalk, stick and ink, etc.
3   Have children read about the artists.

EPISODE 9

Objective: To enrich children's concepts of visual art elements and to extend their frames of reference for portraiture and two- and three-dimensional works of art

Teacher background

1   Know how bronze is cast and procedures and tools used for carving in stone.
2   Know the different materials used by sculptors.
3   Understand different uses of light: physical (sculpture) and painted.
4   Understand the historical framework for the exemplars.
5   Have experience with clay or modeling and sculpture techniques.
6   Know the uses of the opaque projector (see Figure 182, page 267).

Materials

Halftones: William Zorach, *Adam*

               Gaston Lachaise, *Portrait of John Marin*

Reproduction: Rembrandt Van Rijn, *Portrait of a Youth with a Black Cap*

Opaque projector and screen (if halftones of sculpture from this book or other art books are used)

Vocabulary

bronze

bronze casting

granite

William Zorach

Adam

Rembrandt

Portrait of a Youth

   with a Black Cap

Gaston Lachaise

Portrait of John Marin

Instructional procedures

Motivation and instruction: Sensory, multi-sensory experiences; topic discussion

1 Introduce the episode by reviewing what the children have learned about the visual art elements and the use of these elements in their clay work and in exemplars they have seen. Review the terms *portrait* and *profile*, and the differences between two- and three-dimensional works of art.

2 Have the children demonstrate their understandings by selecting various two- or three-dimensional objects in the room.

3 Mention various objects and have the children classify them as two- or three-dimensional. Include children's own work and exemplars they have seen.

Exemplar:

1 Introduce the exemplar in Figure 129 (use an opaque projector if necessary) by asking the children what kinds of tools a sculptor would have to use on granite, the material used by this artist. Explain that the sculptor, as well as the artist who draws or paints, has been interested in representing heads of people. Have children describe the simple forms used by sculptor to depict hair, eyebrows, and the pupils of the eyes in his representation of man. Discuss the relationship between the simple forms and the title of the sculpture. Ask the children to tell how the stone might feel if they touched it.

2 Introduce the exemplar shown in Figure 130 by discussing with the children the different materials that might be used by sculptors to make three-dimensional objects. Explain that the artist whose work is shown in Figure 130 also created a three-dimensional head using

Figure 129
William Zorach, *Adam,* 1948

Granite boulder, 11½ × 10½ inches

Figure 130
Gaston Lachaise, *Portrait of John Marin,* 1928

Bronze, 12½ × 9 × 10 inches

a material called *bronze,* and that since bronze is a metal it is rarely carved or chiseled. Instead, a mold is made from clay, plaster, or wax and the bronze is cast in the mold. (Explain this in more detail, if necessary.) Have the children compare the differences between the two heads, particularly with reference to the use of more detail on the bronze work. Ask the children to describe the way the two different sculptures might feel.

3 Direct the children's attention to the way that light strikes the pieces of sculpture. Help them to notice that since these are solid forms and are three-dimensional, light shining on them creates shadows. Explain that the sculptor uses light to enhance the forms he creates.

4 Introduce the exemplar shown in Figure 131 by discussing with the children the artist's interest in light. Explain that since the painter works on a flat surface, usually canvas or paper, he must capture this quality of light by paint and color. Ask children to describe the painting in terms of light and color.

Figure 131
Rembrandt Van Rijn, *Portrait of a Youth with a Black Cap,* 1666

Oil on canvas, 31¾ × 25½ inches

5 Display all exemplars at the children's eye level and have them compare and contrast them in terms of materials used, two- and three-dimensional works, possibilities that some materials have which others do not (Rembrandt could use fine lines for the hair and eyebrows because of the material he used), and the artists' interest in light.

Expected outcome

Children should:

1 Have increased understanding of the differences between two- and three-dimensional works of art.
2 Know the different materials used by sculptors and painters.
3 Understand artists' use of light.
4 Understand that throughout the years artists have been inspired by the same subject matter, but have represented it in different ways with different materials.

Related activities

(Visual exercises, books, poetry, related activities in other subjects)

1 Many children will want to do further research on bronze casting.
2 Whenever possible, direct the children's attention to the way light strikes objects in the room at different times of the day. Help the children to see that artists have also been interested in this and have used light in their two- and three-dimensional work.
3 Stimulate children to read about the artists.

EPISODE 10

Objective: To introduce the concept of "original print"

Teacher background

1 Have creative experiences in print making, including linocuts.
2 Be acquainted with the differences and similarities in print-making procedures for linoleum and woodcuts.
3 Understand the ways artists can create different shapes and textural and transparent effects by making several printings on the same print.
4 Be familiar with safety precautions involved in cutting linoleum.

Materials

Precut pieces of battleship linoleum or 3M Printmaker Plate

Linoleum cutters
Variety of papers in assorted colors
Reproductions: Kihei Sasajima, *Woodland Stream*
                John Talleur, *The Veronica*
Water-soluble or oil-base printing ink
Brayers
Spoons or baren

Vocabulary

print making   linoleum print
print   brayer
original print   baren
woodcut

Instructional procedures

Motivation and instruction: Sensory, multi-sensory experiences; topic discussion

Part I.

1 By the intermediate level children should have had numerous print-making experiences: vegetable printing, monoprints, gadget printing, cardboard printing, etc. Introduce the episode by reviewing the various print-making experiences which children have had, the visual art elements they used in these activities, and the relief effects created.

2 Introduce the term *linoleum* and explain that this will be another material they will use for print making.

3 Demonstrate the preparation of a linoleum block for printing by: (a) designing on paper, (b) transferring the design to the linoleum, (c) cutting the lines with various cutting tools and noting how various textures can be created by the instruments, (d) inking the prepared linoleum, (e) printing on paper. Care should be taken to demonstrate proper procedures and cautions to be exercised during the cutting process. Explain that the print will be the reverse of their prepared design.

4 After the preliminary demonstration, stimulate the children to think about what designs they might like to create. Designs can be inspired from objects in nature or from some activity which children have experienced. After they have marked off their papers to coincide with the size of the block, motivate the children to think in terms of line, size, shape, and texture.

5 After the designs are completed, stimulate the children to think about a color which will suit their particular design.

6 Supervise the printing process and hang the prints to dry.

7 Display all the prints.

Part II.

1   Stimulate the class to talk about their prints in terms of the use of the visual art elements and design.

2   Introduce the term *original print* by asking the class how many prints they think could be printed from their linoleum blocks. Explain that these are all called original prints.

Exemplar:

1   Introduce the first exemplar by telling the class that photographs or halftones can also be made from original prints, such as the one seen in Figure 132. Explain that this is a woodcut and that the process used to make it is similar to linoleum printing, but that the artist has used wood and wood-cutting tools. The printing process itself is much the same.

2   Explain that the artist must state the total number of original prints printed from a wood block and that this total constitutes a series. He must also tell what number each print is in the series. Direct children's attention to the number to be found under the signature of the artist. This exemplar is the first original print from a series of eighty, as shown by the notation 1/80. If this halftone of the original print were the twentieth, it would be written 20/80.

3   Stimulate the children to discuss the print in terms of how the artist has used the visual art elements to create different textures for his subject matter and how he has solved his problem in ways similar to ones they have used with their linoleum prints.

Figure 132
Kihei Sasajima, *Wood-land Stream*

Woodcut, 75 × 23½ inches

Figure 133
John Talleur,
The Veronica

Color woodcut

4 Introduce the exemplar in Figure 133 by asking the children to explain how they think this artist created textures that look very different from those of Kihei Sasajima's *Woodland Stream*. Ask the children if the artist created all his textures by using cutting instruments. Help them to understand that some of the texures are created by using the natural texture of the wood.

5 Ask the children to explain how they think the artist created different values and shapes that look transparent. If they are unable to do this, explain that this artist is known for his color woodcuts. He often uses numerous wood blocks designed for a specific color, and original prints of this kind sometimes have as many as twenty printings on the same print.

6 Have the children compare the two works in terms of number of printings used, use of visual art elements, and subject matter.

7 Help the children understand that artists use the visual art elements differently according to how they wish to solve their problems and create different effects. Lead the discussion into understanding how both original prints convey a different message and different moods, feelings, and atmosphere.

8 Lead the discussion into the differences among the various art exemplars which children have learned about: original paintings, reproductions, original prints. Encourage them to talk about the difference between a reproduction and an original print, and ways in which an original print can be identified.

Expected outcome

Children should:
1 Be able to identify an original print by number and series.
2 Know the difference between a linocut and a woodcut.
3 Know the difference between an original painting, reproduction, and original print.
4 Know that artists can create many different effects using the same materials.

Related activities

(Visual exercises, books, poetry, related activities in other subjects)
1 Conduct research on the history of print making and make reports to the class.
2 Read books on print making.
3 Discuss the responsibility that artists have to maintain their integrity concerning the number of prints printed from the original plate.

FURTHER READINGS

Suggested readings for this chapter are given on pages 97 and 98.

11

Intermediate Level: Environmental Climate

AWARENESS OF PRESENT AND FUTURE

The following episodes constitute an episodic cluster which deals with the present and the future. Although the present world bears evidence of the impact of non-aesthetic man, it also shows evidence of the products of aesthetic man—products indicative of a better future. Children need to become aware of these contributions. The way the world will look in the next quarter or half century will depend, to a large extent, on the way teachers work with children today.

Many people are apprehensive about what the future will be, with its increased technological advancements, and long for a return to the "good old days" in which life was slow-paced and values were relatively constant and stable. Although many adults, including teachers, are nostalgic for the past, the children with whom they work are not. Children are future-oriented, and may be less fearful and anxious about what is to come. Their imaginative thinking includes trips to outer space, and enables them to envision innovations and creations for the future which deal with things other than space travel. It is the responsibility of the teacher to capitalize on the interest and imagination which children have about the present and the future so that they can become better prepared for it.

203

In preparing children for the future, teachers can capitalize on another group that is future-oriented, the contemporary designer-craftsmen and artists whose imagination may be equated with that of children. The products of the creative abilities of this group are built upon the past, executed in the present, and intended for use now and in the future; they constitute a source of environmental exemplars which can be used for helping children to become more aware of the future and of the need for planning for it. These exemplars are products of the culture of twentieth-century man, but their use, along with the learning procedures developed for enhancing the visual perception of children, can help children appreciate the heritage of the past as well as the possibilities for the future. They will also help children reinforce their understanding of the visual art elements, for these remain constant while the innovations man creates with them are ever-changing. For these reasons, the following episodic cluster is presented for use on the intermediate level.

EPISODE 1

Objective: To enrich children's concepts of the contributions of industrial designers

Teacher background

1 Know that functional objects for everyday use are designed on a drawing board or through some other design process.
2 Understand that objects have to perform a function and meet the requirements of the user, but that the two need not be isolated from the aesthetic.
3 Understand the relationship between art and the use of objects.
4 Understand that designer-craftsmen are often future-oriented.
5 Know the kinds of materials used by designer-craftsmen.
6 Know the names and works of the designer-craftsmen.
7 Understand the objects in historical perspective.
8 Know the uses of the opaque projector (see Figure 182, page 267).

Materials

Industrial design products exemplars:
  Henry Dewenter, Household Blender
  Luigi DeBenedetto, Thermo-Spoon

Keck-Craig Associates, Condiment Caddy
John Kapel, Hostess Cart of Walnut and Formica
William Curry, Porcelainized Aluminum Ware
Opaque projector and screen, if exemplars are shown from this or other
books (see Figure 182, page 267)

Vocabulary

industrial design	thermo
porcelainized	Henry Dewenter
functional	Luigi DeBenedetto
refinement of line	William Curry

Instructional procedures

Motivation and instruction: Sensory, multi-sensory experiences; topic discussion

1 Introduce the episode by asking children to explain the role that designers play in their lives. Mention objects which children use every day and help children understand that these were originally designed by industrial designers, so named because their products are mass-produced by industries for sale to the public. Use something as ordinary as a spoon, and ask children to tell about the use of the visual art elements in its design.

2 Ask the children what things they consider when they are buying products, in addition to cost. Introduce the term *functional* and help children understand that the industrial designer is interested in function and design: products should be useful and pleasing to the eye. Ask them what would happen if the bowl of a spoon were flattened— i.e., what would happen to its function. Emphasize the relationship of design and use by asking similar questions about well-known objects.

3 Ask children what kinds of objects, in addition to the everyday ones already mentioned, are used by industrial designers. Explain that the industrial designer not only designs for the present, but also anticipates the future in his work; he designs spacecraft and articles for use inside the craft. He is concerned with the future world as well as the present.

Exemplar:

1 Introduce the exemplar shown in Figure 134 by asking the children to explain the functions of the blender, thermo-spoon, and condiment caddy. Ask what these products can do to make life easier and more pleasant. Direct the children's attention to the designer's use of the visual art elements. Have them express the sensory experiences which

Figure 134
Henry Dewenter, Household Blender; Luigi DiBenedetto,
Thermo-Spoon; Keck-Craig Associates, Condiment Caddy

might be derived from the use and handling of the products. Ask
them to express their feelings and imaginations in describing the way
they would like to have objects look and feel.

2 Introduce the exemplar in Figure 135 by asking children to tell the
various uses of the cart to make our lives easier, and to tell how the
industrial designer has combined functional qualities and design.
Help children understand that the designer has a tendency to design
very simple products. Have them notice the lines, textures, sizes, and
shapes used by the designer, and by painters and sculptors.

3 Have children describe the articles on the cart and have them tell who
is responsible for the design of the articles. Have them describe
utensils that are used in their homes for the preparation of food.
(Children may make a guessing game out of this; one child describes
the articles, and the others guess what it is and how it is used.)

Figure 135
John Kapel, Hostess
Cart

Walnut and formica

4   Introduce the exemplar in Figure 136 by asking the children to describe the utensils shown. Ask them to tell how these are different
from utensils used during Colonial times or other periods in history
so they will understand that the industrial designer keeps pace with
changes in technology and in society. Ask them to tell how technological changes influence the industrial designer. Explain that these
utensils are made primarily of aluminum and are covered with
poreclain, a superior quality of china from which dishes are often
made. Ask children to explain why the designer has not used a lot of
decoration.

Figure 136
William Curry,
Porcelainized
Freezer

Expected outcome

Children should:

1   Know the role that the industrial designer plays in their daily lives.
2   Understand that changes in technology and ways of living bring changes in industrial design products.

Related activities

(Visual exercises, books, poetry, related activities in other subjects)

1   Encourage children to look at magazines in which the products of the industrial designer are displayed or advertised. Provide them with old and new magazines so that comparisons can be made between products of the past and of the present in terms of the use of the visual art elements.
2   Since children at this level are often engaged in studies of people of other times and places, many research projects can be conducted on the functional products used by these people.

EPISODE 2

Objective: To develop children's understanding of the relationship between forms they have created and forms created by industrial designers

Teacher background

1   Have experience in making paper sculpture.
2   Know techniques for paper sculpture: folding, tearing, scoring, and cutting.
3   Understand analogies between forms created in paper sculpture and works of designer-craftsmen.
4   Understand the history of lighting.
5   Know the uses of the opaque projector (see Figure 182, page 267).

Materials

Detail paper
Construction paper—various colors
Knives
Scissors

Rulers

Elmer's glue

Halftones: Ben Gurule, Radial System Chandelier
          Howard Miller Clock Company, Plastic Lamp

Opaque projector and screen, if exemplars from this or other books are
   used (see Figure 182, page 267)

Vocabulary

scoring	Ben Gurule
shaping	chandeliers
light patterns	plastics
paper sculpture	ornaments

Instructional procedures

Motivation and instruction: Sensory, multi-sensory experiences; topic discussion

1 Prepare children for an art activity using paper sculpture:

   a Demonstrate what can be done by cutting, folding, scoring, or
      curling detail paper and construction paper. Describe the inter-
      esting forms that can be created from paper. Introduce the term
      paper sculpture and explain that all the visual art elements—line,
      size, shape, texture, form, and color—are used in creating forms.

   b Ask children to tell the ways in which paper sculptures can be
      used: Christmas tree decorations and room decorations that move
      either as a part of mobiles or as decorations in themselves.

   c Have children select materials for paper sculpture. Stimulate
      them to create interesting forms for their sculpture.

   d As the children are working, motivate them to use the visual art
      elements and to develop techniques in scoring, cutting, and folding.

   e When the sculptures are finished, hang them on a string in the
      room. Ask the children to describe their works in terms of use of
      the visual art elements and the light and dark patterns created
      when light strikes them. Some of the children's work may look
      like the sculptures shown in Figures 137 and 138, which represent
      two different approaches used by children in creating with paper.

Exemplar:

1 Introduce the exemplars shown in Figures 139 and 140 by explaining
   that designers have been interested in experimenting with paper and
   similar materials to create different forms. Ask the children to tell
   what kinds of materials could have been used to make the forms
   shown in Figures 139 and 140, and to describe the uses of these forms.

Figure 137
Intermediate Level

Figure 138
Intermediate Level

Explain that these have been made from plastic, a material which can be molded into interesting forms. Have children compare these forms with the ones they created. Help them see the relationship of one shape to another, the repeating of shapes, and the light patterns created by the shapes in the lamps and chandelier.

2 Ask children to describe the different kinds of lamps which they have seen and the qualities that make some more interesting to look at than others. Ask them to understand that the designer, like the artist, is influenced by lines, shapes, forms, and colors found in nature.

Figure 139
Ben Gurule, Plastic Radial System Chandelier

Figure 140
Plastic Lamp

Expected outcome

Children should:

1 Be aware of the forms and shapes that the designer has used in different kinds of lamps.
2 Understand the relationship between their own paper sculptures and the more complex shapes and forms created by designers for functional uses.
3 Be able to equate forms in nature with those developed by designers.
4 Be able to compare the lamps shown in the exemplars with those currently being used in homes and public buildings.

Related activities

(Visual exercises, books, poetry, related activities in other subjects)

1 Discuss the different kinds of lights that are used for specific purposes, such as reading, television viewing, eating, decoration only, etc. Discuss how the purpose of the light helps to determine its design.
2 Many children will be interested in doing research on the history of lighting from the discovery of fire to modern lighting systems. Some may want to do special projects within this large topic, such as a study of the history of the design of the electric light bulb, direct and indirect lighting, candle making, etc.

EPISODE 3

Objective: To develop children's visual skills so they can see analogies between nature and architecture

Teacher background

1 Understand analogies between structures in nature and in architecture.
2 Know contemporary movements in architecture.
3 Know antecedents of these movements.
4 Understand changes in architecture and their relationship to changes in society.
5 Know the uses of the opaque projector (see Figure 182, page 267).

Materials

Examples of children's paper sculpture from the art activity in Episode 2
Several large pine cones

Materials

Halftone closeup of pine cone

Halftones: Marina City Apartments, Chicago

Opaque projector and screen, if halftones from this or other art books are used (see Figure 182, page 267)

Magnifying glass

Vocabulary

architectural structure

design and structure in nature

light and shadow

Marina City Apartments

Instructional procedures

Motivation and instruction: Sensory, multi-sensory experiences; topic discussion

1   Select some complex paper sculptures done by the children in which structural qualities are easily recognizable, such as those shown in Figures 141 and 142.

Figure 141
Intermediate Level

Figure 142
Intermediate Level

2 Introduce the episode by explaining that the paper sculptures have been selected because they are basic structures; they have structural qualities and can stand alone. Ask the children how the forms in these sculptures could be used for architectural designs. Stimulate them to use their imagination to describe buildings which would be shaped like their sculptures and to plan what building materials they might use.

3 Ask children to compare the types of homes that primitive people lived in with present-day dwellings, particularly skyscrapers. Encourage children to hypothesize about homes in the future. Ask them how it would feel to live in a skyscraper so high that the landscape could be seen for many miles from all angles. What would be the advantages and disadvantages of living in a skyscraper city where people live, work, shop, and play in the same building?

4 Show the halftone of the pine cone in Figure 143. Ask children to tell how this kind of "design and structure in nature" could be used in architecture. How could different sections and layers of the pine cone be used? Help children understand that they have used an object in nature as a source of inspiration for planning a building, and that architects are also inspired by natural objects because nature has structures which can be used in architectural designs.

5 Pass around the pine cones and a magnifying glass so that children can examine the structure closely.

Figure 143

Figure 144
Orlando R. Cabanban, Hedrich-Blessing, Marina City Apartments

Figure 145
Marina City Apartments
(Closeup)

Exemplar:

1 Introduce the exemplar in Figure 144 (use an opaque projector if necessary) by asking the children to compare the two towers with the pine cones and their own paper sculptures. Ask what objects in nature these towers remind them of. The responses could include: corncob, beehive, fish scales.

2 Introduce the exemplar in Figure 145, a closeup of the Marina City Apartments, and ask children to describe the structural qualities and the architect's use of the visual art elements. Ask them to compare the architect's use of visual elements with that of painters and sculptors, and to tell why the architect designed the building in this way.

3   Have children find other architectural structures near the building and compare them with the apartments in terms of use of visual art elements, relative time they were built, use. Help them understand that as times change, new forms of architecture are developed. Have them hypothesize about possible architectural structures of the future on earth or other planets.

Expected outcome

Children should:

1   Be aware of the similarities of structure in their own work, in natural forms, and in architectural structures.
2   Understand the need for thinking about and planning for future buildings and cities.

Related activities

(Visual exercises, books, poetry, related activities in other subjects)

1   Provide children with opportunities to look at books and magazines on architecture so they can compare styles of different eras.
2   Encourage them to read such books as: *A World Full of Homes* by William A. Barnes, *Cities* by Lawrence Halpin, *Farm on Fifth Avenue* by Elizabeth Naramore, *Forms and Patterns in Nature* by Wolf Strache, *My Skyscraper City* by Penny Hammond and Katrina Thomas.
3   Show the film *Around My Way*, Contemporary Films, Inc.
4   Play the record *Sounds of My City* (New York), Folkway Records.
5   Since social studies at the intermediate level is often concerned with other people and places, many children will want to do research on the topic: Architecture in Other Places and Other Times.

EPISODE 4

Objective: To enrich children's concepts of visual art elements and to extend their frames of reference for furniture and interior design

Teacher background

1   Understand the difference between style and taste.
2   Understand that furniture is designed by designer-craftsmen.
3   Understand why changes in furniture occur: economic, aesthetic, and functional.

4   Know the visual art elements used by designer-craftsmen.

5   Understand the historical development of furniture.

6   Know the uses of the opaque projector (see Figure 182, page 267).

Materials

Halftones: (Attributed to) Thomas Dennis, New England Court
              Cupboard

   Interior, Philip Johnson House, New Canaan, Connecticut

   Interior, Herman Miller Furniture Company

   Sam Maloof, Rosewood Rocker

Opaque projector and screen, if halftones from this or other books are
   used (see Figure 182, page 267)

Vocabulary

interior design	antique
interior designer	relief
furniture designer	

Instructional procedures

Motivation and instruction: Sensory, multi-sensory experiences; topic discussion

1   Introduce the episode by reviewing with the children their understandings of the design of everyday products and the use of the visual art elements by the designer.

2   Ask children to identify products used today that were not in existence 10, 50, or 100 years ago. Ask them to describe changes which have been made in products that were in existence during these times. Why have new products been developed and why have changes been made in existing ones? Why will products designed in the future be different from those used today?

3   Ask children to explain how new materials invented by scientists have helped designers. Have them name as many of these materials as they can and associate each material with certain products. Have them hypothesize about materials which may be available in the future and why these will be available.

Exemplar:

1   Introduce the exemplar in Figure 146 by reviewing the word *antique.* Some children may know people who collect antiques and can explain why these are often very valuable. Have the children identify the piece of furniture in Figure 146 and ask them to find the many repeated shapes, sizes, and forms in it. Review the word *relief*—projection from a flat surface or background for ornamentation. Direct

Figure 146

(Attributed to) Thomas Dennis of Ipswich, American New England Court Cupboard, c. 1638–1706

Oak and white pine, 45¼ inches wide × 21¼ deep × 58½ high

children's attention to the various reliefs in the cupboard and the ways they are repeated. Have the children locate geometric shapes and patterns and help them see that repeated shapes and patterns are part of the design of the cupboard.

2 Ask children to tell why antiques are a link to the past. How do they help us understand the past? Will our furniture ever be classified as antique?

3 Review the word *contemporary* and contrast it with antique. Show the exemplar in Figure 147 and have the children find the differences between the furniture shown and that used in the past. Ask children to explain why the antique cupboard has so much surface decoration,

Figure 147
Philip Johnson House (*Interior*), New Canaan, Connecticut

while the contemporary furniture has a simple design. Explain that the furniture in the house was designed over 25 years ago by Mies van der Rohe, but that it is still considered to be contemporary.

4 Have the children notice differences between this house and houses of the past. Today, man often wants to have the outside of his house become part of the inside, and the architect, Philip Johnson, accomplished this by building a rectangular house with glass walls.

5 Direct the children's attention again to the interior of the house, and discuss the work of *interior designers.* Explain to the children that interior designers are responsible for designing the interiors of houses, schools, churches, and public buildings, and that they usually work with the products of other designers. As is true of all designers, they make use of the visual art elements, and are primarily concerned with color, placement, and over-all arrangements that are visually pleasing.

6 Introduce the exemplar shown in Figure 148 by asking children to explain the differences between a place to work and a place to live. How do these differences make a difference in design? Discuss the similarities between a place to work and a place to live. Help children understand that the placement, arrangement, and visual impact of furniture are important in a home or in an office, as shown in Figure 148. Explain that works of other artists can be found in both home and office. Direct children's attention to the sculpture, planters, and painting which are found in the exemplar and which might also be used in a home. Review the painter's use of the visual art elements in painting. Have children compare the furniture designer and the interior designer in terms of their use of visual art elements and space and the differences in materials they work with.

Figure 148
Interior

Figure 149
Sam Maloof, Rocker

Rosewood with leather
upholstery

7 Introduce the exemplar shown in Figure 149 by asking children to describe chairs they have seen which are similar to this one. Is there anything about this chair that suggests a link with the past? Explain that designers are often influenced by what has been done in the past, but that they discover new and sometimes better ways of designing furniture to fit the needs of people today. Have the children notice how the designer has created pleasing lines by using wood in ways that are almost sculptural. Ask them to describe the lines that have been used, and to see how one line leads into another because of slight curves. Ask children to explain how the designer has used the natural grain of the wood in his design.

8 Have the children describe the kind of furniture they would like to have if they could choose their own. What qualities would they consider in making a selection?

Expected outcome

Children should:

1 Understand the changes in design of furniture and interiors to meet the changing needs of man.

2 Be able to discriminate between the needs of man at home and at work.

3 Be able to compare the designers' use of visual art elements with their use by painters and sculptors.

4 Understand that works of art are a part of the everyday environment and are not just for museums.

5 Have developed deeper understandings of time concepts by their comparisons of the old and the contemporary.

6 Understand that people have always expressed their preferences in the things with which they surround themselves and that preferences differ.

Related activities

1 Stimulate children to talk about the kinds of furniture, sculpture, and paintings they would like to live with, and to explain why they would choose them.

2 Invite an interior designer to talk with the children about his work.

3 Invite an architect to talk with the children about his work.

4 Provide the children with magazines and books displaying photographs of contemporary architecture and furniture.

5 Some children will want to do research into the designs of furniture used in other times and/or other places.

EPISODE 5

Objective: To introduce children to automobile designers as designer-craftsmen

Teacher background

1 Understand that automobiles are designed for public taste and consumption and that motivational research indicates what the public at present will buy.

2 Understand planned obsolescence as it is related to contemporary economics.

3 Know that children at the intermediate level are interested in designing cars and that they have experience in this, such as designing cars for a soap box derby or assembling model cars.

4 Understand the processes and the number of people involved in designing an automobile.

5 Know sculptural forms.

6 Understand that a car can be a work of art.

7 Have experience in modeling with clay.

8 Know the uses of the opaque projector (see Figure 182, page 267).

9 Before this episode is presented, children should have had experiences in designing a car for the future. Children at this level are

interested in future means of transportation and this interest should be directed toward aesthetic understandings. Pen and ink or pencils should be provided for this activity, and children should be stimulated to think of the visual art elements while they are designing.

Materials

Halftones showing progressive stages in the design of an automobile
Opaque projector and screen, if halftones from this or other books are used (see Figure 182, page 267)

Vocabulary

automobile designer   stylist
sculptor-modeler   render
fiberglas

Instructional procedures

Motivation and instruction: Sensory, multi-sensory experiences; topic discussion

1   Have children describe the automobile designs they have made and explain why they included certain design features.

2   Ask children to compare their designs with automobiles currently available and with older automobiles. What changes can be noted?

3   Ask children why changes are constantly being made in the designs of automobiles. Why don't we find one design that is functional and pleasing and keep it year after year?

4   Have children refer again to their automobile designs and relate these to future cars. Ask them where they might find similar designs. Explain that many designs that have already been made will not be seen for many years because the designer works ahead of his time, just as the painter, sculptor, ceramist, and architect often does. Help them understand that designers and artists are frequently ahead of the rest of the population in the designs and works of art that they create.

Exemplar:

1   Introduce the halftone in Figure 150 by asking the children what stage of automobile designing it might represent. Why is this first drawing board sketch important? Help them understand that hundreds of such sketches are turned out as a new automobile design is begun, and that hundreds more are made as its details and special features are developed. Ask children to explain what visual art elements are used in the sketches and what effects the designer strives for.

Figure 150

2 Show the halftone in Figure 151 and discuss what has happened to the sketch that the children saw in the preceding exemplar. Explain that this is a model done in clay by a sculptor-modeler and is one-fifth the size of the automobile. Direct the children's attention to the size of the man and the size of the model.

Figure 151

3   Introduce the halftone in Figure 152 by explaining that a model, such as that shown in Figure 151, is changed and/or approved by the stylist (one who is concerned with the appearance and design of the automobile). It is then modeled in clay in actual size by the sculptor-modeler. Ask the children to explain why this clay model would be helpful in evaluating the design. What skills does the sculptor-modeler need in order to adapt a two-dimensional sketch into a three-dimensional model? In what ways does the experimental car look like a piece of sculpture? Have the children compare the simple lines in the model with other products and exemplars they have studied.

4   Introduce Figure 153 and explain that after the clay model has been approved by various stylists, it is turned over to technicians who design the model in fiberglas and include all mechanical innovations. The mass production of automobiles comes from this design.

Figure 152

Figure 153

5 Ask children to describe the car of the future. Would their designs be helpful for this car? Would their designs be acceptable to automobile manufacturers? Why are some cars preferred over others? What visual art elements used by automobile designers can be compared with those used by other designers and artists?

Expected outcome

Children should:
1 Know that automobiles and other products are the result of hundreds of sketches made by designers.
2 Understand that the designer uses all the visual art elements in planning designs and that they have also used these in their designs.
3 Understand why automobile designs are changed so frequently.
4 Understand that designers and artists are usually years ahead of their time and that their innovations cannot always be understood by people today.

Related activities

(Visual exercises, books, poetry, related activities in other subjects)
1 Many children will enjoy reading *The Automobile Book* by Ralph Stein.
2 Many children will want to assemble a picture history of the automobile, and will enjoy reporting about changes that have been made.
3 Children should consider the question of merchandising or selling the products of designers: a pleasing and harmonious design is not the only thing that manufacturers consider. What other factors may enter into their choice?

EPISODE 6

Objective: To introduce concepts of urban renewal and city planning as they relate to the use of visual art elements and to planning for future living *

Teacher background

1 Have experience in sketching and rendering sketches in watercolor.
2 Understand the limitations of watercolor.

---

* This episode is presented in four parts to show the logical breaking points for presenting it to children.

3 Know simple construction procedures involving the use of boxes, milk cartons, etc., to represent houses and buildings.

4 Understand how to plan and manage group activities.

5 Understand analogies between design principles in nature and in works of art and their uses in designs for city planning.

6 Understand contemporary innovations which involve movements of growing populations.

7 Know major city planning and renewal projects and the reasons behind them.

8 Understand the problems which have prompted the need for urban renewal.

9 Understand the role of politics in city planning.

10 Develop a sensitivity to the non-aesthetic environment.

11 Understand contemporary social and economic problems.

12 Know the uses of the opaque projector (see Figure 182, page 267).

Materials

Watercolors

Brushes

Paper

Brown or white wrapping paper

Milk cartons

Tempera paint

Green sponges

Reproduction: Edward Hopper, *Early Sunday Morning*

Halftones: Before and After, Philadelphia City Planning Commission
    Downtown Plan for Springfield, Missouri
    New Ideas in Land Planning, Springfield, Missouri

Opaque projector and screen, if halftones from this or other books are used (see Figure 182, page 267)

Vocabulary

urban renewal

city planning

city planner

landscape

Edward Hopper

Early Sunday Morning

beautification

Instructional procedures

Motivation and instruction: Sensory, multi-sensory experiences; topic discussion

Part I.

1 Select a section of the city with which the children are familiar and which is in need of urban renewal. This may be a neighborhood in which children live, the downtown area, or any feature of the landscape. List specific items in this section that need to be renewed or renovated: houses, store buildings, parking lots, etc.

2 Introduce the episode by discussing the section selected. Ask questions to determine what the children know and remember about the section: What is the condition of the buildings? How could the section be described?

3 Assign to each child one or more of the items from the list compiled in question (1), and have him make an "on the spot" pencil sketch of the item or items. Discuss the specific things that children are to look for and record in the sketches. (This may be done as homework; or the class can make a field trip to the section and sketch while they are there.)

Part II.

1 When the pencil sketches have been completed, review watercolor and its use with the children, and have them render their sketches in watercolor. Many of their watercolors may look like the one in Figure 154, which shows many features in need of renewal.

2 Display all the watercolors. Have the children describe their work and the condition of the section they have sketched and painted.

Figure 154
Ten Year Old

Figure 155
Edward Hopper, *Early Sunday Morning,* 1930

Oil on canvas, 35 × 60 inches

Exemplar:

1 Introduce the exemplar shown in Figure 155 by reviewing the steps the children went through in recording their impressions of the section of the city: they first observed, studied, and then recorded their impressions. Explain that artists often paint impressions of what they see in neighborhoods, as the artist has done in Figure 155, and that they too observe, study, and then record their impressions.

2 Discuss the paintings done by the children in terms of changes that could be made. Why would such changes be necessary or important?

Part III.

1 Have children tell the changes they would like to make in what they originally saw and recorded and why they would like to make these changes. Let them do another sketch or painting in which they include their suggested changes.

2 Display the sketches or paintings beside the first ones, and ask children to describe the improvements they have made and to explain why they have made them.

3 Introduce the terms *urban renewal* and *beautification.* Explain that city planners are concerned with constructing new buildings, repairing or renovating other buildings, creating parks, improving the landscape, etc.

Figure 156
Washington Square East, Philadelphia, January 1961

Figure 157
Washington Square East, Philadelphia, 1962

4 Stimulate the children to talk about the kind of place they would like to live in. Ask questions that will lead them to suggest where they would like to have their parks, what kind of parks they need, where they could get the space for parks, what landscaping they would like, etc.

5 Have children bring in newspaper clippings about urban renewal and city planning projects.

6 Introduce the halftones shown in Figures 156 and 157 by explaining to the children that city planners are already doing something about urban renewal, as shown in these before and after halftones of a section in Philadelphia. Have the children compare the two scenes and describe the changes made in buildings and landscaping. Have them express the way each makes them feel.

7   Ask children to compare the way the city planner, the architect, and the landscape architect have used the visual art elements. Help them understand that differences in texture, repeat patterns, lines, size, shape, form, and color can be combined in ways that provide us with more aesthetic surroundings, and that everyone wants pleasant surroundings in which to live.

8   Introduce the halftone shown in Figure 158 by explaining that city planning encompasses urban renewal, or the improvement of existing areas, and planning for the city, whether it is large or small, old or new. Figure 158 shows such a plan for downtown Springfield, Missouri. Have children discuss the problems of renovating an old city as compared with those of planning an entirely new city.

Figure 158

DOWNTOWN PLAN for SPRINGFIELD · MO.
LADISLAS SEGOE & ASSOC. · Urban Renewal Division · Cincinnati · Ohio 1963

9   Discuss the plans which many cities now have for better spacing of buildings, parks, etc., and the fact that these plans are blueprints for the future so that they will have more pleasant places to live in when they are adults. Encourage the children to talk about how it would feel to walk from one section of a city to another with a different but well-planned vista in each section. Discuss the importance of having such pleasant places to walk; it is likely that people will not be allowed to drive their cars through certain sections of the city, but will walk through these sections just as we walk through shopping centers today.

Part IV.

1 Prepare for a group activity for making a model community using a reproduction, such as *Park Near Lucerne* by Paul Klee, as a guide.

    a Stimulate children to think of the importance of planning for new cities for the future so that all people on earth will have places to live.

    b Provide children with a large piece of wrapping paper, milk cartons, tempera paint, brushes, and green sponges (for trees).

    c Discuss the use of the reproduction *Park Near Lucerne* as a small city plan, since the lines and shapes located within the reproduction provide an already well-organized composition for placement of houses, parks, etc. Help children visualize houses, parks, and buildings placed along the lines.

    d Compare this with the housing development in Springfield, Missouri, shown in Figure 159.

Figure 159

    e Stimulate children to plan their own model community and to make a model of it.

    f While the children are working on their group project, motivate them to think in terms of parks, architecture, landscape, and the over-all aesthetic feeling of their city.

Expected outcome

Children should:

1 Be aware of the problems that face those responsible for city planning and urban renewal.

2 Understand that the solutions to these problems affect their lives today and their future.

3 Have developed some feelings about aesthetics in their community, and should have insight into the ways that other cities have solved the problem of "before" and "after."

4 Understand the reasons for planning for the future.

5 Understand the need for aesthetic behavior as this relates to cities: respect for property, etc.

6 Have insights into ways that they would work with city planners.

Related activities

(Visual exercises, books, poetry, related activities in other subjects)

1 Provide the children with opportunities to design imaginary cities of their own in their painting or drawing activities.

2 Many children will want to visit libraries and museums where there are original plans for some of our older American cities.

3 Some children may be interested in studying the history of their town to see how it has grown, and to determine how much planning has been a part of this growth.

EPISODE 7

Objective: To introduce concepts of architectural sculpture and murals

Teacher background

1 Have experience in planning and executing a mural using colored chalk, chalk and sugar water, or tempera paint.

2 Understand the function and place of a mural: a mural has a message.

3 Understand the placement of paintings and murals on walls of architectural structures.

4 Understand the use of visual art elements in a mural.

5 Know the difference between free standing sculpture and architectural sculpture.

6 Understand the use of both in enhancing a building.

7 Understand trends in the use of both of these.

8 Understand architectural sculptures in historical perspective.

9 Know the uses of the opaque projector (see Figure 182, page 267).

Materials

Reproductions: *Methethy with His Daughter and a Son,* Egyptian
            Sculpture
            Pablo Picasso, *Guernica*

Halftones: Antoine Pevsner, Sculpture, General Motors Building
            Bernard Frazier, Sculpture for Federal Building

Opaque projector and screen, if halftones from this or other books are
used (see Figure 182, page 267)

Vocabulary

architectural sculpture   Antoine Pevsner

mural   Bernard Frazier

relief sculpture   *Guernica*

Instructional procedures

Motivation and instruction: Sensory, multi-sensory experiences; topic discussion

1 Introduce the episode by reviewing with the children the differences
between relief sculpture and sculpture in the round.

2 Ask the children to tell of ways that man has made buildings more
aesthetically pleasing. Introduce the term *architectural sculpture* as
one way buildings have been enhanced.

3 Discuss how the early Egyptians, Greeks, and Romans often used
sculpture as a part of their buildings, and lead the discussion into the
introduction of the first exemplar.

Exemplar:

1 Introduce the exemplar shown in Figure 160 by explaining that this
is a very old example of relief sculpture used by the Egyptians about
2450 B.C. Have the children find the variety of shapes used by the
Egyptians in carving this relief sculpture from limestone. Direct the
children's attention to the simplicity of line used by the designer-
craftsmen. A review of frottage may be helpful so that the children
can see that rubbings can be taken from relief sculpture of this kind.

2 Discuss the problem confronting contemporary architectural sculptors. Unlike the Egyptians or people in other past periods of history,
modern man is usually walking hurriedly or driving past buildings and

Figure 160
Methethy with His Daughter and Son, Egyptian, Late V Dynasty, c. 2450 B.C.

From Sakkary (Round Unis Pyramid, south of causeway); polychromed limestone re-lief, 56¼ × 30 inches

Figure 161
Bernard Frazier, Architectural Sculpture for Federal Build-ing, Tulsa, Oklahoma

does not have or take time for more than a quick glance at the sculp-ture. Explain the way architectural sculptors have solved this prob-lem today: they have created forms which are meant to be looked at by a person who is walking quickly or driving past the sculpture. The forms have been created so that the viewer, if he glances at the sculpture two or three times, sees different views and gets the feeling that the sculpture is moving, although it is stationary.

3 Introduce the exemplar shown in Figure 161 by explaining to the children that it is an example of sculpture created for modern man.

It is designed to be viewed in two glances by a person in a moving car, and for this reason the sculpture, which is a part of the building, is carved in two distinct profiles. Ask the children to tell how they would get different views of the sculpture if they were driving past it. How would the car's movement affect the view of the sculpture?

4 Have children describe the way telephone poles seem to move as they drive past them, or the way they seem to feel movement when they stand beside a moving train.

5 Introduce the exemplar shown in Figure 162 by reviewing the use of sculpture to complement and add an aesthetic touch to the building. Help children understand that this sculpture has many forms which seem to move as a person walks in and out of the building or past the sculpture. Discuss the scale of the sculpture in relation to the size of the man. Help the children see the way the sculptor has used natural light to enhance the forms. Have the children talk about the different shadows created by the sculptural forms at different times of the day.

6 Ask children to explain the uses of architectural sculpture.

Figure 162
Antoine   Pevsner,
Sculpture for General Motors Building, Detroit, Michigan

Figure 163
Pablo Picasso, *Guernica*, 1937

Oil on canvas, 11½ × 25⅔ feet

7 Introduce the exemplar shown in Figure 163 by explaining that the architect not only uses architectural sculpture on the outside of the building, but that he also allows space for murals on walls inside the building to beautify it. A mural is usually a painting on a two-dimensional surface, such as a flat wall, which depicts a story. The story can be about early Indians and pioneers, early Egyptians, or anything the artist chooses. The mural shown in Figure 163 is a story which deals with man's inhumanity to man. Help the children to see that the story is important, but that the way the artist has used all the visual art elements is important too. Have the children describe the mural in terms of line, shape, size, texture, repeated shapes and textures, color, and placement of objects.

8 Have children identify murals they have seen in buildings and compare them with ones that they have made.

Expected outcome

Children should:

1 Understand the use of architectural sculpture.

2 Know that different kinds of architectural sculpture are used.

3 Know that murals are often used to enhance interiors of buildings.

4 Reinforce their understanding of two- and three-dimensional works of art.

5 Develop an historical framework for the types of architectural sculpture given in the episode.

Related activities

(Visual exercises, books, poetry, related activities in other subjects)

1 Children who have not had an opportunity to create a mural will learn from this activity. Provide them with wrapping paper, colored chalk and sugar water or tempera paint. Children are often interested in depicting stories from social studies.

2 Have children bring in newspaper clippings, books, and magazines which show sculpture and murals as a part of buildings.

3 Many children will enjoy doing research on Egyptian sculpture; reasons for having it, where it is found, etc.

EPISODE 8

Objective: To develop children's visual skills to see analogies between nature, their own creative products, and architectural forms

Teacher background

1 Understand analogies between natural forms and structures in ordinary objects and their implications for design.

2 Understand that nature and art are related.

3 Know the technological discoveries of man which enable him to innovate new forms.

4 Understand how commonplace objects can become uncommon.

5 Understand future needs of man's ever-changing world.

6 Know the uses of the opaque projector (see Figure 182, page 267).

Materials

Examples of children's paper sculpture (if applicable)
Halftone enlargement of egg

Halftones: Charles Deaton, The Sculpture House, Colorado
Charles Deaton, Model of Key Savings and Loan Building, Englewood, Colorado
Eero Saarinen, TWA Building, *Interior,* New York

Opaque projector and screen, if halftones from this or other books are used (see Figure 182, page 267)

Vocabulary

innovation   interior
sculptural form   Charles Deaton
concrete shell   Eero Saarinen
exterior

Instructional procedures

Motivation and instruction: Sensory, multi-sensory experiences; topic discussion

1 Introduce the episode by reviewing some of the paper sculpture that the children have recently produced and the various forms they have created by scoring and turning their flat pieces of paper into three-dimensional pieces. Some of the examples may look like the one shown in Figure 164. Review other designers, such as architects, who are also interested in such forms. Explain that the knowledge developed by man in structure and the new building materials which are now available have enabled him to create new buildings using these forms.

Figure 164
Intermediate Level

2 Help children to identify objects in nature which are beautiful and simple, such as an egg.

3 Use the opaque projector, if necessary, and show an enlarged halftone of an egg, as seen in Figure 165. Have the children describe the thin strong shell of the egg. Discuss how the light strikes this simple form and makes its texture more evident. Stimulate the children to talk about the use of such common forms as a source of inspiration for creating or innovating new forms in architecture. Ask the children if houses have to be square or rectangular. What other geometric shapes and simple forms can be used?

Figure 165

Exemplar:

1 Introduce the exemplar shown in Figure 166 (use the opaque projector, if necessary) by having children describe the form of this house. Ask what materials might have been used. Help children to understand that this house in Colorado was constructed from concrete, which can sometimes be sprayed onto a steel form. Help the children see the architect's use of all the visual art elements: line, form, size, shape, texture, repeat pattern, color. Have them describe the sweeping view of the mountains which can be seen by the occupants of the house. Encourage the children to find the relationships between the form of the egg and the architectural form created by the architect.

Figure 166
Charles Deaton, The
Sculpture House, Colo-
rado

Figure 167
The Sculpture House
(Closeup)

2 Introduce the exemplar shown in Figure 167 by having the children
note the similarities between this house and three-dimensional forms
they have studied. The house can be seen from various angles and
each angle creates another light pattern and presents an interesting
view to the observer.

3 Many children will immediately equate the shape of this house with
a "flying saucer." The teacher should capitalize on this imaginative
expression, and ask children to tell about new forms of architecture
that can be expected in the future because 'of man's desire to create
different forms for homes using the visual art elements and new materials which will be available.

4 Introduce the exemplar shown in Figure 168 by discussing man's need for new forms for office buildings as well as homes. Explain that this is a model made before the building was built, and that architects plan and make scale models just as automobile designers do, or just as the children make small-scale models of airplanes.

5 Help the childern see the resemblance between the office building and the house in terms of line, form, texture, size, shape, color, pattern, and function. Encourage the children to tell how it might feel to be inside such a structure.

6 Lead directly from the preceding discussion into the introduction of the exemplar shown in Figure 169. Explain to the children that this

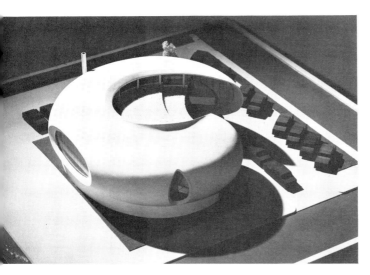

Figure 168
Charles Deaton, Model of Key Savings
and Loan Building, Englewood, Colorado

Figure 169
Eero Saarinen, TWA Building
(*Interior*), New York

is the work of another architect who has also experimented with new concrete forms. Have the children describe the interior of the building and the way that the light creates different and interesting patterns inside at different times of the day. Explain that the architect is just as concerned about the inside or interior of the building as he is about the exterior. Help the children notice how the various curves, lines, and shapes are repeated throughout the interior to create interesting relationships. Stimulate the children to express how it would feel to live inside a three-dimensional piece of sculpture, and equate that with the interior shown here.

Expected outcome

Children should:

1   Be aware that the architect is constantly searching for new and different ways to express himself, although he uses the same visual art elements that man has employed throughout history.
2   Have had their imaginations stimulated concerning future forms for architecture.
3   Recognize that common objects, such as an egg, can be used as a source of uncommon imaginative innovations.
4   Reinforce their understandings of the visual art elements so that they can interact more knowledgeably and aesthetically with the works of artists and designer-craftsmen.

Related activities

(Visual exercises, books, poetry, related activities in other subjects)

1   Direct the children's attention to shapes and forms found in nature and commonplace objects.
2   Many children will want to design their own homes and should be provided with this opportunity. Encourage them to develop imaginative forms with watercolor, tempera, or pen and ink.
3   Provide children with good books on architecture so that they can see examples of forms which may be used in the future.
4   Some children may want to do research on the changing styles of homes throughout history and the reasons for the changes.

ANALYSIS OF THE EPISODES

An analysis of the selected learning experiences for the intermediate level reveals that by the time children are halfway through this level in school they should have become well acquainted with the visual art elements given in the basic structure for art in the nursery and elementary schools. The understanding of these elements is used to develop richer concepts of and for vocabulary, art history, design, and symbols; and these, in turn, provide an extended frame of reference (or richer concepts of and for) the works of the artist, the designer-craftsman, and the natural environment. Each time a new episode is presented, children are·called upon to use the visual art elements in a different and/or extended frame of reference. This progression is comparable to that used in the other disciplines.

An analysis of the media processes reveals that these are used to help children develop an extended frame of reference for the works of artists and designer-craftsmen and the natural environment. This does not mean, however, that episodes based solely on the media processes should be excluded from children's learning experiences, for, as we know, richer symbols are derived from the way children use the visual art elements. Exemplars and media processes should be used together to reinforce each other. Episodes which do not always deal with the media processes were presented because the learnings derived from them are not commonly used in teaching procedures for art today.

Those who are schooled in art history as an area of specialization will question the apparent disregard for art history, but an analysis of these episodes shows that art history is not disregarded or neglected. In fact, children are being well prepared for it through the enrichment of concepts of the visual art elements and the comparisons made between the old and the new in many of the episodes. Whenever possible, works of art have been placed in an historical framework: frequent references are made to historical events with which children are familiar. Concepts of the past are enriched to include works of artists and designer-craftsmen. Teachers will also notice many possibilities for the use of time lines to reinforce the developing sense of chronology at this level, and to draw attention to the significance of art in the history of mankind.

Equal emphasis has been placed on preparing the child for the world of tomorrow. The second episodic cluster, which makes use of environmental exemplars designed for use in the present and in the future, should help children become noticers of the environment and to be aware of future possibilities for it.

FURTHER READINGS

Suggested readings for this chapter are given on pages 97 and 98.

12

Supplementary
Aesthetic Experiences

INTRODUCTION

Although the exemplars used in the preceding episodes are perhaps the most important ones children will have as far as learning experiences are concerned, they are not the only ones to which children will be exposed. There are other exemplars to be used in the classroom which are a part of traveling art exhibits from art museums, mobile art units, and the school's private art collection. Children will also be taken to museums and galleries to see works of art which cannot be brought into the room. Although these exhibits cannot substitute for a planned program of aesthetic education, their use can be very important in supplementing this program. Exhibits of the works of artists and designer-craftsmen can enrich aesthetic education, particularly if they are used as culminating activities presented after the completion of an episodic cluster.

TRAVELING ART EXHIBITS

Within recent years many excellent exhibits and displays have been assembled for use in elementary classrooms. There are indications that these will be developed in even larger numbers and will be available to more schools. Almost every reputable museum and gallery and several commercial companies have developed traveling art galleries in the form of packaged or mobile units rented to schools. Often, imaginative and informative audio-visual installations accompany the exhibits. The exhibits are usually planned according to themes or schools of art, or are composed of informative displays of the visual art elements which can be found in nature.

In addition to these traveling units are exhibits developed by art administrative and supervisory personnel. Various photographs, reproductions, and sensory aids are assembled and circulated from the main office into the schools. Since the basic purpose of any exhibit is to help children develop aesthetic understandings, some of the most meaningful displays are those designed by school personnel, because these can be planned as a part of the total curriculum. The effective use of these exhibits places a responsibility on art administrative personnel as well as on teachers. Informative workshops need to be held so that the use of the exhibit can be discussed and its relationship to the curriculum stressed. Without a close working relationship between the classroom teacher and the art educator, even the best circulating exhibits may do little more than consume time.

The use of traveling art exhibits, whether from museums, commercial companies, or the art administrator's office, is recommended and encouraged. The exhibits should be used, however, to complement and enrich the curriculum by providing exemplars to supplement the ones already included for use with instructional procedures.

THE SCHOOLS AS FINE ART COLLECTORS

Within recent years, many schools have initiated programs in which art administrative personnel have become art collectors for the schools. Although there are certain positive features to this practice, there are also negative ones. In many school systems, the original remains in the art administrator's office and is not used in the classroom. Sometimes children get only an occasional glimpse of the original work as the administrator or art teacher carries it from class to class; it is never left in one room for any length of time. When original works are used in this way, there is little chance that they will contribute to aesthetic understandings.

In addition, the original works obtained for the collection are often those of local artists and artisans, and are not always good works of art. A few good local works are always desirable because children need to see handsome originals done by people whom they can meet. However, it is a questionable practice to base an entire program on originals executed by local artists whose works have never been purchased by a museum for its permanent collection. The money might be better spent on quality reproductions, books, art films, good audio-visual materials, and more frequent trips to art museums and galleries. Many school systems which have enough money to purchase original works of art and all the instructional aids they need, have found it advisable to use the consultant services of museum curators and their professional associates for selecting the originals to be purchased.

THE ART MUSEUM AND ITS FUNCTION

Art museums have two main functions: to collect works which are representative of our art heritage and to display these acquisitions to the public. Recently, museums have also assumed another function, that of educating the public in art. Since public education in this country has not yet produced a large population capable of an intelligent use of a culture center, such as a museum, the museums have taken over this role and have developed programs designed to help make museum visitors, including children, visually literate. In assuming this task, museum directors are making it easier for the schools to carry out their part of the responsibility.

Although the major purpose of museums and galleries, as far as children are concerned, is to bring the children into contact with works of art, many museums now provide children with opportunities for creative art activities. Some of the most meaningful art experiences for children take place in classes sponsored by education directors in museums and galleries. These directors have understood the importance of the media processes in helping children develop a frame of reference for an exemplar, and almost all the museums engaged in this kind of activity have excellent programs.

One of the most delightful innovations to be made by museums in recent years is the development of special sections for children, sometimes referred to as Junior Galleries. These excellent exhibits and displays designed for children are also frequently used by adults in their search for visual literacy. The exhibits often include sensory materials and aids, and informative audio-visual installations that enable children to learn more easily about those works on exhibit and to develop a

Figure 170
Junior Gallery and Creative Arts Center, William Rockhill Nelson Art Gallery, Kansas City, Missouri

frame of reference for them. Such a gallery is shown in Figure 170. Notice that audio-visual installations are provided for the children and that all reproductions, prints, and originals are displayed at the children's eye level. Numerous other children's galleries, among them the Chicago Art Institute's Children's Museum, are to be found throughout the country. This innovation by the museum directors can help teachers enrich children's aesthetic education.

The Visit to the Art Museum

Schools located close to an art museum often take advantage of this center. All too often, however, the children who visit art museums are those whose parents have an interest in original works of art and wish to expand their children's aesthetic education. Therefore, very few children are involved in special programs sponsored by museums, and few even visit one. It is apparent that public education must assume this responsibility. Although the schools may not be able to involve children in all the programs sponsored by a museum, they can assume the responsibility of taking children to visit one.

Visits to the museum, when they are made, are sometimes conducted before children have had an opportunity to develop a frame of reference for the works of art they are to see; as a result, children may not interact with them empathically and intelligently. It is little wonder that they sometimes remember the bus ride to and from the museum more than they remember the museum itself and what they saw. This need not and should not be the case; visits to the museum are valuable educational field trips and can be used to good advantage.

The museum visit is probably best used as a culminating activity which follows and reinforces an episodic cluster completed by the children in the classroom. In order for children to profit from this activity, careful planning must be made and instruction given in the classroom before the visit. Planning far in advance for the museum visit will help children discover the wonder, excitement, and enjoyment—which are rightfully theirs—of the museum or gallery. The planning and the instruction should be directed toward three important objectives:

1 To help children understand the function of the museum and develop a positive attitude toward it.
2 To help children develop a frame of reference for what they will see.
3 To help children prepare for the trip itself.

Accomplishing these objectives may require the use of three or four specially designed episodes. However, the results of careful planning and instruction will be evident when the children are taken for a visit to the museum. The suggestions presented below for each of these objectives have been found helpful to teachers in developing the episodes needed.

Helping children understand the function of the museum and develop positive attitudes toward it.   The attitudes which children form about art museums may be the result of their early experiences with them.   These experiences are usually very limited and do not always help children understand the function of museums or stimulate them to want to return.   In other places children visit, such as the zoo, this difficulty does not arise.   Children generally visit the zoo more often and understand that animals are kept in the zoo because they are rare and/or undomesticated.   Children have a background for understanding the zoo—and its inhabitants.   Their knowledge of museums is not nearly so extensive, and they need to be helped to discover that the works of art and artifacts found in the museums are equally "special" and are housed in a special place so that they can be enjoyed by all.   Comparisons with a zoo need not be made, but understandings and positive attitudes can be established by pointing out the relationships between the known and the unknown, and by providing children with experiences and background for the trip to the museum.

A wise investment for a teacher in preparing children for the museum is the purchase of a museum's catalog for use as a guide in the classroom.   Most art museums have catalogs which explain their function and purpose, and provide useful information such as biographical sketches of the artists, discussions of schools of art, photographs of major works of art in the permanent collection, and architectural photographs of the museum itself.

In helping children to understand the museum it is desirable to start with the architectural structure of the building itself, both exterior and interior.   Children need to become familiar with the structure; for a first visit, this is most important.   The teacher can acquaint the children with the museum by using the opaque projector and the museum catalog.   Children can be helped to discover that the architecture of a museum is determined by its function—to provide galleries for exhibit purposes—and that its structure is designed accordingly by the architect, as shown in Figure 171.   The museum building, as an example of architecture, can be discussed in terms of the visual art elements which children will be acquainted with if the basic structure for teaching art has been used.   They should also understand that museums are not alike, an understanding which can be developed and reinforced by showing the architectural structure of other museums, such as the Whitney Museum, shown in Figure 172.   Both are exemplars of contemporary architecture, but are completely different in their design.

Figure 171
Philip Johnson, Sheldon Art Gallery (East Entrance), University of Nebraska, Lincoln, Nebraska

Figure 172
Marcel Breuer and Associates, Whitney Museum of American Art, New York

Once again, children will be able to understand that architects use the visual art elements in their designs, but that each one uses them differently. In addition, children should be told that there are many museums in this country, and that each is different in architectural design.

After the children have had an opportunity to develop a frame of reference for the buildings which they will see, a visual experience of what they can expect to find on the inside should be presented to prevent the formation of the attitude that museums are "stuffy." The first visit for children is an important experience, and they should know what they will see. For example, Figure 173—which can be shown in the classroom by using the opaque projector and the museum catalog— shows that the interior of the museum is a home for original works of art, and that these are always hung on the walls if they are two-dimensional or displayed from many sides if they are three-dimensional or pieces of sculpture. The children's attention can be directed to the various textures to be found in the building itself. In Figure 173, for example, they should notice that the walls are covered with white carpet against which works of art are displayed. Once again, to extend their frame of reference for museums, an exemplar of a museum's interior should be used to establish the idea that not all museum interiors are the same. Showing the interior of the Guggenheim Museum (Figure 174) will help children see some of these differences. From their visual experiences, however, they should also develop the understanding that although museums do not look alike they serve the same function—the display of original works of art. Children should also understand that there are a large number of museums, that each one houses different collections, and that many of these can be visited when trips are made to other parts of the country.

Figure 173
Philip Johnson, Sheldon Art Gallery (*Interior*), University of Nebraska, Lincoln, Nebraska

Figure 174
Frank Lloyd Wright,
Guggenheim Museum
(*Interior*), New York

Helping children develop a frame of reference for what they will see. After children have had an opportunity to use their knowledge of the visual art elements in learning about the architecture of museums, and have understood the function of a museum, they are ready to develop a frame of reference for the exhibit they will see. Perhaps the best kind of preparation for the teacher in helping children develop this frame of reference is to visit the museum herself. Such a procedure is recommended for all field trips, and is especially important for a museum trip. A teacher who has seen at firsthand the exemplars that the children will see can do a better job of preparing them for their museum experience.

It is not enough, however, for the teacher to be able to tell the children about what they see; visual experiences are needed as part of the preparation. Again, materials that are available from museums can be used to good advantage for this visual preparation. Most museums have postcard reproductions of the works in their permanent collection, works which the children will see on display. Another good investment for the teacher is the purchase of postcard reproductions of the works the children will see. These reproductions will help extend the children's frames of reference. The opaque projector can be used for showing the cards, and discussions centered on the children's understandings of the visual art elements can be conducted. This is a very important step in the preparation, for children should see reproductions of the works of art before they see the originals. Some teachers feel that this practice detracts from the experience of seeing the original, but quite the reverse is true; when children know what to expect, aesthetic understandings can be increased. The use of postcard reproductions also serves as a way of helping children distinguish between originals and reproductions.

The particular exhibit that the children will see is determined by the teacher, with the assistance of the art supervisor and museum personnel. It is much wiser to give children a limited but studied exposure to a few works of art, instead of a survey tour of everything to be seen in the museum. Many school systems provide at least four to six museum visits during the elementary school period, and these are carefully planned and synchronized with what is being studied at school. Other school systems make the mistake of spending a complete day at the museum, usually in the spring, and children sometimes leave with a strong dislike for the museum. Limiting the works to be seen at the museum will give children an opportunity to study them and apply what they have learned in the classroom, and will prepare them for future visits.

Helping children prepare for the trip to the museum. Field trips can be an important part of children's learning experiences, but very often they become experiences of chaos and confusion, particularly on the bus. It is not enough to prepare children for what they will see when they get to the museum; they must also be prepared for the trip itself. The teacher can help children prepare for the trip by learning about the places of interest to be seen along the way. The teacher will find it helpful to inquire about the route the bus will take, follow this same route, and make notes of buildings, parks, construction sites, and other features which will be of interest to the children. Many teachers have even found it helpful to plan the trip with the driver so that different routes may be taken going and coming, and so that places of specific interest to the children will be included on each route. If the teacher can help in such planning, buildings of unusual design, new recreational centers under construction, or areas where urban renewal is in progress are features to include in the trip. This kind of planning can make the trip itself exciting and informative for the children.

Conduct on the bus is sometimes a problem. Teachers who have included the children in the planning of behavior and conduct, both during the trip and in the museum, have found that better behavior can be achieved. Children need to know what is expected of them, and they are quite capable of setting the limits, with teacher guidance, for these expectations.

Evaluation. Trips to the museum, like all learning experiences, should be evaluated. After the trip, the teacher should discuss with the children what they saw, discovered, and learned. In this way, the children are involved in the evaluative process, and the teacher is able to determine the outcome of this learning experience. Evaluation is important because it determines the direction of the succeeding learning experiences for the children, and serves as preparation for the many follow-up activities which should result from the museum visit. For while the museum trip is a culminating activity, it is not the end of aesthetic education.

FURTHER READINGS

Christensin, Erwin O. (Ed.). *Museum Directory of the United States and Canada.* Washington, D. C.: Museum Association of America, 1961.

Hiller, Carl E. "Art in the Museum," *Education and Art.* New York: UNESCO, 1953.

Low, Theodore. *The Educational Philosophy and Practice of Art Museums in the United States.* New York: Teachers College Press, Columbia University, 1948.

Munro, Thomas. *Art Education: Its Philosophy and Psychology.* New York: The Liberal Arts Press, 1956.
Chapter 25, "The Art Museum and Creative Originality."

III

PREPARATION
AND PLANNING
FOR TEACHING ART

13

Using Visual Media
To Enhance
Visual Perception

INTRODUCTION

Within the past twenty-five years, scientific technology has provided teachers with a variety of visual media designed to enhance teaching procedures. Slide projectors, opaque projectors, film projectors, and other media enable teachers to use procedures heretofore impossible, and increase the possibilities for effective learning. These media will be improved as technological innovations and developments are made. Such innovations will also bring completely new media to the classroom, some of which will be developed as a result of suggestions and assistance from teachers. Since visual media are important materials for the program presented in this book, suggestions for their use are given in this chapter. Media that have been found to be particularly useful in helping children enhance their visual perception and acquire appreciative skills are dealt with. Although these media were never intended to replace the teacher in the classroom, they can assist her in doing a more effective job.

REASONS FOR USE

Since a knowledge of art elements and a knowledge of the works of artists and designer-craftsmen and the natural environment are a part of the basic structure, the use of visual media serves an important function. Through these media children can discover aspects of their environment which heretofore have been missed or unconsciously passed over, and can see the interrelationship of all the visual art elements as they exist in nature. In this way their frames of reference can be extended for use in other experiences with exemplars in which the children see man's use of art elements. Many meaningful opportunities are provided for children to develop skills of seeing, and, subsequently, skills of appreciation, as the enlarged worlds of nature and the visual arts are projected for their viewing and study.

DEVELOPING TECHNIQUES

There are three main steps that teachers can follow to develop techniques for using visual media. First, become familiar with media by using them. It is not enough to read about their uses or to listen to someone explain them. One learns the uses of visual media by using them, experimenting with them, and learning their possibilities and limitations.

Second, implement the suggestions given for the various media in this chapter. No attempt has been made to go into detail concerning all the uses, but those which have been found to be effective are presented.

Third, build on these suggestions with individual variations. These can come from the children as well as from the teacher, since they too can learn to use the media and can discover possibilities for their use.

VISUAL MEDIA AND THEIR USES

The 2 x 2 Slide Projector

The 2×2 slide projector, a common piece of equipment in most schools, serves many important functions in the enhancement of children's visual perception. Two of these functions are outstanding. First, this type of projection enables children to enrich concepts from the basic structure by showing the interrelationships of all visual art elements as they exist in organic and inorganic objects. This is done through the use of transparencies made from small particles barely discernible to the naked eye. Such transparencies are, perhaps, one of the best ways for children in nursery and elementary schools to learn about line, repeated lines into textures, shapes, sizes, and even color.

Teachers of early primary children can make their own transparencies since it is very simple procedure. At the primary and intermediate levels even the children can make their own, and the construction of these provides another way for them to enhance their perception. There are many ways to make the transparencies, but the following procedures have been found to be helpful.

Materials for the transparencies should be assembled. These materials should include:

1 Minute particles of: lemon peel, tomato skin, leaves, stamen, pistils, pollen, cucumber cross-sections, yarn, netting, fabrics, insects, colored cellophane, etc.
2 2 × 2 slide mounts (these may be purchased at any camera supply house).
3 Medium-weight acetate precut for 2 × 2 slide mounts.
4 Clothes iron for sealing.

Figure 175 shows these materials.

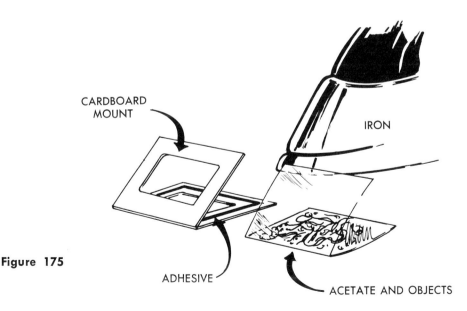

CARDBOARD MOUNT

IRON

Figure 175

ADHESIVE

ACETATE AND OBJECTS

The procedures for using these materials are: (1) place any one or combination of the minute particles between a folded piece of precut acetate; (2) place this in a 2 × 2 mount; and (3) with a warm iron press the edges of the photo mount to seal. When this procedure is completed, the slide is ready for showing.

For variation, thin rubber cement may be added to the slide between the acetate. When the heat from the projector hits the slide, the rubber cement will expand and move, giving the effect of looking at amoeba under a microscope. Many other materials may also be used for effects of this nature. Heat from the machine does not destroy the slide or cause it to deteriorate. Figure 176 shows the projection of a simple transparency made by children.

Figure 176

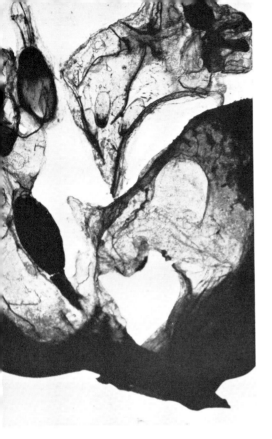

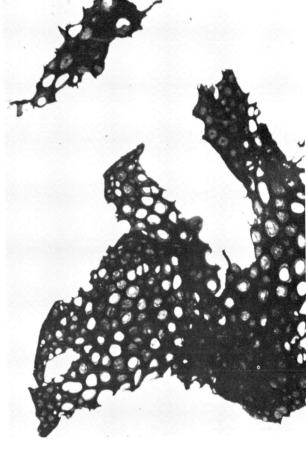

Figure 177
Cucumber Slice

Figure 178
Orange Peel

So that children will become more skilled in looking and in relating this experience to learnings in art, teachers have found it helpful to make a series of transparencies encompassing a visual art element developed from simple to complex. For example, a simple line in one slide can become two or more lines in another, followed by others which show texture, repeat pattern, size, shape, and color. The teacher can then end with an exemplar which has all the same qualities shown in the slides. Transparencies may also be used to show analogies between art elements found in commonplace objects and in works of art. For example, the details of a cucumber slice and an orange peel (Figures 177 and 178) can be revealed to children by transparencies. Comparisons can then be made with exemplars. Or, a simple window screen composed of shapes, texture, and repeat pattern can help children understand architectural structure, such as that used by Philip Johnson in his design of the Seagram's Building in New York.

The 2 × 2 slide projector can also be used to show the works of artists and designer-craftsmen, a use which is commonly found in college art history classes. In elementary classrooms, however, it is doubtful that the necessarily short projection time will allow children to study and reflect about the exemplar in relation to the visual art elements. In most cases large color reproductions serve this purpose better. However, although these are usually available for paintings, they are not always available for other exemplars. This is particularly true for exemplars of architecture, silver, crystal, ceramics, sculpture, city planning, textiles, and photography. Slides of exemplars from these areas can be used to fill this void.

When cartridge projectors are used, series of slides can be arranged sequentially and shown quickly and easily. It is also quite simple to return to slides with which children might need more time.

The 2 x 2 Filmstrip Projector

Quite often the 2 × 2 slide projector comes equipped with a filmstrip attachment and is easily converted for showing filmstrips. Commercial filmstrips are available for classroom use, including ones which explain the visual art elements as well as those which help give children a knowledge of works of art.

The Overhead Projector

The overhead projector, a fairly recent addition to visual equipment for classrooms, is used in increasing numbers in schools. It is a very versatile projector, even though its use is limited to materials which are transparent. One use of the overhead is the projection of written or typewritten acetate copies. For example, when a brief biographical sketch of an artist is needed, the teacher may select one from a file of transparencies which she has made for just such purposes. This is a time-saving procedure since it does away with the writing of the material on the chalkboard. Such transparencies also make available information which might not be found in other resource materials in the school.

The overhead projector may also be used to help children discover various textures, weaves, and patterns which are to be found in textiles.

The projection of textiles readily assists children in seeing the relationship of lines, textures, and patterns; when they see the textile enlarged on a screen and have this viewing supplemented with concrete tactual experiences with the textile, they are able to discover, understand, and experience the work of the designer-craftsman. This kind of projection offers the teacher another way to help children enrich concepts by showing how the designer-craftsman has used line, shape, repeat pattern, color, and differences in textures.

In addition to showing fabrics, the overhead may be used by the children for composing with colored acetates and textiles, such as burlap. With theatrical jelled acetates, children can learn light color theories by using overlappings; they learn that green is created when yellow and blue overlap. Different textured textiles can be used to provide contrast.

The children in Figure 179 are learning about shapes, sizes, color, and composition by using the overhead. Such experimentations can also help children understand positive and negative space. Experiments of this kind can be used as follow-up activities for children who finish their art or other activities ahead of the others. This freedom to experiment with yarns, fabrics, and acetates gives children an independent work activity which leads, hopefully, to constructive learnings. In many cases, children even learn respect for each other, since they have to take turns in using the overhead.

Figure 179

It has already been pointed out that children need a variety of materials with which to work in the media processes. Children are natural innovators and are enthusiastic about experimenting with visual media, and the overhead projector lends itself well to such innovations. For example, when a child has completed his work, he may enjoy the activities described above, or he may enjoy drawing with a felt-tipped pen or grease crayon on acetate and seeing his drawings projected as the child in Figure 180 is doing. Teachers have found that felt-tipped pens are the best for this procedure since the ink is easily removed by holding the transparencies under a faucet. Children are, of course, delighted to use colored inks. Grease crayons are excellent, but can be removed from the transparency only with a paper towel or solvent.

Transparent objects, both organic and inorganic, are also projected with great clarity on the overhead. Figure 181 shows the use of the overhead with simple objects found in nature. Here again, children are able to see design qualities inherent in nature and are able to become consciously aware of nature and design, an awareness which might not be realized without the use of such enlargements.

A particularly exciting use of the overhead projector by children is creating with reflected light. This technique, which is described below, can easily become another "gimmick" used in the classroom unless correlation is made between this procedure and learnings that primary children are acquiring in science. Light color theory, which is the basis for creating with reflected light, is dealt with in certain science programs.[1] The understandings developed in science can be used to help children create and understand art processes.

The materials needed for creating with reflected light are:

Overhead projector

Screen

Colored acetate—primary colors from light color theories [2]

Ferrotype photographer's plate or convex makeup mirror, or any high mirror-finish plate such as certain cookie sheets

Record player

Record—ballet music, such as Tchaikovsky's "Swan Lake," has been found to be very useful for this procedure

[1] John Navarra and Joseph Zafforoni, *Today's Basic Science, Book One* (New York: Harper & Row, 1963), pp. 116–22.

[2] *Ibid.*, p. 122.

Figure 180

Figure 181

The procedure for creating with reflected light includes the following points:

1 The overhead projector is reversed so that the image is reflected away from the screen.

2 Colored acetate is placed on the stage of the projector. Various combinations of colors can be used. The reflection of the acetates need not be focused.

3 The child uses the mirror plate to catch the image from the projector and to reflect it on the screen. If the plate is flexible it can be bent to create different colorful images on the screen. If enough plates are available, two or three children can work at this together.

4 Music is used during the activity to help children determine rhythm and images.

The preceding description of uses for the overhead projector does not begin to exhaust the possibilities for this piece of equipment. As teachers work with the projector, they will develop other techniques. For teachers who are fortunate enough to have an overhead projector in their rooms permanently, or for long periods of time, the following suggestion may be helpful. The projection screen may be placed at a 45-degree angle in a corner of the room with the overhead placed nearby for focused projection. Such an arrangement allows for freedom of movement in the room without disturbing the setup of the projector.

The Opaque Projector

The opaque projector is, at best, a somewhat cumbersome piece of equipment to use in the classroom. It is hoped that future technological innovations will make this projector as easily manipulated as the overhead. Even though the projector is difficult to move around, it has many important uses in the classroom.

Unlike the overhead, which projects transparencies, the opaque projects materials that are opaque. Thus, with this projector, teachers can show visual and written content from many sources, such as books on art. The projection shown in Figure 182 is a small exemplar taken from an art book, and there are many such books available. Also, full-color exemplars found in periodicals may be shown. Photographs of textures, line, shapes, and color may be shared with all the children instead of a few at a time. And children enjoy seeing their small ink or crayon drawings projected and enlarged on a screen.

Figure 182

A degree of caution needs to be exercised in the use of opaque projectors. Those available at the present create a great deal of heat and will ruin the projected object if it is shown too long. With practice, teachers can soon develop their own timing and techniques with the opaque.

The 8-mm Movie Camera and Projector

During recent years, many people have become home movie fans and have developed techniques which are sometimes very professional. Recently, many teachers have found that the use of the movie camera is an excellent way to bring environment into the classroom or to isolate interesting features in the environment for children to discover, experience, and study. Many creative teachers, for example, have made movies of various textures, patterns, colors, and shapes which exist in the environment but which are rarely observed by children. Others have made films of art collections in museums and have brought the museum into the classroom. While there are many excellent commercial films available for educational purposes, the simple 8-mm movie camera can provide experiences needed for individual classrooms. Teachers and art personnel can make specific films which aid in teaching the basic structure or which deal directly with the immediate environment of the children. Indeed, it is an unusual art educator who has not made at least one experimental film for the enhancement of perceptions of movement or color. In some cases, even students have become involved in the making of films. Art clubs for students at the junior high school level have made experimental films which almost rival the more sophisticated works of the professional film producers. The learnings derived by the students in making their own films showing movement, texture, line, shape, and color, and the interest of the students in using newer media, are gratifying to teachers. Films made by teachers and/or students are not meant to replace commercial films, but do serve the role of supplementing them.

Children in elementary classrooms are also capable of producing their own films through activities which are both rewarding and exciting. The simple processes used by children do not require a movie camera, but involve only the use of leader film. A variety of interesting and aesthetic effects can be created by having children work directly on film in the following way:

1 Draw directly on the film with pen and ink, colored felt-tipped pens, or tubed watercolors.
2 With a sharp pointed instrument, scratch directly on the film, as shown in Figure 183.
3 Perforate the film with pins to create interesting light patterns.

Figure 183
Scratching or Drawing Directly on Film with Colored Inks

Children need such opportunities to develop their visual awareness of how films are made, and they are stimulated by seeing their own film run in the classroom. It is possible to elaborate on the procedures above by having children make simple figure animations without the use of a camera. The exposed film can usually be obtained from home movie enthusiasts, including teachers. White leader film can be purchased for a nominal cost from camera or movie supply shops.

When commercial films or ones prepared by children and/or teachers are shown to children, there are certain procedures which should be followed. Films are to be used as a part of instructional procedures, and children should not be encouraged to equate these with recreation or fun time. This often happens in the use of commercial films which have to be ordered from companies or from the audio-visual center. Since schedulings from both are often delayed or untimely, films are sometimes used which have little connection with what the children are studying. Also, when a film arrives, it is sometimes shown to all the children in a particular grade level with little regard for the curriculum. Insightful and exciting films are available, and proper use of them contributes to the learning process.

The Isolator

The isolator, shown in Figure 184, is so named because it isolates specific parts of the environment for easier study and observation by children. The isolator consists of a simple 12″ × 18″ white posterboard or piece of construction paper, with a 2″ × 2″ hole cut in the middle.

Figure 184

Very often, when children or adults are asked to look at a spot in the grass or earth and to tell what they see, they reply that it is grass or earth. This is not unusual because the complexities of our culture have dulled the conscious sense of vision and people have become only unconsciously aware of their environment. The isolator, by separating small sections of grass or earth from the total environment, enables children to discover, analyze, and enjoy the wonders of the world through concentrated looking. Additional enhancement can be obtained by using a magnifying glass with the isolator, which is also shown in Figure 184.

The Simple Camera

Photographs made with a simple camera are another way of isolating unique texture, structures, and patterns from the environment so that they can be studied by children. Figure 185 shows an effective use of the camera to obtain photographic visuals for classrooms. The use of the camera constitutes another procedure for helping children bring their unconscious awareness into conscious awareness.

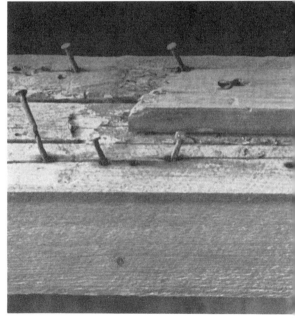

Figure 185

Educational Television and Video Tapes

While some school systems are just now experimenting with closed-circuit educational television, many schools have had such programs in operation for a number of years. Those art educators who have pioneered this area have had numerous obstacles to overcome, particularly since many children associate educational television with the entertainment television seen at home. Children tend, at first, to look upon it as another show, and carry over listening habits more appropriate for entertainment television. Other obstacles, such as programming, use of personnel, and timing, are being dealt with, but much remains to be done before educational television reaches its full potential.

As with all the media discussed here, television was never meant to replace the teacher, but is intended to supplement and enrich the curriculum offered by the teacher. Television teachers must therefore work closely with classroom teachers so that what is presented will fit in with the total curriculum and apply to what is being studied at the moment. Those who are knowledgeable in the field of educational television have, through their own experimentation, developed guides with teachers, and present programs which are informative and usable.

Figures 186, 187, and 188 show the potential for using television to enhance the visual perception of children. Children are exposed first to an object in nature, as shown in Figures 186 and 187. This is followed by exposure to an exemplar, as shown in Figure 188.

Television can be used as a tool for curriculum enrichment, and can become one of our most valuable tools in helping children enhance their visual perception: it is this medium, more than all the others, which can bring into the classroom those visuals, understandings, experiences, and exposures to exemplars which teachers do not have time or opportunity to prepare. Figure 189 shows this use. With the technical advances made recently in color television, it may be possible for an insightful television teacher to take literally thousands of children through an art gallery to see exhibits of works of art.

In contributing to the enhancement of visual perception, educational television programs should follow simple guidelines such as the following:

1 Use the basic structure for art in the elementary school.
2 Plan and execute television programs which implement this basic structure at the time it is needed.

Figure 186

Figure 187

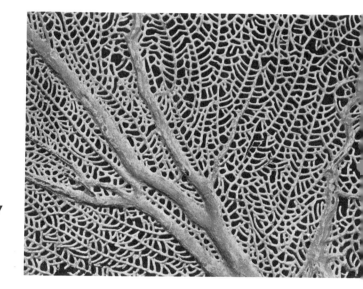

Figure 188

3   Develop with classroom teachers those instructional procedures which are to precede and follow the telecast.

4   Develop evaluative procedures to insure that the telecast is enriching the curriculum in ways that the classroom teacher cannot do.

At the present time, commercial film and publishing companies are very much concerned with providing educational television films for use in elementary school classrooms. While these will be most professional in nature, it is questionable whether they will fulfill the need for enhancing children's perception. To do so, commercial companies will need to have on their consultant staff art educators who are concerned with the basic structure for art, and who are knowledgeable about children at different age levels and their capabilities for discovering, learning, and understanding. The use of commercially prepared educational films for telecasting is no guarantee that children will acquire appreciative skills and become visually literate. However, with proper direction, such films may even surpass many of the closed-circuit television programs being used today. Commercial companies have an opportunity to do more at this moment to promote visual literacy than was thought possible even ten years ago.

PROGRAMMED INSTRUCTION

In recent years, many devices have been developed for encouraging independent study by children in school. Generally these are classified as programmed materials, and include textbooks and various kinds of teaching machines. Although programmed materials have been used mainly for reading, mathematics, science, and social studies, any discipline is adaptable in some form or other to programming. Visual media which can be used in programmed instruction for the body of knowledge of art will probably be developed in the near future. However, it must be developed out of experimentation and research, with the same careful exploratory procedure that has been used for the other disciplines. Programmed instruction should not be thought of as a way of replacing the teacher, but, rather, as another way of helping to cope with individual differences in classrooms.

SIMPLE SENSORY AIDS

Basic to instruction in many disciplines is the use of concrete sensory aids to assist children in the mastery of difficult concepts. Comenius was one of the first educators to recognize the value of real objects, or the visual representation of them, in helping children learn better. Other great names in the history of education also advocated the use of concrete materials, including Pestalozzi, Froebel, Seguin, and Montessori. Although the aids advocated and used by each were by no means identical, all were designed to help children manipulate and discover, increase their perceptions of the world, and facilitate their learning.

Today's classrooms, especially those for young children, contain an array of learning aids—concrete objects designed to help children learn better. Many of these would not seem at all strange to the early pioneers, since their aids have served as a basis from which present ones have been developed. Counting rods, counting frames, blocks, geometric insets, balls, cylinders, cones, and tactile materials are currently used aids developed from earlier models to serve today's children.

Many of these same aids, with or without modifications, can be used for learnings in art. Aids developed specifically for art education may also be useful for other disciplines. Those presented in this section have been found effective in helping young children develop frames of reference for exemplars and for symbol enrichment in creative activities.

Tactile Sensory Aids

Figure 190 shows simple tactile sensory aids. These are 4″ × 4″ squares which are covered with a variety of materials, including sandpaper, netting, and acrylic paint, to encompass varying degrees of roughness and smoothness. Each square has its match in texture, but all are the same color since different colors tend to detract from the concrete tactual experience. These squares are to be used to help children enrich their concepts of rough and smooth, and gradations of roughness and smoothness, so that their frames of reference for exemplars may be extended. Similar squares with different coverings may be used to enrich concepts of hard and soft.

Figure 190

Auditory Sensory Aids

Figure 191 shows simple auditory aids constructed from small containers which hold different ingredients (sand, pebbles, seeds) graduated from loud to soft. Each sound cylinder has a match, and in finding the matching pair, children enrich their concepts of loud and soft.

Figure 191

Olfactory Sensory Aids

The olfactory aids shown in Figure 192 consist of two vials, one containing oil of amber and the other oil of rose geranium. Oil of amber is a yellowish-to-brown translucent fossil resin which has a rather unpleasant odor. Oil of rose geranium is produced from the distillation of finely chopped leaves of geranium plants, and has a pleasant odor. The use of the olfactory sense is, in part, based on the culture or subculture in which one lives, and what is pleasant to one person may not be to another. However, the odors used for the olfactory sensory aids are usually found to be pleasant or unpleasant. These aids can contribute to the formation of art concepts.

Figure 192

Visual Sensory Aids for Size, Shape, Color, and Repeat Pattern

Figure 193 shows a series of shapes in primary colors derived from the circle, square, rectangle, and diamond. These are used to help children enrich concepts of size, shape, color, and pattern in logical sequence. Such aids are common to mathematics as well as to art, and teachers have used them to excellent advantage in helping children develop a frame of reference for numerous exemplars. These aids are

Figure 193

particularly useful, since they are closely related to that stage in children's symbol development when representations consist of geometric shapes.[1]

Visual Sensory Color Aids

The matched color sets, as shown in Figure 194, help children to become aware of color relationships and to distinguish between colors. These can be used in numerous ways in visual exercises to enhance the perception of colors, and to make judgments and discriminations about colors.

[1] Viktor Lowenfeld, *Creative and Mental Growth* (New York: The Macmillan Co., 1957), p. 111.

Figure 194

Other Sensory Aids

Many sensory aids available are not in permanent form. For example, lemon extract and sugar cubes can be used for the gustatory sense to enrich concepts of sweet and sour. Other sensory aids which may be used very effectively for visual abstractions of concrete experiences are objects which are already a part of the room: display units, cabinets, desks, windows. Such aids are constantly available to children and teachers.

DISCRETION IN THE DEVELOPMENT AND USE OF SENSORY AIDS

Any sensory aids which are developed for and used by children should be consistent with the development of children and basic learnings in art and other subjects. Manipulative devices designed solely for manipulation may be questioned. Any kind of aid, sensory or otherwise, needs to be tested in practical situations with enough follow-up to insure that perceptual learnings have taken place. Some materials suggested for use today seem to be no more than manipulative tools, with little relationship to basic art learnings. Examples are the numerous cube and jigsaw puzzles developed recently from exemplars. Children should not be given exemplars in free form or cube sections which have no relationship to the composition or structure of the original. Since each part does not constitute a meaningful whole, it is doubtful that the distortion of the exemplar enhances the children's sensitivity to it.

Puzzles can be excellent teaching devices when used in connection with the basic structure. For example, exemplars which can be cut or cubed so that each part constitutes a meaningful whole as far as visual art elements are concerned offer possibilities for useful teaching aids. This limits the number which can be used, but some works of art would certainly fall into this category. Care must be exercised in creating and using puzzles of exemplars since children should become capable of interacting with the aesthetic qualities of the whole composition and should become aware of the creative use of art elements in parts of the composition which achieve the aesthetic.

FURTHER READINGS

Dale, Edgar. *Audio-Visual Methods in Teaching*. Rev. ed. New York: Holt, Rinehart and Winston, Inc., 1954.
Audio-visual aids and their use.

Erickson, Charlton W. H. *Administering Audio-Visual Services*. New York: The Macmillan Co., 1959.
Illustrations showing proper storage of prints and reproductions (pp. 282–83). Chapter 10, on systematic evaluation, can be of help to teachers and audio-visual directors.

Freedman, Florence B., and Esther L. Berg. *Classroom Teacher's Guide to Audio-Visual Material*. Philadelphia: Chilton Co., 1961.
Chapter 5, ideas for use of audio-visual aids for art education and the other areas of the curriculum.

Fry, Edward B. *Teaching Machines and Programmed Instruction*. New York: McGraw-Hill Book Co., 1963.
Chapter 1, introduction to programmed instruction and its implications for the curriculum.

Schultz, Morton J. *The Teacher and Overhead Projector*. Englewood Cliffs, N. J.: Prentice-Hall, Inc., 1965.
Ideas, uses, and techniques concerning the projector.

Thomas, Murray, and Sherwin S. Swartout. *Integrated Teaching Materials*. Toronto: Longmans, Green and Co., Inc., 1960.
Chapters 7–11, 21. Helpful suggestions on the proper use of audio-visual materials in the classroom.

Wittich, Walter A., and Charles F. Schuller. *Audio-Visual Materials: Their Nature and Use*. 3d ed. New York: Harper & Row, 1962.
Chapters 2, 4, 6, 8, 12–14. Well illustrated for informative use of effective audio-visual materials.

14

Those Who Teach Art

INTRODUCTION

The teaching of art in nursery and elementary schools requires the same background necessary for teaching any subject: knowledge of the content and an understanding of children and the ways they learn. In addition, those who teach art should have a background of general education so that they can understand what is being done in other areas and see relationships between art and these subjects. To develop art education programs which meet the objectives described in Chapter 1, competency in each of the above categories should be a requirement for classroom teachers, special art teachers, and art supervisors. There are, however, differences in the kinds of competencies which may be required for each of the groups and, therefore, in the type of professional preparation needed by each group.

PROFESSIONAL PREPARATION

Elementary Classroom Teachers

Although it would be ideal if art were taught by special teachers, particularly in the intermediate grades, at the present time art education is largely in the hands of the classroom teacher. Certainly the classroom teacher is capable of teaching art, but she does not as a rule have a background in art comparable to the background she has in other areas, or to that of the special teacher. This background can be developed if the classroom teacher takes course work in art and art education at the undergraduate level. Specifically, art requirements should include:

1 History of art: A course or courses dealing with the historical development and contemporary movements in painting, sculpture, architecture, ceramics, silver, industrial design, landscape design, and urban planning.
2 Fine arts: A course or courses designed to assist prospective teachers in developing adequate performance with the visual elements in the media processes.
3 Art education: A course or courses which encompass a study of literature in the field, the art media process for children, motivational procedures, a study of individual differences, the creative development of children, curriculum organization, and procedures for implementing the basic structure for the enhancement of visual perception.

In addition to these suggested requirements, prospective teachers should have courses which are already a part of most teacher education programs, especially ones in child psychology and the psychology of learning. With this kind of preparation, teachers should be able to carry out a prescribed program developed by the art supervisor or coordinator. A more extensive preparation in art should also contribute to an enriched background for the social studies, language arts, and other content in the curriculum, and should provide a better understanding of the cultural contributions of art and their relationship to man's past, present, and future. Course work does not insure successful teaching, but it does provide an important prerequisite for successful teaching—a knowledge of the subject being taught and an understanding of those to whom it is taught.

Special Art Teachers

The fact that increasing numbers of school districts are employing special art teachers indicates that there is a demand for specialists who have had a major concentration in art. In some respects the professional preparation of the special art teacher should be no different from that for the classroom teacher; both need to understand children and be familiar with the content of art and with procedures to be used for presenting it to children. Since the art teacher has different kinds of responsibilities from those of the classroom teachers, especially in planning art programs and serving as a consultant to other teachers, there should be some differences in professional preparation.

The undergraduate program for the special art teacher should include course work in the same three areas described for the classroom teacher. In every category, however, the specialist should have more courses and should have the opportunity to become competent in art history and fine arts studio. In art education, the student should have courses which will prepare her for working with teachers and children. The student-teaching experience, which is also a part of art education, should include teaching on every level (kindergarten through sixth) of the elementary school, and should last for a minimum of eight weeks.

Art Supervisors

Art supervisors should have preparation beyond that required for the special art teacher. Because art supervisors are responsible for developing art programs in the entire school district and for coordinating personnel, as well as for working directly with children, they need a more extensive and intensive background. Since it is almost impossible for all the professional preparation for the art supervisor to be obtained on the undergraduate level, a master's degree should be required. The program for this degree should include work in the fine arts and art education. Advanced work in art education should include a study of the administration of art education programs and the supervision of personnel, both specialists and classroom teachers. Art supervisors should also have graduate level courses in child psychology and the psychology of learning.

WHAT IS EXPECTED OF THOSE WHO TEACH ART

Scholarship, philosophy, and theory are extremely important in art education, just as they are in any area of the curriculum. These mean little, however, if the teacher cannot implement what she has learned in the classroom, for it is through the implementation of what has been learned in course work and through experience that effective teaching is demonstrated. The implementation of theory into practice is the basis for evaluating those who teach art.

Art directors and supervisors seem to have developed their own criteria for evaluating the effectiveness of both elementary classroom teachers and art teachers. In some school systems, this evaluation consists of a formalized checklist by which every teacher is evaluated, while in other systems it is even more subjective, with each evaluator using his own rating scale. Evaluational procedures differ and are highly individualized, but all are attempts to determine whether or not teachers, through knowledge, initiative, sensitivity, and ingenuity, meet a standard of excellence.

In spite of the differences which may be found on rating scales used by administrators, there seems to be agreement on many of the skills, competencies, and attributes that characterize effective teaching. As the art administrator or supervisor evaluates and rates, he attempts to find answers to questions which include such characteristics. In general, these questions may be grouped into four categories, which cover the full range of teaching ability: (1) preparation and planning, (2) management of the art activity, (3) classroom control, and (4) interaction with children. Much of what is expected of those who teach art is included in the questions presented below.

Preparation and Planning

1 Has a meaningful objective been developed for the art episode and is this understood by the children?
2 Have all necessary materials been assembled before introducing the art activity?
3 Has consideration been given to all children in the room and have individual differences been attended to?
4 Have provisions been made for evaluation during and after the episode?

Management of the Art Activity

1 Have children learned to take care of their art materials?
2 Have children participated in developing a routine for passing out materials for different kinds of activities?
3 Have desks or tables been arranged suitably for the activity?
4 Has consideration been given to individual and group needs for materials?
5 Have children learned to take turns in passing out materials and cleaning up?

6　Have precautions been taken to insure an easy clean-up, i.e., the use of newspapers for painting and clay work?

7　Have materials been stored so that they are easily accessible to children?

8　Have materials—scissors, brushes, crayons, etc.—been stored so that they can be visually inventoried?

9　Have all the necessary materials been prepared for the episodes?

10　Have children learned to evaluate routine procedures, such as passing out paper?

11　Have children been provided with smocks or old shirts when these are needed?

12　Have children learned efficient clean-up procedures?

13　Have children learned respect for the classroom and the school building?

Classroom Control

1　Do children know what is expected of them?

2　Have routine procedures been established for and by children on the first day of school?

3　Do children understand the routine procedures?

4　Have children been involved in setting up standards for conduct?

5　Has information about each child (home background, interests, level of aesthetic development, etc.) been obtained and studied?

6　Is the art episode appropriate for the children?

7　Have the best media and/or materials been selected for the episode?

8　Have children been included in planning the episode, whenever possible?

9　Is the work interesting and challenging?

10　Have procedures been re-evaluated as needed?

11　Has motivation reached each child?

12　Have activities been planned for those who finish ahead of others?

Interaction with Children

1　Has the motivation reached all children?

2　Have individual differences been considered?

3　Have the motivational procedures been successful?

4　Have children responded well to the teacher and to the activity?

5　Have the needs of children been met?

6　Have children been enthusiastic about the art activity?

The answers to these questions can be used to determine whether or not the teacher has reached the standard of excellence expected of all teachers. It is not enough, however, for the prospective or beginning teacher to know those areas which art supervisors are evaluating; she must know how to prepare herself so that she can make the transition from theory to practice in the classroom and achieve a high rating.

PERFORMANCE IN THE CLASSROOM

In developing skills for implementing theory in the classroom, the teacher can use procedures which help facilitate the transition from theory to practice. Unfortunately, these procedures are frequently overlooked because it is believed that a good teacher can learn to teach without being subjected to the details of planning and managing a room, and that these practical aspects of teaching are unrelated to the creative aspects. It is true that many good teachers learn to teach without having instruction in the routine aspects of teaching; it is also true that management may be less rewarding to a teacher than the creative elements of teaching. However, to overlook routine procedures in planning is to invite poor instruction by causing or encouraging classroom environments of confusion and disorder where order could have prevailed, and to cause a potentially good teacher to be unsuccessful. Sensitivity to these procedures and an understanding of ways to utilize them in the classroom can help create optimum teaching and learning situations, and, hopefully, can help the teacher attain a standard of excellence in both.

Prospective and experienced teachers may find that the criteria used to evaluate their performance as teachers can more nearly be met by a mastery and understanding of the following areas.

Knowledge of What Is Being Taught and the Ability to Teach It

Art administrative personnel have a right to expect beginning elementary classroom teachers and art teachers to be knowledgeable in the field of art education. Basically, this knowledge consists of an understanding of the basic structure for art, but teachers should also understand the relationship which exists between art and the other disciplines—the nucleus of commonalities. Teachers who understand these relationships are better able to help children discover them and enrich their concepts. Of the two groups of teachers—classroom teachers and art teachers—classroom teachers are often more capable of seeing these relationships, but all should be able to do this. Being a specialist in an area does not exempt one from giving some attention to other content areas. Children need direction toward the discovery of relationships, and the teacher should have the knowledge to provide this direction.

A knowledge of the content is useless if teachers do not also have an understanding of children. Teachers need to be aware of the levels or stages of development of children, and the sequence or pattern of growth and development. Teachers also need to understand each individual in the classroom, since all children do not pass through each stage in exactly the same way and no one child is always at the same stage of development physically, socially, emotionally, intellectually, and aesthetically. Teachers need to be sensitively aware of each child and his development so that they may effectively help the child to learn and use the knowledge in the art curriculum.

It is possible for a person to have a knowledge of content and an understanding of children and still not be able to teach well; the ability to perform well seems to be dependent upon many indefinable qualities. These are enhanced through education and experience, particularly when directed toward improving techniques for more effective teaching.

Preparation and Planning

Basic to effective teaching is the preparation necessary for any lesson presented to children. Procedures for planning art learning experiences have been presented elsewhere in this book. Suffice it to say here that planning is essential so that consideration can be given to every aspect of the experiences: children, objectives, materials, procedures, and evaluation. This is a time-consuming procedure, especially since some preparation (such as ordering films) must be done days in advance, but it is warranted because of its effectiveness in achieving the goals of art education.

The real test of the ability to teach is the way plans and preparations are used with children, i.e., the teaching procedures used to implement the plans. Naturally this is the hardest part of all. Effective procedures for art are not those which can be labeled "cookbook" approaches, in which there is little more than a mixture of children and media. Instead, effective procedures are the special ways to teach art which can be learned in art education classes and discovered through working with children. Many experienced teachers, through their own daily research in the classroom, have found ways of teaching that help children learn more easily and more effectively. This kind of research or experimentation requires initiative, but it is an initiative which administrators expect.

Making Maximum Use of School Time

An insightful teacher knows that some of her best teaching is done at unusual times and places. For example, a good teacher may use that interlude just before the bell rings to enrich concepts. While children are waiting, the teacher may ask them to determine how many are wearing red, blue, or green. From this simple experience children can find out and learn about different kinds of red, blue, or green. Concepts of line, size, shape, texture, and form can be enriched through similar procedures. An insightful teacher rarely misses an opportunity to add to her children's experiences and understandings, and is particularly sensitive to incidental opportunities in which this may be done.

Classroom Management

Classroom management does not just happen; it is developed through thoughtful critical planning by the teacher and the children. The value of good management can be learned through trial and error, but often both children and teachers suffer, and effective learning may be handicapped. A better approach is to provide the prospective teacher with guidance and direction in the ways of good classroom management while she is still in college, as well as during the beginning teaching period.

Teachers should not be expected to teach alike or to manage their classroom in the same way. Each classroom requires a planned procedure of management which is unique to that classroom. There are, however, some ideas which may be of help to all teachers in all classrooms, and which are recommended for teachers to try. Effective classroom management may be more easily achieved if consideration is given to routine procedures for the art activity itself.

During the art activity, teachers must consider children, materials, and the activity. These three components can be harmonious or chaotic; the difference lies in the ability of the teacher to manage all three. Classrooms and children differ, and what will work with one class will not necessarily work with another. Experience should help the teacher learn when to vary procedures so that teaching truly becomes an art. Since specific recommendations will not apply to all situations and to all teachers, it would be futile to make long lists of do's and don'ts. Instead, teachers can learn to manage and can evaluate their own managerial procedures by answering the questions given earlier.

Many of these questions are centered on things that children have learned to do in the art activity. There is much that children can learn in just such routine procedures, and they should always be involved. Children need to feel that the room is truly theirs and that they have certain responsibilities for maintaining order within the room. They derive a sense of pride and accomplishment, as well as a measure of self-discipline, from participating in these activities. Teachers should not do work that children can do and can learn from doing.

Classroom Control

The answers to the questions presented earlier, including those under "Managing the Art Activity," can assist in achieving good classroom control. All these questions should be answered during each activity because classroom control must be constantly evaluated so that variations may be made as needed. Close attention should be paid to the influence of the teacher's concept of control or discipline on the children's respect for laws, rules, and regulations. Children need not grow up with an unhealthy attitude toward rules and regulations. Modern society depends on such regulation, and since the school is responsible for contributing to the good of the whole of society, there should be a carryover from the procedures established in the classroom to the larger society. Not only the larger society but the individual himself should feel some benefit from ordered freedom. Good mental health requires that children develop respect for law and order early in life. Man constantly tries to order his environment, and to do so effectively he must depend upon established values developed by all social agencies. Control in the classroom can be conducive to helping the child become a disciplined adult who can contribute to society.

The ability to effect good classroom control often makes the difference between success and failure for a beginning teacher. Classroom control should not be confused with the rigid routine and silence considered desirable in earlier years, nor should it be considered as something attainable only through rules and regulations laid down by the teacher. Classroom control is achieved through the use of effective teaching procedures which reach all the children, and through the establishment of standards of conduct by the children and the teacher. Developing effective teaching procedures for art is no more difficult than it is for other subjects, but because of the nature of art activities, and the emphasis placed on creativity and discovery, it may be more difficult to establish standards for conduct.

As with other items mentioned in this chapter, it is not possible to lay down specific procedures to be followed by teachers in developing and maintaining classroom control. Each teacher must develop those procedures which are most effective for her. Answering the questions listed in this chapter may assist the teacher in effecting and maintaining good classroom control.

The Ability to Interact with Children

It is difficult to define specifically what is meant by "the ability to interact with children." This is a quality readily discernible to those who observe and/or evaluate teachers, but it is not as easily described in terms of specific attributes. It would seem safe to say, however, that basic to any attribute is the teacher's self-concept. Teachers who are able to interact well with children are usually those who have achieved self-confidence and self-realization in the classroom. These qualities, in turn, lead to the development of a teaching personality which enables one to interact with others and to adjust successfully to new situations. Interactions include not only those with children in the classroom, but those with parents, administrators, supervisors, and other colleagues. The test of one's ability to interact is, therefore, not confined to classroom teaching situations, both routine and unusual. It also includes routine and unusual situations outside the classroom, such as parent conferences and meetings.

There is no agreement on what a teaching personality is, so there is ample room for deviations. If there were not, the spontaneity, creativity, and ability that are unique in a teacher would be lost. Yet, each teacher should be aware of her own personal attributes—her strengths and weaknesses—and should constantly attempt to improve and strengthen herself toward the end result of an effective teaching personality.

Care and Use of Art Materials

Ideally, every elementary school should have a room designed as an art education center to which children could be taken for aesthetic education. Such a room could include permanent equipment, such as audio-visual installations, specially designed furniture, kilns, sinks, display areas, and adequate storage space. Centers of this kind are being built, but at the present time most art classes are held in regular classrooms, and much of the equipment mentioned above must be brought in for classes.

Regardless of the type of room used, certain materials must be a part of the program and must be taken care of. Teachers are expected to take proper care of art materials and to teach this to children. For the art program suggested in this book, the materials for which teachers and children are responsible would include, in addition to the equipment given above:

1 Paints—tempera, watercolor, fingerpaints, acrylics.
2 Brushes for different painting techniques.
3 Paper—different sizes, surfaces, weights, colors.
4 Adhesives and solvents.
5 Yarns, fabrics, fibers.
6 Clay, linoleum, metal, wire, cardboard, woods.
7 Brayers, hammers, vises, saws, nails.
8 Materials for matting, mounting, and framing children's work, reproductions, and prints.

Teaching aids should include:

1 Sensory aids for the enhancement of the auditory, gustatory, olfactory, tactile, and visual senses.
2 Teaching portfolios for line, color, texture, size, shape, and form.
3 Teaching portfolios of halftones which encompass historical developments and contemporary movements in architecture, industrial design, ceramics, sculpture, textiles, silver, urban and city planning.
4 250 reproductions (color and halftones) which encompass historical developments and contemporary movements in drawing, painting, and print making.

5 Reference books:
   a Source books on media processes.
   b Source books on drawing, painting, architecture, sculpture, industrial design, ceramics, textiles, print making, silver, urban and city planning.
   c Dictionary of art vocabulary.
   d Biographical sketches of artists and artisans.
6 Periodicals.
7 Films and filmstrips dealing with art media processes, biographical sketches of artists, drawing, painting, architecture, industrial design, ceramics, textiles, print making, silver, urban and city planning, line, color, texture, size, shape, form, design, composition, nature, children's art.

Procedures for caring for art materials and equipment may be developed by using the following suggestions.

Storage of art materials and visuals. Most contemporary elementary schools are equipped with adequate storage space, provided this space is used properly. In schools where little or no storage space is available, teachers will have to become innovators and create space from boxes and crates. In some schools there will be a central storeroom or special artroom, and it is usually the responsibility of the elementary art consultant or art teacher to plan storage of art materials in this area.

Regardless of where the storage space is, in the classroom, the special artroom, or a central storage center, orderly storage procedures should be used. Figure 195 shows one orderly arrangement which makes the materials readily accessible and easily inventoried. Notice that tempera paints are stored according to colors, a system which makes them easily obtainable, even by a child. Paper in stored in a similar orderly arrangement by size, kind, and color. Such an arrangement saves time and effort with materials, thus making more time available for teaching.

Figure 195 includes only those materials considered expendable, but storage provisions must also be made for non-expendable items: brushes, rulers, scissors, etc. Proper storage facilities should be arranged for non-expendable items so that teachers can tell at a glance whether or not all the materials are accounted for and in good condition. The facilities shown in Figure 196 allow for easy accessibility and inventory. Again, the figure merely shows one possibility for storage. Different systems can be devised to make the most of available space. Well-planned storage, whatever system is used, should

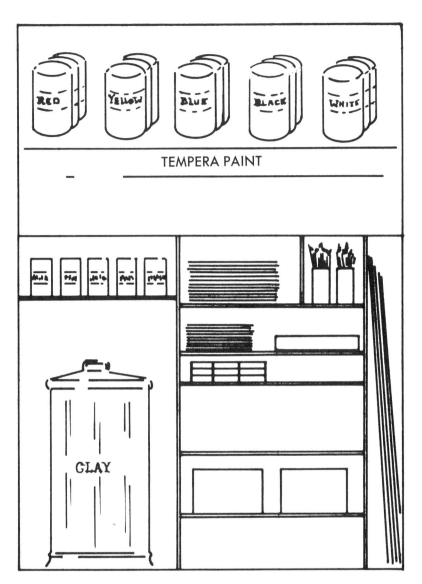

Figure 195
Storage of Art Materials

Figure 196
Storage of Non-expendable Materials

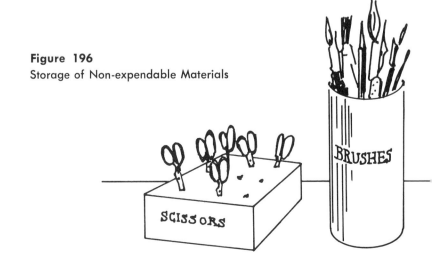

facilitate good teaching, but concern for this should not supersede instruction itself. Management of this kind is one developed efficiency for making teaching easier.

Care of other materials. Storage of materials is just one aspect of the care and use of materials. Some pieces of equipment, such as the kiln, are expensive and less easily cared for. However, instructions and directions for loading and firing are included with such equipment. Less expensive materials should also have proper care and attention. Among the more common ones used in art programs are brushes and paints. Although brushes are considered expendable, they will last quite some time if proper care is given to them. To insure their durability, they should be rinsed after every use. Teachers have found that as many as ten or twenty can be rinsed at the same time under a faucet with good water pressure. After rinsing, each brush should be shaped by hand so that the original contour can be retained.

Liquid tempera paints must be tightly sealed or they will dry out very quickly. All paint jars and containers must be kept clean. Before a jar is closed, excess paint should be removed from both the lid and container to prevent the paint from caking and to save time at the next lesson.

Good managerial procedures also include routines for quick inventory. The teacher should learn to exercise a "counting measure" for non-expendable materials: scissors, brushes, rulers, hammers, and modeling tools. Such an inventory is easily made if the suggested procedures for storage are followed. Careful inventory of all materials will help both the children and the teacher become more aware of the proper use of materials and the need to conserve them whenever possible. Children need a variety of materials to create, but a waste of materials is inexcusable even in our affluent society. Regard for and care of materials cannot be taught directly, but they can be developed in children if they are presented as an inherent part of the instructional and managerial procedures.

WHAT TEACHERS SHOULD EXPECT FROM ART SUPERVISORS

Art administrative and supervisory personnel have a right to expect beginning and experienced teachers to meet the standard of excellence in performance. Similarly, teachers have a right to expect a certain performance from those who supervise them. Such expectations may be summarized in the following points.

Art supervisors should have:

1 Insight, understanding, and a conscious awareness of the elementary classroom teacher's situation.

2 Specific guidelines regarding expectations of the elementary teacher.

3 A contemporary and sound elementary school art curriculum which encompasses recent developments and objectives.

4 The ability to give guidance in implementing the art curriculum.

5 The ability to give help when it is needed in meetings, workshops, etc. Particular attention should be given to keeping teachers up to date.

6 Adequate art materials and equipment.

7 An adequate number of exemplars.

8 The ability to give constructive criticism aimed toward teacher improvement and improved teaching procedures.

9 The ability to give the teacher reasons for approval or disapproval.

10 A sense of humor, dignity, and a respect for the teacher.

Such expectations imply that supervisors, as well as teachers, must constantly evaluate themselves and their programs. Only through evaluation by all who have contact with children can schools achieve their potential in the educational process.

FURTHER READINGS

National Art Education Association. *Planning Facilities for Art Instruction.* Washington, D. C.: The Association, 1961.

15

Creating
a Room Environment
for Art Education

INTRODUCTION

Every child has a right to be educated in a room which is visually stimulating and conducive to learning. Creating such an environment is, perhaps, easier to do in contemporary schools—which have been designed for today's educational programs—than it is in older buildings. A stimulating environment can be achieved in any classroom, however, if the teacher is attentive to features in the room which can be used to facilitate learning, particularly those which can be organized for visual interpretation. Certain features of the classroom can be used by a creative teacher to enhance learning and to make teaching procedures more effective. Because this should be a creative activity for the teacher, no formulas can be given, but there are some suggestions which may help to spark teacher creativity.

ACCEPTING CLASSROOM LIMITATIONS

A positive attitude toward the limitations of the classroom, though difficult to develop, is necessary for creating a learning environment for art education. Some classrooms will not have sufficient storage or exhibit space, but it is often possible to improvise for these in ways that can enhance the environment. Storage procedures have been presented in the preceding chapter; modifications of the suggestions can be made to fit many classrooms.

When there is not enough exhibit space, more can be provided by using wallboard, beaver board, free-standing easels, or portable folding screens. These can be covered with burlap or other materials of neutral color, thus creating a background for displays that may be even more pleasing than bulletin boards. Also, these can be moved to different places in the room as needs arise.

Classroom furniture can usually be rearranged in many different ways. The checklist given in the preceding chapter provides some hints on the importance of different arrangements, both for effective learning and for a pleasing atmosphere.

Perhaps one of the most difficult limitations for the teacher to accept is the color of the room. The color may not be one that the teacher prefers or even likes, but the creative teacher can devise ways of making the most of this. She can, for example, use color relationships on bulletin boards which complement the color of the room, or she can overcome a drab room by using color on bulletin boards and other display areas.

CHANGING THE ROOM ENVIRONMENT

The first visual impact which a room has on anyone who enters it is one of conscious awareness—awareness of the visual qualities of the room. When a teacher moves into a classroom, she is consciously aware of every object in it and creates an environment because of this awareness. However, after having been in the classroom for a time, she can become less aware of it—items and objects become commonplace and she is not actively conscious of them. A change in the room environment can cause her to become alert again, allowing the completion of the cycle from unconscious awareness to renewed conscious awareness.

In many classrooms, conscious awareness is seldom restored. The learning environment is allowed to remain unchanged, and children and teachers are deprived of a chance to enhance visual perception through the classroom environment. There are several ways to create changes in the room environment so that awareness can be renewed. These include: (1) applying the principle of balance, (2) displaying visuals, (3) creating bulletin boards, and (4) creating displays for all subjects.

Applying the Principle of Balance

Two types of balance may be used in classrooms: formal and informal. The principle of formal balance and the practical application of the principle are shown in Figure 197. Formal balance is frequently used and certainly has a place in the classroom, but overuse of it may cause the room to become dull, uninteresting, and uninviting. Hence, the rate at which both the teacher and the children become unconsciously aware of the room may be increased.

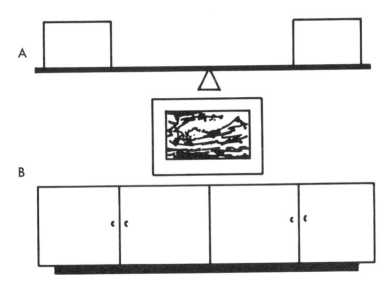

Figure 197
Formal Balance

Quite often informal balance is more interesting and will hold children's interest longer. Informal balance is based on the principle of the offset fulcrum for distributions of different weights. The principle of informal balance and its practical application, shown in Figure 198, can be applied to each component of the classroom so that furniture

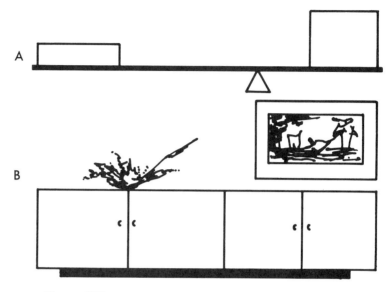

Figure 198
Informal Balance

arrangement, bulletin boards, and the use of color on bulletin boards and in visuals can become a part of a totally balanced classroom.

Applying the principles of balance is just one way for the creative teacher to help the children become consciously aware of their environment. In this respect, the teacher becomes a designer who works not on paper but with objects in the room. As she designs, she becomes an innovator who creates a learning environment which can contribute to the enhancement of visual perception; she helps children apply art learnings to the room itself.

Displaying Visuals

Visuals encompass all materials that can be seen and that enhance the subject with which they are used, i.e., exemplars, photographs, pictures from magazines, children's artwork. Creative teachers will find many different kinds of visuals to use for different subjects and will find several ways of displaying them. Some visuals will be used only temporarily while others will become a part of permanent collections, but all visuals need to be displayed by mounting or matting so that they are isolated from their environment and can be easily seen by the viewer.

Procedures for mounting. For visuals that are to be kept, the following mounting procedures have been found to be expedient and useful:

1 Select a sturdy mounting material such as heavy construction paper, poster board, or medium-weight mat board.

2 Exercise judgment in selecting the color for the mounting. White always enhances any visual, but sometimes color is desired. If color is to be used, select one which appears in the visual so that it will be picked up and enhanced.

3 Allow enough area around the visual to isolate it sufficiently from the environment. It is usually desirable to allow at least a 2-inch area around the visual.

4 Allow a greater area at the bottom of the visual than on the other three sides.

5 Use a good adhesive to mount the visual. Liquid plastic-based adhesives which dry clear seem to be best suited to this purpose. Along with this, a clear acetate can be used to cover and protect the visual.

Figure 199 shows exemplars which have been mounted for display use with children in classrooms.

Figure 199

A

B

BACK

Figure 200
Matting Procedures

Procedures for matting. Permanent matting is usually done in the office of the art administrator. Not all visuals need to be permanently mounted or matted. Every child, however, needs to see his creative art product in an attractive mat at one time or another, and teachers will find that other visuals are enhanced by a mat. Series of precut mats have been found to be useful for the temporary display of visuals. The most common sizes are those which take 9 × 12″, 12 × 18″, 18 × 24″, and 24 × 36″ visuals, and of these the 12 × 18″ and 18 × 24″ are used most often. A quick way of using these precut mats is:

1 Select medium-weight mat boards and prepare a series of mats for the sizes given above.
2 Select mat boards that are white or neutral tones.
3 Leave 3 inches on the three sides and 4 inches on the bottom.
4 For a mat to be used with a 12 × 18″ visual, the visual frame should be cut 11 × 17″. This allows one inch for tentative pinning or matting.
5 Visuals can be pinned to the bulletin board and the mats hung over the top pins (Figure 200A). Or, if desired, masking tape can be used to fasten the corners of the visual to the mat on the back side (Figure 200B).

Precut mats facilitate the arrangement of displays and can be used for a number of years. The constant use of mats requires that they be cleaned occasionally with a kneaded eraser. Aesthetic qualities and standards are impossible to achieve in displaying visuals unless mats that truly enhance them are used.

In their efforts to innovate and be creative, teachers sometimes go too far in mounting and matting visuals. Too much innovation has led teachers to use frames of curled paper, shadow construction paper, or rolled paper for two-dimensional visuals, and even to display two-dimensional visuals as three-dimensional. Although innovative, such framing practices do not always enhance the visual, and, in some cases, the frame actually becomes more important than the visual. The viewer's perception of the visual can be distorted, and its importance can be reduced. Two-dimensional visuals should always be displayed as such in simple mountings.

Creating Bulletin Boards

Every teacher is expected to create arrangements of attractive displays in rooms and hallways, and to assist children in creating them. Since both space and time in schools are limited, care should be given to the construction and use of bulletin boards, and only those which really contribute to the children's education should be used.

Bulletin board displays are basically a form of visual instruction and should be informative in content; they should convey an idea from one of the subject areas: science, social studies, language arts, mathematics, music, creative movement, or art. The idea should be presented in a way that is stimulating and exciting to children—adult concepts should not be the subject matter for displays. Anything used in displays should not only contribute to the intellectual development of children, but should add to aesthetic learnings and sensitivities. To accomplish this dual purpose both teachers and children need to develop pleasing arrangements which will enhance the content displayed. The following guidelines will help in this.

Selecting a topic or theme for the information to be presented and composing a heading or caption. An economy of words should be employed in the caption; it should be just long enough to convey the message of the display. Captions are an introduction to the theme and the informational material which follows explains it.

Teachers often spend hours in cutting letters for captions when commercially prepared letters of cardboard or plastic could be used. These come in a variety of sizes and colors that are eyecatching, legible, and aesthetically pleasing. In fastening the letters (or any other material) to the board, it is better to use pins or staples, since these are less obtrusive and tend not to detract from the whole effect.

Quite often illustrative material requires written explanation. This can be done in an aesthetically pleasing way by using a primary typewriter or manuscript writing. Too often the use of manuscript writing is discarded after children have made the transition to cursive, but it should be retained for use with display materials. Explanatory information can also be obtained from periodicals or duplicated from books and other sources.

Using judgment and discrimination in selecting visuals. Visuals have long been used for instructional purposes when communication is impossible because of language and cultural barriers. The visuals used in classrooms should also be selected because they can communicate a specific topic or theme, particularly since visuals often carry greater powers of communication than the printed word. There are so many

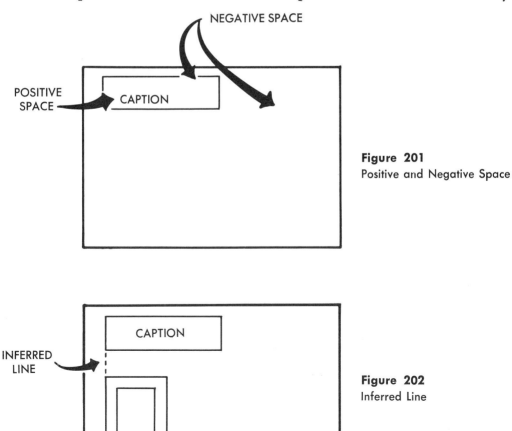

Figure 201
Positive and Negative Space

Figure 202
Inferred Line

visuals available today that it is especially important to select them carefully, not only for their informational value but also for their aesthetic qualities. The most attractive bulletin boards are those with visuals selected and grouped according to related colors, differences in size, and principles of good composition.

Arranging visuals into an aesthetic unit. A unified unit, such as an aesthetically pleasing bulletin board, is sometimes difficult to achieve. It can be done, however, if teachers keep in mind that any effective display involves the use of the visual art elements of color, line, size, texture, and shape in the categories of grouping, inferred line, and space.

In addition to the selection of the visual and illustrative materials and captions, the teacher needs to select a dominant color and to plan a group of visuals with regard to color and balance of positive and negative space. With the grouping or groupings in mind, the actual composition can be started. Since bulletin boards are usually perceived from left to right, they are best composed in this manner. A teacher can become adept at arranging displays if she learns to design while she works; it is not necessary to make preliminary sketches. Working sketches are time-consuming and often have little relationship to size as it is realized on the board. Designing while working makes it possible to create, to become visually astute, and to eliminate the necessity for making accurate measurements—measurements which may later prove visually misleading. Figures 201, 202, 203, and 204 illustrate the working procedures involved in such designing. By utilizing grouping, inferred line, and space, an aesthetic unit can be created.

Figure 203
Inferred Line and Space

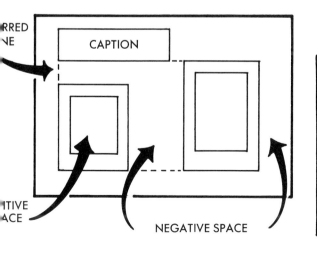

Figure 204
Aesthetic Unit

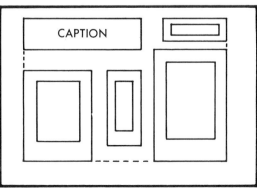

Although many bulletin boards are created by the teacher for a specific learning purpose, children should also have opportunities to develop displays. At the intermediate levels, particularly, there are countless times when children should be involved in the planning and execution of bulletin boards. Participation of this kind provides children with another chance to use judgments and discriminations in the selection of visuals and in the organization of visual art elements into aesthetically pleasing arrangements. They are also given the chance to acquire and use the knowledge which comes from the basic structure and to apply this with reference to inferred line, dominance, balance, and positive and negative space.

Creating Displays for All Subjects

Within any classroom there are items which do not change except in their arrangement: furniture, storage space and units, equipment, and the general architectural structure of the room. There are, however, features which should be changed and changed often if visual perception is to be enhanced. These include the displays presented earlier in this chapter and learning aids related to art and to other content areas.

Living things—plants, animals, and fish—should be a part of every classroom. These become features of the total environment, but can also be isolated for closer study. Exhibits arranged for other subjects may also contribute to art education. For example, the study of natural science can make many contributions to art. Displays of rocks, seashells, coral, woods, and fur can help children learn about texture as they explore and manipulate objects. Although such materials are available in kit form, there is no reason why a teacher cannot assemble them herself.

In each classroom there should also be a display or displays of enlarged and unusual photographs of texture, line, pattern, values, and colors which are created by nature. Excellent photographs are available from industries, conservation societies, and periodicals. The teacher may also be able to provide these from her own collection of photographs.

In all classrooms children should have opportunities to manipulate objects, to see enlarged sections of objects in two-dimensional displays, and to see a fine arts exemplar in which the artist has used the same elements. Figure 205 shows how experiences with texture in an incidental but somewhat teacher-directed way can provide a good fol-

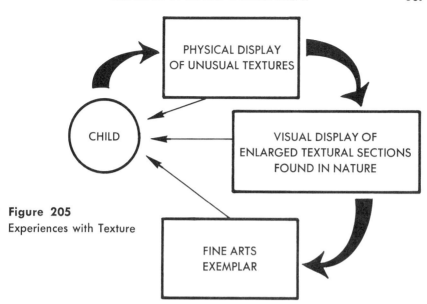

Figure 205
Experiences with Texture

low-up for preceding episodes. Each child is given the opportunity to see relationships independently, to abstract these into the visual, and to contribute to the enhancement of the visual.

Children need opportunities to continue learning on their own, and such learning reinforces directed learning. Exhibits and displays should, of course, be limited in scope so that children are not bombarded with too many stimuli. It is better to change exhibits often and to exhibit less, since too many items confuse children and restrict rather than expand opportunities for enhanced visual perception.

FURTHER READINGS

Burgert, Robert H., and Elinor Meadows. *Eye-appealing Bulletin Board Ideas.* Dansville, N. Y.: F. A. Owen Publishing Co., 1960.

Weseloh, Anne Douglas. *E Z Bulletin Boards.* San Francisco: Fearon Publishers.

16

Process and Scope
of Art

INTRODUCTION

The basis for the art education program presented in this book has considered children, art, and art experiences together in the belief that these three must be combined if an aesthetically pleasing world for tomorrow is to be achieved. The theoretical foundations and their implementation have brought these components together in such a way that an understanding of art, and hence the enhancement of visual perception in children, should be the end result.

CHILDREN AND THE PROCESS

Art education offers unique possibilities for children to learn and to express their learnings and feelings. Although it is not the only part of the curriculum which contributes to children's understandings or to the enhancement of their creativity, it is one which presents children with the same problems that confront the adult artist and designer-craftsman and which calls upon children to solve their problems using the same content and techniques as the adult. In other words, in art children use the visual art elements to express their understandings, reactions, and emotions. This, of course, does not mean that the work of children can be equated with that of adults; but the problems and the problem-solving procedures are comparable. Art offers even more than this to children; it offers or should offer them the chance (1) to understand the works of artists and designer-craftsmen and how they have contributed to and enhanced the environment in ways that cannot be equated with any other area, and (2) to be aware of possible contributions which they themselves make through their own artwork and/or through understanding what others have done.

Since it is not likely that many of the children who have art education in elementary school will go on to become artists and designer-craftsmen, it would seem that considerable attention should be given to helping them understand the world of art—the problems that artists have solved and will solve in the future. These include problems not only in visual art elements, but in such areas as sociology, political science, and economics; for as the population increases and as technological changes increase in scope and speed, the art problems of the future will be centered more and more around persons who are capable of responding aesthetically to proposed changes. It is not enough for more buildings to be constructed; those that are built should be truly worthy of the natural foundation on which they are imposed and should add to the lives of those who use them or are exposed to them.

Perhaps the crux of the program presented here is that the children who are in our schools today will be the adults of tomorrow—an obvious statement but one which is frequently overlooked in education. And, although the full extent of the influence of educational programs has not been measured, it can be assumed that what is presented to children in school and what is learned by them will to a large degree determine what that future world will be.

Inherent in the program suggested in the preceding chapters is the involvement of children in the creative or expressive aspects of art. Creative art activities also have the potential to contribute to the world of tomorrow. Not only do these offer children many outlets for expression and personal satisfaction in non-verbal ways, but they can also contribute to children's growth and development, intellectually and aesthetically, as well as creatively. Children's art expression coupled with problem-solving activities can make the unique contributions of art education far-reaching.

For the expressive and learning aspects of the process of art to become realities in classroom situations, recognition must be given to the individuality of each child, both in his expressive intent and in his ability to comprehend and internalize the understandings or learnings to be acquired about and through art. The art expression and learning potential of children, and the ways these are interrelated and interwoven, should be a concern of everyone who works with children in art education. Children and the process are inextricably linked. Guidance in the process can help them learn to see and comprehend the world of art—its past, present, and future—and its relationship to the total environment.

THE SCOPE OF ART

The scope of art education has often been vaguely and loosely defined, or defined in various ways. In this book the scope has been based on the existing knowledge in the arts and has been expressed in terms of the art concepts which exist within that knowledge and which can be presented to children. The four parts of the knowledge—the visual art elements, production, vocabulary, and the works of artists and designer-craftsmen and the natural environment—are related to each other because all are derived from the major art concepts of line and color and because all art concepts are interrelated through line and color. Identifying the art concepts which can be presented to children limits the scope of art to a manageable content, but it also frees the content so that the full potential of art education can be realized in schools. Understanding the content as it has been defined here enables teachers to realize what art education is all about and to recognize the various things children can learn.

The scope that has been given is based on the assumption that knowledge in art is as important as knowledge in any other subject. The body of knowledge of art which has been accumulated throughout history represents an important facet of man's life—the aesthetic—and involvement in and understanding of the aesthetic provides an opportunity to help children understand man, and themselves, more fully. Part of this knowledge includes nature and the natural environment. Nature is not, of course, a part of art, but many of the art products made by man are superimposed on nature and much of the inspiration for art products as well as the use of design elements comes from nature. Structural design elements can be found in nature by children who have developed seeing skills. This would seem to make an understanding of and sensitivity to the natural environment important to any art education program.

The knowledge of art which is acquired through the formation and enrichment of art concepts should help children learn to see and to interact empathically with art products and nature. Knowledge by itself has not made man what he is, but man's use—or misuse—of knowledge has. The way that knowledge in the scope of art is used partially determines and enhances the creative process which yields the end-product that becomes a part of the world of art.

ART EXPERIENCES: SEQUENCE

The sequence of the content of art education should be based on both children and art so that the learning experiences developed and their placement will be appropriate to the children and to art. The learning experiences, or episodes, should be arranged sequentially so that art concepts can be returned to again and again in increasingly complex and sophisticated ways. The sequential arrangement of episodes rests, in part, upon the children's ability to comprehend, but it also is determined by the content itself and the objectives to be achieved with that content. With enhanced visual perception as the major objective of the art education program outlined here, episodic learnings arranged sequentially from simple to complex should sharpen children's perceptual abilities by capitalizing on the many ways children can learn about art. These include media activities, discussions, and other procedures which help children learn to look at and learn about art. Any procedure which is used should, of course, be designed to enable the children to make discoveries so that concepts and symbols can be enriched.

THE TEACHER IN THE PROCESS

Although art curricula are often developed by professional art educators, the real art curriculum is the one developed by the teacher and used day by day in the classorom. Thus the curriculum that really counts is the one the teacher uses; what she selects determines what she considers to be important for children to learn. To make this classroom curriculum effective and important, teachers must assume the same responsibilities for art education that are assumed for other areas: they must focus on the children they are teaching and the subject being taught.

Teachers must, first of all, know their children—their total growth and development patterns, and their growth and development in art. Knowing the level of art development of each child enables the teacher to understand the symbols being used and when and how these symbols can be enriched. Levels of development in art also include the understandings or degree of awareness that children have developed for the works of artists and designer-craftsmen.

A knowledge of children and their level of art expression and understanding provides teachers with a part of the background for enhancing creative self-expression, for selecting exemplars to be used with children, and for implementing procedures to deal with both of these effectively. The analogies which can be drawn between children's expression and the expressive intent of artists constitute one criterion for selecting exemplars and for developing teaching procedures. The exemplars, which are to be chosen from those in museums and galleries, can be effective in enhancing children's visual perception when they are used after appropriate learning experiences.

The experiences used with children, both for their expressive intent and for interactions with exemplars, are ones through which teachers—by their judgments and discriminations about the use of visual media and other aids, coupled with appropriate procedures—can help children achieve the objectives of art education and, in a sense, the objectives of all education. Implicit in the objective of enhancing the visual perception of children and of making them sensitively aware of their environment is the all-encompassing goal of the total educational program: that of developing well-informed, enlightened citizens who can cope with and add to society.

Art education has unique contributions to make to the child and to his society in meeting both its own objectives and the more general one of the total educational program. The effect of this contribution depends upon the way teachers select content from art and direct it toward the objectives; the process must lead to the desired product. If children can become adults with visual perception enhanced beyond that of many people today, the aesthetic behavior which has been stressed in this book may become an integral part of their lives and will be reflected in the society created by them.

Scope and Sequence
for Art Education

The listing of content on pages 314–23 is organized according to grade placement to provide for the formation and enrichment of concepts that are derived from:

1 Knowledge of visual art elements
2 Knowledge of production (art media processes)
3 Knowledge of art vocabulary
4 Knowledge of works of artists, designer-craftsmen, and the natural environment

As in the text, the Early Primary Level includes nursery school and kindergarten, Primary Level includes grades one, two, and three, and Intermediate Level includes grades four, five, and six.

Line

Introduction of straight and curved lines and other lines derived from them.

Introduction of closure of line to make shapes: round, square, triangle, rectangle, free-form. (The visual discrimination of these shapes is basic to mathematics, science, and reading readiness at this level.)

EARLY PRIMARY LEVEL

Activities for the visual recognition of the use of lines by artists and designer-craftsmen and of lines to be found in the natural environment.

Introduction of use of repeated lines to create textural qualities.

Correlation of these learnings with other areas of the curriculum: creative movement, mathematics, science, music, etc.

Art media activities to give children who are in the scribbling stage opportunities for expression.

Study of lines which form structural qualities to be found in minute particles in nature.

Activities for visual recognition of lines used in many symbols: letters of the alphabet, directional lines, maps, written scores in music, mathematics, traffic signs, and those used by the child as he paints, draws, or works with clay. Particular attention is given to the child's use of base line and symbols created from line: symbols for man, house, cat, etc., in his creative art activities.

PRIMARY LEVEL

Use of line by children to interpret feelings evoked by sound waves and rays from the sun.

Extended visual exercises for recognition of lines used in: jewelry and silversmithing, sculpture, ceramics, painting, architecture, interior design, commercial layout, crystal, industrial design products, and the environmental climate.

Visual exercises for comprehension of use of line by contemporary designers.

Visual exercises to show the relationship between structural qualities in nature and structural qualities in architectural design.

Study of lines used in relief in sculpture and in furniture.

Visual exercises for comprehension and interpretation of lines used by architects in architectural drawings, blueprints, city planning, and all phases of environmental climate.

INTER-MEDIATE LEVEL

Use of line by children in designing three-dimensional space stabiles.

Use of line by children in planning, sketching, and constructing a model city.

Correlation of sociology, economics, and technology with the aesthetics of city planning and urban renewal.

Art media activities designed to motivate children to use lines to create illusions of space (perspective) in their drawings and paintings.

Visual exercises for comprehension and interpretation of lines used by artists to create illusions of space.

Color

Introduction of primary colors.

Introduction of use of color to enhance shape.

Visual exercises designed to enable children to use knowledge of colors and shapes in interpreting the artist's use of color and shape: Mondrian's *Broadway Boogie-Woogie.*

Games for matching a variety of colors.

Activities designed to help children recognize primary colors in their environment: paintings, commercial layouts, etc.

Painting activities that require children to use primary colors.

Correlation of art and science through study of light color theory.

Study of secondary colors derived from primary color pigments.

Creative activities using reflected light as an art media.

Visual exercises designed to help children comprehend works of contemporary artists who are creating with light.

Introduction of value of colors, both primary and secondary.

Visual exercises designed to help children recognize differences in value of color used by artists and designer-craftsmen.

Art media activities designed to help children use and understand differences in color value.

Introduction of warm and cool colors.

Correlation of sound and mood to evoke feelings toward color.

Introduction of intermediate colors derived from primary and secondary colors, using both light and pigment color theories.

Introduction of color relationships and the effect one color has on another, e.g., activities planned from Josef Albers' approach to color.

Use of auditory stimuli to evoke the use of intermediate colors in children's art work.

Introduction of intermediate color values and their interrelationships.

Study of artists' and designer-craftsmen's use of all colors.

Study of colors and their meanings as used by various cultures.

Study of colors used in consumer products and advertising to promote sales.

Introduction to the sociological, psychological, physiological, and aesthetic aspects of color.

Study of the historical changes in the use of color.

Shape (Dominance)

EARLY PRIMARY LEVEL

Introduction of closure of lines to make round and square shapes.

Visual exercises which show the enhancement of round and square shapes with primary colors.

Introduction of shapes derived from round and square shapes: rectangle, triangle, and free-form.

Activities to help children discriminate visually the various shapes used in common objects, such as food, by integrative uses of olfactory, gustatory, tactile senses.

Visual exercises to help children comprehend the use of these shapes in the work of artists in painting and architecture.

Correlation of the study of shapes with mathematics, science, and reading readiness programs.

Games developed to help children discriminate shapes tactually and to develop intersensory integration.

PRIMARY LEVEL

Motivation for use of shapes by children in their art media activities.

Activities designed to motivate children to enrich the symbols used in their art expression with art media and to discuss them.

Visual exercises which show the enhancement of shapes with secondary colors and value.

Introduction to frottage using shapes.

Visual exercises to help children comprehend the use of shapes in the work of artists in painting, collage, print making, frottage, and relief sculpture.

Visual exercises to help children comprehend the use of shapes in common objects designed by the industrial designer.

Study of repeated shapes to be found in minute particles in nature.

INTER-MEDIATE LEVEL

Introduction of shapes enhanced by intermediate colors and values and study of color relationships which visually affect shapes.

Introduction of the use of shape, color, and size to create perspective and feelings of space.

Study of shapes to be found structured in nature and their relationships to architectural structure.

Art media activities designed to help children use free-form shapes, and correlation of these activities with shapes used in contemporary architecture.

Visual exercises to help children make aesthetic discriminations about the use of shapes by industrial designers, city planners, architects, and artists.

Size (Dominance)

Visual exercises to help children discriminate between big and little basic geometric shapes.

Visual exercises to help children discriminate among various sizes of basic geometric shapes.

Activities designed to help children discriminate the use of shapes of various sizes in their immediate environment and in the works of artists.

Correlation of perception of sizes with reading readiness and mathematics.

Activities designed to help children develop conscious awareness of space: up, down, above, below, etc.

Extension of activities given in early primary level, with emphasis placed on the use of various art exemplars.

Introduction of the relationship of size to space.

Activities designed to help children extend conscious awareness of space.

Art media activities to help children recognize and use shapes of various sizes to create illusions of space (perspective).

Art media activities to help children use shapes of various sizes to create feelings of space, and to comprehend artists' use of these shapes, particularly in painting.

Introduction of size as a factor in developing rhythm and dominance as these are used in children's art expression and as they are found in the works of artists and designer-craftsmen and in the natural environment.

Study of the relationship of size to space and the function of space as used in rooms, buildings, homes, etc.

Activities which evoke aesthetic feelings of space.

Correlation of size and space with learnings in social studies and science.

Study of the sociological, economic, and psychological impact of space on man.

Texture ───

Tactual exercises to help children discriminate rough and smooth.

Tactual and visual exercises to help children discriminate rough and smooth objects found in the immediate environment and in the works of artists: painting, sculpture, architecture.

EARLY PRIMARY LEVEL

Thermal activities to help children discriminate between hot and cold.

Tactual activities to help children discriminate among hot, cold, hard, soft, rough, smooth.

Taste games to help children discriminate textural qualities in food.

Tactual, thermal, and visual exercises to help children discriminate among varying degrees of roughness, smoothness, hardness, softness, heat, cold, etc.

Matching games for tactual, thermal, auditory, and visual discriminations.

Study of various ways to create texture in art activities, such as stipple, cross-hatch, frottage, etc.

Visual abstraction activities to help children discriminate qualities of texture.

Study of aesthetic uses of texture by architects and artists.

Study of texture created by repeat pattern of three-dimensional forms.

PRIMARY LEVEL

Use of auditory stimulation to evoke children's use of texture in art media activities.

Use of sound (music, etc.) to help children use the auditory sense to discriminate aesthetic tactile qualities.

Introduction of art exemplars which depict auditory and tactile qualities and which evoke aesthetic response from children, e.g., *Sounds Across the River* by Jimmy Ernst.

Study of uses and relationships of different kinds of texture in weaving, sculpture, painting, architecture, print making, and city planning.

Study of simulated and different textures created as a result of technological advances.

INTER-MEDIATE LEVEL

Study of relationship of texture to color and their effect upon each other.

Study of man's needs which have led to the development of various textures: clothing, aesthetics, etc.

Study of function which determines texture and its aesthetic qualities.

Art media activities designed to stimulate increased use of texture by children in their art expression.

Visual exercises for the perception of texture in nature.

Pattern (Rhythm) ————————————————————————————

Introduction of repeat pattern created by repeated lines.

Introduction of repeat pattern created by repeated shapes.

Introduction of repeated shapes used to create visual textures.

Visual exercises to help children discriminate artists' use of repeated lines and shapes to create repeat patterns and texture.

Activities to show the auditory and visual relationships of pattern and rhythm in creative rhythms and musical scores.

Introduction of repeat patterns found in: mathematics, nature, clothing, reading readiness materials, architecture, and common objects in the immediate environment.

———

Visual exercises to help children understand the use of repeat pattern of lines, colors, shapes of different sizes, and forms to create texture.

Activities designed to help children understand that repeat pattern is used by painters, sculptors, printmakers, architects, weavers, and commercial layout artists.

Introduction of simple print-making techniques—gadget and vegetable—to create repeat patterns.

Other art activities designed to help children "see" the use of different kinds of repeat pattern in their art work.

Extended activities in the auditory and visual perception of patterns.

———

Introduction of the conscious use of repeat pattern as a design element.

Introduction of counterpoint repeat patterns and their relationships.

Introduction of counterpoint patterns found in art, music, nature, and architecture.

Study of the use of repeat patterns enhanced with color as elements of design in merchandising.

Study of the sociological, physiological, and psychological impact of the use of repeat patterns to develop aesthetic feelings.

Study of the use of repeat patterns to show rhythm.

Study of rhythms of living organisms and how these have been interpreted by artists.

Art media activities designed to motivate children's use of repeat pattern as a design element.

Visual exercises for the perception of pattern.

Activities designed to help children discriminate aesthetically among various repeat patterns.

———

Form ───

EARLY PRIMARY LEVEL

Introduction of the differences between flat shape and solid form.

Art media activities designed to have children make solid forms (clay work) and flat shapes (collage).

Visual exercises to help children understand the differences between the work of the painter and the sculptor.

PRIMARY LEVEL

Introduction of the differences between two- and three-dimensional forms in children's art activities and the works of artists and designer-craftsmen.

Introduction of repeated solid forms to create texture, e.g., solid forms in orange peel and sandpaper.

Art activities designed to help children discriminate between solid forms and non-solid forms.

INTER-MEDIATE LEVEL

Introduction of the relationship between form and shape.

Introduction of the difference between form and solid form in children's artwork, in the work of artists and designer-craftsmen, and in the natural environment.

Art media activities which help the children distinguish between form and solid form in their own artwork and which help them distinguish between the two in the work of artists and designer-craftsmen and in the natural environment.

Introduction of the controversy concerning distinctions between shape and form.

Symbols ————————————————————————————————

Motivation for enrichment of symbols (schema) that children are using in their art expression (only after children have reached the "naming of scribbles" stage).

Activities which use art media processes and children's symbols so that children can comprehend symbols derived from the natural environment as well as those used by artists and designer-craftsmen (only after children have reached the "naming of scribbles" stage).

Activities for interacting with non-objective symbols used by artists and designer-craftsmen.

————————————————————————————————

Motivation for enrichment of symbols (schema) that children are using in their art expression through the use of the visual art elements.

Motivation for developing new symbols as children need them.

Activities which use art media processes and children's symbols so that children can comprehend symbols derived from the natural environment and those used by artists and designer-craftsmen.

————————————————————————————————

Motivation for enrichment of symbols (schema) through knowledgeable and creative application of *all* visual art elements by children in their art expressions.

Study of symbols developed by artists and designer-craftsmen to portray aesthetically truths, ideals, and feelings.

Study of symbols used in commercial advertising.

Study of sociological, psychological, and aesthetic use of symbols in various cultures.

Design ————————————————————————————————

EARLY PRIMARY LEVEL

No conscious approach to design is to be introduced with the media process to children at this level.

Exposure to exemplars created by artists and designer-craftsmen which use good design principles.

———————————————————————————————————————

PRIMARY LEVEL

Introduction of the conscious use of design through the creative use of gadget and vegetable printing.

Exposure to more complex exemplars created by artists and designer-craftsmen which use good design principles.

———————————————————————————————————————

INTER-MEDIATE LEVEL

Visual exercises to help children develop aesthetic judgments about good and poor design in: sculpture, painting, jewelry and silversmithing, ceramics, weaving, commercial layout, architecture, graphic processes, city planning, and industrial design products.

Art media activities which encompass knowledgeable and aesthetic use of all principles of design.

———————————————————————————————————————

EARLY PRIMARY LEVEL

Vocabulary ————————————————————————————

Art vocabulary introduced in accordance with the learning situations and stage of development of children at this level.

———————————————————————————————————————

PRIMARY LEVEL

Art vocabulary introduced in accordance with the learning situations and stage of development of children at this level.

———————————————————————————————————————

INTER-MEDIATE LEVEL

Art vocabulary introduced in accordance with the planned learning situations and stage of development of children at this level.

———————————————————————————————————————

History of Art

Activities to help children distinguish between original works of art and reproductions of them.

Activities which help children identify names of artists and designer-craftsmen and their works of art. These evolve from exemplars used in learning activities.

Introduction of the chronology of art through activities which help children distinguish between works of art from the past and contemporary works.

Introduction of simple comparisons of different ages and styles of works of art with exemplars used in learning activities.

Use of time lines to show the development of man's cultural heritage.

Correlation of works of art with movements in history and cultures being studied in social studies.

Correlation of works of art with periods in music history.

Visual exercises to help children distinguish between an original print and a print.

Visual exercises which help children compare different artists' use of visual art elements—style.

Activities which help children interpret the expressive intent of artists and designer-craftsmen.

Recommended Readings

BOOKS ON ART EDUCATION

Anderson, Warren H. *Art Learning Situations for Elementary Education.* Belmont, Calif.: Wadsworth Publishing Co., Inc., 1965.
Selected learning situations to promote visual literacy in children.

Barkan, Manuel. *Through Art to Creativity.* Boston: Allyn and Bacon, Inc., 1960.
An evaluation of art activities in self-contained classrooms.

Bealmer, William, *et al. Children Learn and Grow Through Art Experiences.* Springfield: Office of Superintendent of Public Instruction, State of Illinois, 1958.
Resource guide for elementary art teachers.

Cole, Natalie Robinson. *Children's Arts from Deep Down Inside.* New York: The John Day Co., 1966.
Accounts of children and their art expression.

Conant, Howard, and Arne Randall. *Art in Education.* Peoria, Ill.: Chas. A. Bennett Co., Inc., 1959.
Characteristics of art teachers and recommendations for professional preparation.

D'Amico, Victor. *Creative Teaching in Art.* Rev. ed. Scranton, Pa.: International Textbook Co., 1960.
Creative aspects of child art.

de Francesco, Italo L. *Art Education: Its Means and Ends.* New York: Harper & Row, 1958.
Philosophical and theoretical concepts for art education.

Eisner, E., and David Ecker. *Readings in Art Education.* New York: Holt, Rinehart and Winston, Inc., 1966.
Compilation of articles related to research and trends in art education.

Kaufman, Irving. *Art and Education in Contemporary Culture.* New York: The Macmillan Co., 1966.
Chapter 15, "Redirection in Art Education."

Knudsen, Estelle, and Ethel Christensen. *Children's Art Education.* Peoria, Ill.: Chas. A. Bennett Co., Inc., 1957.
Classroom art experiences and art media.

Linderman, Earl W., and Donald W. Heberholz. *Developing Artistic and Perceptual Awareness.* Dubuque, Iowa: Wm. C. Brown Co., 1964.
Chapter 6, "Starting a Beginning Art Program." Art as study and appreciation.

Lowenfeld, Viktor. *Creative and Mental Growth.* 3d ed. New York: The Macmillan Co., 1957.
Chapters 3, 4, 5, 6, and 7. Children's growth and development in art expression.

McKee, June King. *Preparation for Art.* Belmont, Calif.: Wadsworth Publishing Co., Inc., 1961.
Relationship of psychological and anthropological principles to art education.

McIlvain, Dorothy S. *Art for the Primary Grades.* New York: G. P. Putnam's Sons, 1961.
Art activities and their uses for primary grades.

Smith, Ralph A. (Ed.). *Aesthetics and Criticism in Art Education.* Chicago: Rand McNally and Co., 1966.
Aesthetics in art education.

ART MEDIA TECHNIQUES

La Mancusa, Katherine C. *Source Book for Art Teachers.* Scranton, Pa.: International Textbook Co., 1965.
Reference for all media processes for elementary school teachers.

Lord, Lois. *Collage and Construction.* Worcester, Mass.: Davis Publications, Inc., 1958.
Sources of materials and their use of collages.

Loughran, Bernice B. *Art Experiences: An Experimental Approach.* New York: Harcourt, Brace & World, Inc., 1963.
A variety of materials and their relationship to the visual art elements.

Mattil, Edward. *Meaning in Crafts.* 2d ed. Englewood Cliffs, N. J.: Prentice-Hall, Inc., 1965.
Practical guidebook for methods, procedures, and materials for craft projects.

Moseley, Spencer, *et al. Crafts Design.* Belmont, Calif.: Wadsworth Publishing Co., Inc., 1962.
Practical guidebook for methods, procedures, and materials for craft projects. Excellent section on paper and its uses.

Pattemore, Arnel W. *Printmaking Activities for the Classroom.* Worcester, Mass.: Davis Publications, Inc., 1966.
Materials, procedures, and different print-making techniques for children.

Randall, Arne W. *Murals for Schools.* Worcester, Mass.: Davis Publications, Inc., 1962.
Procedures and materials for making murals.

Rainey, Sarita R. *Weaving Without a Loom.* Worcester, Mass.: Davis Publications, Inc., 1966.
Procedures for using a variety of yarns and fibers in a variety of processes.

BOOKS ON UNDERSTANDING ART

Anderson, Donald M. *Elements of Design.* New York: Holt, Rinehart and Winston, Inc., 1961.
A study of the visual elements of art.

Blake, Peter. *God's Own Junkyard.* New York: Holt, Rinehart and Winston, Inc., 1964.
An architect's view of man's non-aesthetic contributions to the natural environment.

Brodatz, Phil. *Textures.* New York: Dover Publications, Inc., 1966.
Photographs of closeups of textures.

Canaday, John. *Keys to Art.* New York: Tudor Publishing Co., 1963.
Description of ways to help people see and understand the works of artists.

Capers, Roberta M., and Jerrold Maddox. *Images and Imagination.* New York: The Ronald Press Co., 1965.
An introduction to art written for general readers.

Chase, Elizabeth A. *Famous Artists of the Past.* New York: Platt & Munk, Publishers, 1964.
A book of selected artists with whom the author believes children should be familiar.

————. *Famous Paintings.* New York: Platt & Munk, Publishers, 1964.
A selection of paintings with which the author believes children should become acquainted.

Emerson, Sybil. *Design: A Creative Approach.* Scranton, Pa.: International Textbook Co., 1953.
Visual elements of art and the experimental process for using these.

Faulkner, R., E. Ziegfeld, and G. Hill. *Art Today.* Rev. ed. New York: Holt, Rinehart and Winston, Inc., 1963.
Resource book for works of artists and designer-craftsmen.

Feibleman, James K. *Aesthetics: A Study of the Fine Arts in Theory and Practice.* New York: Duell, Sloan and Pearce, 1949.
A source for learning about art and aesthetics.

Freedman, Leonard (Ed.). *Looking at Modern Painting.* New York: W. W. Norton & Co., Inc., 1961.
An aid to assist the general reader in understanding the work of modern artists.

Janson, H. W., and Dora Jane Janson. *The Picture History of Painting.* New York: Harry N. Abrams, Inc., 1957.
Source for selecting exemplars.

Kepes, Gyorgy. *Language of Vision*. Chicago: Paul Theobald, 1944.
A foundation for the development of seeing skills.

Kuh, Katherine. *Art Has Many Faces*. New York: Harper & Row, 1951.
Description of many ways to look at art.

Levi, Julian. *Modern Art: An Introduction*. New York: Pitman Publishing Corp., 1961.
Ways to help the general reader look at modern art.

Lowry, Bates. *The Visual Experience*. Englewood Cliffs, N. J.: Prentice-Hall, Inc., and New York: Harry N. Abrams, Inc., 1961.
A comprehensive book on visual experience as it is related to the works of artists.

Lynton, Norbert. *The Modern World*. New York: McGraw-Hill Book Co., 1965.
Includes architecture, city planning, sculpture, interiors, and paintings from the modern world.

McCallum, Ian. *Architecture U.S.A.* New York: Reinhold Publishing Corp., 1959.
Exemplars in architecture with emphasis on various movements and contemporary architecture.

Matusow, Marshall. *The Art Collector's Almanac*. New York: Art Collector's Almanac, Inc., 1965.
Source of works of art and where they can be found.

Moholy-Nagy, Laszio. *The New Vision*. New York: Wittenborn and Co., 1947.
An explanation of principles derived from the Bauhaus movement.

Pasadena Art Museum. *California Design—Nine*. Pasadena: Pasadena Art Museum, 1965.
Collection of exemplars of designer-craftsmen.

Pepper, Stephen C. *Principles of Art Appreciation*. New York: Harcourt, Brace & World, Inc., 1949.
Instruction in the development of aesthetic appreciation.

Schinneller, James A. *Art: Search and Self-Discovery*. Scranton, Pa.: International Textbook Co., 1961.
Information about media processes and works of artists and designer-craftsmen.

The Shorewood Art Reference Guide. Prepared under the direction of the editors of Shorewood Publishers, Inc. New York: Shorewood Reproductions, Inc., 1966.
Selected exemplars, bibliographies, and background information about artists and schools of art for use in elementary schools.

Taylor, Joshua C. *Learning To Look*. Chicago: University of Chicago Press, 1965.
Information on how to look and what to look for.

Wilson, Robert C. *An Alphabet of Visual Experience*. Scranton, Pa.: International Textbook Co., 1966.
A visual presentation of all visual art elements.

PERCEPTION

Allport, Floyd Henry. *Theories of Perception and the Concept of Structure.* New York: John Wiley & Sons, Inc., 1955.
Synopsis of research and theories in field of perception.

Armstrong, D. M. *Perception and the Physical World.* New York: The Humanities Press, 1961.
A study of objects and the perception of them.

Arnheim, Rudolf. *Art and Visual Perception.* Berkeley: University of California Press, 1960.
Psychological and physiological presentation of visual perception.

Boring, Edwin G. *Sensation and Perception in the History of Experimental Psychology.* New York: Appleton-Century-Crofts, 1942.
Review of theories of perception in chronological sequence.

Cantril, Hadley, and Ittleson. *Perception: A Transitional Approach.* Garden City, N. Y.: Doubleday and Co., Inc., 1954.
The psychological process, with emphasis on the transactional approach.

Liebowitz, Herschel. *Visual Perception.* New York: The Macmillan Co., 1965.
Reports of experiments on humans and animals to overcome the inadequacies of the physiological aspects of human perceptions.

Luckiesh, M. *Visual Illusions: Their Causes, Characteristics and Applications.* New York: Dover Publications, Inc., 1965.
Causes of visual illusions.

Sollery, Charles, and Gardner Murphy. *Development of the Perceptual World.* New York: Basic Books, 1960.
Review of theories of perception.

RELATED BOOKS

Anderson, Harold H. (Ed.). *Creativity and Its Cultivation.* Addresses presented at the Intersymposia on Creativity. New York: Harper & Row, 1959.
Some insights into creativity and its development.

Broudy, Harry S., *et al. Democracy and Excellence in American Secondary Education.* Chicago: Rand McNally and Co., 1964.
Although written for the secondary level, this book has some provocative ideas about aesthetic education, the number and use of exemplars, and conceptual development.

Bruner, Jerome S. *The Process of Education.* Cambridge, Mass.: Harvard University Press, 1960.
A presentation of four themes: the role of structure in learning, readiness for learning, the nature of intuition, and the desire to learn and the stimulation of this desire.

Dewey, John. *Democracy and Education*. New York: The Macmillan Co., 1916.
A "classic" in which Dewey proposes that educators and scholars work together so that children can develop advanced ideas from their own experiences.

Hunt, J. McV. *Intelligence and Experience*. New York: The Ronald Press Co.,
1961.
A re-evaluation of the belief in predetermined development, and a challenge
for educators to consider the learning experiences of young children so that
there can be a "higher level of adult intellectual capacity."

Judd, Charles Hubbard. *Education and Social Progress*. New York: Harcourt,
Brace & World, Inc., 1934.
Presentation of a suggestion that the main lines of thought be determined by
authorities so educators can present them suitably to children (p. 263).

Robison, Helen, and Spodek, Bernard. *New Directions in the Kindergarten*.
New York: Teachers College Press, Columbia University, 1965.
These authors present a challenge for selecting content which considers the
intellectual aspect of the development of young children.

Russell, David H. *Children's Thinking*. New York: Ginn and Co., 1956.
A review of research related to children's thinking and learning.

Standing, E. M. *The Montessori Method: A Revolution in Education*. Fresno,
Calif.: The Academy Library Guild, 1962.
The theoretical foundation and the materials and procedures advocated by
Maria Montessori.

Torrance, E. Paul. *Guiding Creative Talent*. Englewood Cliffs, N. J.: Prentice-
Hall, Inc., 1962.
Insights into creativity derived from experimentation in language arts.

Wann, Kenneth, *et al*. *Fostering Intellectual Development in Young Children*.
New York: Teachers College Press, Columbia University, 1962.
A report of action research which shows the processes used by children in
developing concepts and which emphasizes the teacher's role in helping children develop concepts.

Whitehead, Alfred North. *The Aims of Education and Other Essays*. New
York: The Macmillan Co., 1929.
A "classic," with views and comments on education that are timely and provoca-
tive.

CHILDREN'S BOOKS

Barger, Bertel. *Nature As Designer*. Scranton, Pa.: International Textbook Co.,
1966.

Barnes, William A. *A World Full of Homes*. New York: McGraw-Hill Book
Co., 1953.

Beilter, Ethel Jane. *Create with Yarn*. Scranton, Pa.: International Textbook
Co., 1964.

Bright, Robert. *I Like Red*. Garden City, N. Y.: Doubleday and Co., Inc., 1955.

Bulla, Clyde. *What Makes a Shadow?* New York: Thomas Y. Crowell Co., 1962.

Gill, Bob. *What Color Is Your World?* New York: Ivan Obolensky, Inc., 1963.

Halpin, Lawrence. *Cities.* New York: Reinhold Publishing Corp., Inc., 1963.

Hammond, Penny, and Katrina Thomas. *My Skyscraper City.* Garden City, N. Y.: Doubleday and Co., Inc., 1963.

Hughes, Toni. *How To Make Shapes in Space.* New York: E. P. Dutton & Co., Inc., 1955.

Karasz, Mariska. *Adventure in Stitches.* New York: Funk and Wagnall Co., 1959.

Kessler, Ethel. *Are You Square?* Garden City, N. Y.: Doubleday and Co., Inc., 1966.

Kessler, Leonard. *What's in a Line?* New York: William R. Scott, Inc., 1961.

Kirn, Ann. *Full of Wonder.* New York: The World Publishing Co., 1959.

Phillips, Brian. *A Trip to the Zoo.* New York: Lantern Press, Inc., 1962.

Rainey, Sarita. *Weaving Without a Loom.* Worcester, Mass.: Davis Publications, Inc., 1966.

Schlein, Miriam. *Shapes.* New York: William R. Scott, Inc., 1958.

Schneider, Herman, and Nina Schneider. *How Big Is Big?* New York: William R. Scott, Inc., 1950.

Stein, Ralph. *The Automobile Book.* London: Paul Hamlyn, Ltd., 1961.

Strache, Wolf. *Forms and Patterns in Nature.* New York: Pantheon Books, Inc., 1956.

Weiss, Harvey. *Ceramics from Clay to Kiln.* New York: William R. Scott, Inc., 1964.

Wolff, Janet, and Bernard Owett. *Let's Imagine Colors.* New York: E. P. Dutton & Co., Inc., 1963.

———. *Let's Imagine Sounds.* New York: E. P. Dutton & Co., Inc., 1962.

Sources for Exemplars

FILMS AND FILMSTRIPS

American Handicrafts Co., Chicago, Ill. 60605
American Library Colored Slide Co., New York, N. Y. 10011
Associated Films, New York, N. Y. 10016
Bailey Films, Hollywood, Calif. 90028
Charles Besler Company, East Orange, N. J. 07018
Brandon Films, Inc., New York, N. Y. 10019
Contemporary Films, Inc., New York, N. Y. 10001
Coronet Films, Chicago, Ill. 60601
Encyclopedia Britannica Films, Wilmette, Ill. 60091
Film Associates of California, Los Angeles, Calif. 90025
Film Images, New York, N. Y. 10022
International Film Bureau, Inc., Chicago, Ill. 60604
International Film Foundation, New York, N. Y. 10017
Lobett Productions, San Francisco, Calif. 94116
National Film Board of Canada, New York, N. Y. 10022
Neubacher-Vetter Film Productions, Los Angeles, Calif. 90024
Picture Film Corporation, New York, N. Y. 10022
Prothmann, Dr. Konrad, Baldwin, N. Y. 11510
Sante Fe Film Bureau, Chicago, Ill. 60604

COLOR SLIDES

American Library Color Slide Co., Inc., New York, N. Y. 10011
Museum of Modern Art Library, New York, N. Y. 10019
Philadelphia Museum of Art, Division of Education, Philadelphia, Pa. 19130
Prothmann, Dr. Konrad, Baldwin, N. Y. 11510
School of the Art Institute of Chicago, Chicago, Ill. 60603

REPRODUCTIONS AND PRINTS

Artext Prints, Inc., Westport, Conn. 06880
Associated American Artists, Inc., New York, N. Y. 10022
Catalda Fine Arts, Inc., New York, N. Y. 10010
Commerford Gallery, New York, N. Y. 10022
FAR Gallery, New York, N. Y. 10021
Esther Gentle, New York, N. Y. 10017
Metropolitan Museum of Art, Art and Book Shop, New York, N. Y. 10028
Museum of Modern Art, New York, N. Y. 10019
New York Graphic Society, New York, N. Y. 10001
Oestreicher's, New York, N. Y. 10009
Penn Prints, Harlem Book Company, Inc., New York, N. Y. 10003
Prothmann, Dr. Konrad, Baldwin, N. Y. 11510
Raymond and Raymond, Inc., New York, N. Y. 10022
Shorewood Reproductions, Inc., New York, N. Y. 10019
Society for Visual Education, Inc., Chicago, Ill. 60614
University Prints, Cambridge, Mass. 02138
Urban Prints, New York, N. Y. 10022
E. Weyhe, New York, N. Y. 10021

RECORDS AND TAPES

Bowmar Educational Records, North Hollywood, Calif. 91601
Camden Records, New York, N. Y. 10010
Capitol Records Distributing Corp., Hollywood, Calif. 90028
Children's Record Guild and Young People's Records, The Greystone Corporation,
    New York, N. Y. 10003
Columbia Records Education Dept., New York, N. Y. 10019
Folkway Records, New York, N. Y. 10036
Mills Music Company, New York, N. Y. 10019
RCA Victor Educational Sales Dept., New York, N. Y. 10010
Silver Burdett Co., Dallas, Tex. 75201
Simon and Schuster, Inc., New York, N. Y. 10020

Acknowledgments

Albright-Knox Art Gallery, Buffalo, New York: Figure 79 (Room of Contemporary Art Fund).

Courtesy of *Art in America* and Charles Deaton: Figures 166, 167, and 168.

Courtesy of The Art Institute of Chicago: Figures 93, 103 (Mr. and Mrs. M. A. Ryerson Collection); and 89, 110, and 116 (all Helen Birch Bartlett Memorial Collection).

Atkins Museum of Fine Arts, Kansas City, Missouri: Figures 101, 113, 117, 119 (Gift of Mr. and Mrs. Joseph Atha); 123, 127, 131, 146, and 160 (all Nelson Fund, Collection of William Rockhill Nelson Gallery of Art).

Del Michael Studio, Nashville, Tennessee: Figures 6, 7, 9, 11, 13, 14, 15, and 17.

Courtesy of Denver Public Schools: Figure 199.

Courtesy of Bernard Frazier: Figure 161.

Courtesy of General Motors Styling Center: Figures 150, 151, 152, 153, and 162.

Courtesy of Harold Haas, Director of City Planning, Springfield, Missouri: Figures 158 and 159.

The Johnson Collection (*Art: USA*), Racine, Wisconsin: Figures 69 and 108.

Courtesy of the *Journal-World*, Lawrence, Kansas: Figure 1.

Courtesy of Gerald Korte, St. Cloud State College, St. Cloud, Minnesota: Figure 185.

The Metropolitan Museum of Art: Figures 57 (George A. Hearn Fund) and 86 (The Jules S. Bache Collection, 1949).

Courtesy of Herman Miller, Inc., Zeeland, Michigan: Figures 73 (Photograph by Harr, Hedrich-Blessing), 74, 121, and 148.

Courtesy of Howard Miller Clock Company: Figures 104, 105, 106, 107, and 140.

Collection of The Museum of Modern Art, New York: Figures 55 (Gift of Mrs. John D. Rockefeller III), 64 (Gift of Walter P. Chrysler, Jr.), 68, 85 (Gift of Mrs. Simon Guggenheim), 87 (Mrs. Simon Guggenheim Fund), 122 (Abby Aldrich Rockefeller Fund), 125, 126 (Gift of the Advisory Committee), and 163 (on extended loan from the artist to The Museum of Modern Art).

National Gallery of Art, Washington, D. C.: Figures 63 (Andrew Mellon Collection) and 92.

Nesbit Studio, Wichita Falls, Texas: Figures 8, 10, 12, 16, and 18.

Pasadena Art Museum: Figures 81, 96, 99 (Manufactured by Architectural Pottery, Los Angeles, California), 112, 115, 118, 134 (Household Blender, Dewenter Industries; Thermo-Spoon, Gaydell, Inc.; Condiment Caddy, Dispensers, Inc.), 135 (Manufactured by Glenn of California), 136 (Oven "Deslinen" aluminumware, design line), 139 (Manufactured by Modeline of California), and 149.

Courtesy of The Pennsylvania State University: Figures 186, 187, and 188.

Philadelphia Museum of Art: Figures 51 (Louise and Walter Arensberg Collection), 76 (A. E. Gallatin Collection), and 102 (Wilstach Collection).

Courtesy of the Philadelphia Planning Commission: Figures 2, 156, and 157.

© Ezra Stoller, Mamaroneck, New York: Figures 94, 147, 169, 172, and 174.

Courtesy of John Talleur: Figure 133.

University of Nebraska: Figure 189.

University of Nebraska Art Galleries, Sheldon Art Gallery, Lincoln, Nebraska: Figures 53 (University Collection); 59, 78, 100, 114, 128, 129, 130, and 132 (all F. M. Hall Collection); and 75, 80, 82, and 88 (all Collection of the Nebraska Art Association).

Collection of the Whitney Museum of American Art: Figures 61, 109 (both Gift of the Friends of the Whitney), 91, and 155.

Worcester Art Museum, Worcester, Massachusetts: Figure 84.

Yale University Art Gallery, New Haven, Connecticut (Gift of Stephen Carlton Clark): Figure 19.

Index